How Democrats Win The 2020 Election

12 Steps To Victory

David King Keller, PhD

MEDIA TALKING POINTS

- How to Predict 2020 Presidential Election Outcome.
- Overcoming 21 Reasons Democrats Could Lose.
- How Mike Pence becomes our 46th U.S. President.
- Russian 2020 interference: Dems biggest hurdle.
- Trump's claim he can legally murder us: the audio.

- Trump's 20+ (alleged) Federal crimes: Evidence.
- Trump: Putin's Puppet: The evidence.
- The Fatal Flaw in the House Impeachment Strategy.
- The Six Headlines Strategy used to control news.
- Shock-and-Awe-No-Lie-Is-Too-Big-October.

- Trump made average American into slaves for rich.
- 55 Corps: $79B in Profit- Paid No Taxes = T donors.
- How to break the "Trump Trance" gripping 50mill.
- #MoscowMitch and #MassacreMitch.
- Why Republicans are the SPIDER Party.

- Political cartoons that will inform and delight.
- Use of deep fake videos to crush Democratic support.
- Looming Constitutional Crisis: Trump blocks transition.
- 55 Corps: $79B in Profit- Paid No Taxes- rec'd $4.3B in Refunds under Trump's new "tax heist" law.
- How many days a week does the average American works to give their tax dollars as <u>refunds</u> to Corps that make $100 million in profit but pay no taxes?

- "Best Bet" Biden: Strengths / Weaknesses Reviewed.
- Baca v. Colorado could destroy American democracy.
- The 2011 email that cost Clinton the 2016 election foreshadows a 2020 strategy by Trump.
- Democrats should listen to American fears and concerns about illegal immigration and open borders. One solution.
- The number of Americans "Massacre Mitch" and the "Socialist-Republican-Party-Dedicated-To-The-Rich" allegedly kill every year by blocking the re-adoption of the once effective 1994 ban on military assault weapons and high capacity magazines.

- The 12-Step path to a Democratic victory: a strategy that includes celebrities, and unique campaign strategies.
- Some strategies are secret and only available to Joe Biden, Tom Steyer, DNC and Chairs of Democratic supporting PACs.

- Tom Steyer, Sally Susman, George Soros, Barack Obama, Mike Bloomberg, Rob Reiner, Jon Stewart, and YOU: please contact the author.

- To make a difference in our Country's destiny and replace Socialist Republicans providing government welfare for the rich at the expense of everyone else, please contact:
  DrDavidKingKeller@gmail.com

How Democrats Win 2020

12 Steps To Victory

David King Keller, PhD

© 2020 All rights reserved.

Printed in the United States of America.

Purchase of this book or use of this book's contents in any manner is acceptance of Publisher's Terms and Conditions.

Contact publisher for bulk sales and PoliSci textbook sales.
Keller Research Institute, 10950-60 San Jose Blvd, Suite 100, Jacksonville, FL 32257. Email for Phone number.
DrDavidKingKeller@gmail.com

For media interviews or consulting:
send email with "Media" in subject line to:
DrDavidKingKeller@gmail.com

ISBN: 9798651520763

DEDICATION

This book was written for and dedicated to the Democratic leadership.

Tom Perez, Nancy Pelosi, Chuck Schumer, Michael Blake, Bill Derrough, Maria Elena Durazo, Chris Korge, Ken Martin, Grace Meng, Karen Carter Peterson, Jason Rae, Jaime Harrison, and Lorna Johnson. I wrote this book for you. Please give me a few minutes to discuss strategies that I believe must be pursued now to prevent Trump's re-election.

This book is dedicated to all Democrats in the House and Senate.

This book is written for and directed to all decision-makers over Democratic supporting campaign funds and PAC funds because I believe I can deliver a very high ROI on a portion of those funds.

One very enjoyable strategy, not in this book, turns Florida Blue for $24 million. It's a unique tactic that has never been done before. It would garnish significant positive publicity and would aggravate the hell out of Don-the-Con. Other tactics involve a series of TV spots, including one that completely re-brands Trump and his Republican enablers. Also, I have messaging for the Democratic leadership that is effective and not included in this book.

Tom Steyer and Mike Bloomberg, please contact me.

I dedicate this work to all who want to #DumpTrump.

- Thank you, David

DrDavidKingKeller@gmail.com

TABLE OF CONTENTS

"The depth of research in Dr. Keller's two companion books, *Why Trump Won The 2020 Election* and *How Democrats Win 2020,* is worthy of Pulitzer consideration."

— Stephanie Annis, Professional Book Editor

PREFACE

There are four numbers that can defeat the Democrats: 73 million, 127 million, 29%, and 26. We will review these and other obstacles and how to overcome them.

Pain. The majority of us can see, hear and feel the destruction of a great country by a man so selfish that he would crush with potentially lethal force the Constitutional right of peaceful assembly for a photo op.

Over 3,000 hours went into a manuscript that produced this book and its companion book, *Why Trump Won The 2020 Election 21 Reasons The Democrats Lost.* The goal: bring better, saner leadership to America. #DumpTrump.

My original goal was a short treatise to the Democratic leadership on the challenges I thought they were facing and the errors I thought they were making. Not unlike an intervention.

My "short" treatise turned into 600 pages. So, I split the manuscript in half, creating two books.

The first half of the manuscript was intended as a shock-to-the-system-wake-up-call to the Democrats on the dangers they face of losing the 2020 election and why. That companion book has an in-depth analysis on the impact of the Electoral College, third parties, Independent voters and the four polls that can predict an election. That book is titled, *Why Trump Won The 2020 Election, 21 Reasons Democrats Lost.* If you want an unbridled critique of Donald Trump while acknowledging his tactics and political strengths, then it is essential reading.

The second half of the manuscript, this book, is a review on *How Democrats Win The 2020 Election, 12 Steps To Victory*. This book leads with some of the messaging errors of the Democrats that could place them as underdogs in the mind of many Americans. I draw on over five decades of working with the public in politics and a wide range of communication methodologies in a number of different industries. Based on that background, I present *12-Steps to Victory*. These are actions that I believe must be included in a successful 2020 campaign by the Democrats.

After George Floyd was murdered, I pulled out content on racism from the manuscript, expanded on it, and turned it into a short 40-page book dedicated to George Floyd, Breonna Taylor, and Ahmaud Arbery titled, *Racism and Racial Resentment, Their Role In Trump's Election*. The second byline to that book is *Black Lives Matter*.

The fourth title in the quartet pulled from the original manuscript is titled, *Trump's 25 Alleged Federal Crimes, The Statutes and The Evidence*.

The Democrats have got to change their 2016 strategies, tactics, and mindset to win in 2020. Many are now being lured into the belief that Trump is done. He'll lose in a landslide. Remember, that's what we thought in 2016. Trump has an ace up his sleeve, and I describe it in "Chapter 5 – Trump's Nuclear Option To Win 2020". If you read nothing else, read that. That way, you won't be completely shocked if he wins.

Out of love for my Country and a desire to replace all the Republicans who have enabled Trump's horrific actions, I stopped my life and dedicated it to creating these four books.

In this book, we examine how to overcome the four numbers listed above that can spell doom to Joseph Biden and down-ticket Democrats.

◆ ◆ ◆

This book is a wake-up call to Democrats, Independents, and Republicans with a conscience.

Donald J. Trump's lawyer, William Consovoy, told a U.S. Federal Judge in the Second Court of Appeals on October 23, 2019, that Trump had the legal right to murder any one of us and could not be held accountable as long as he was President. Listen to the audio: https://www.vox.com/2019/10/23/20928680/nothing-could-be-done-trump-fifth-avenue-immunity-mazars-vance; also at https://bit.ly/3ijNo4k.

Ample public evidence allegedly proves Trump broke over twenty Federal laws detailed later in this book including:

Title 18 USC 201 – Bribery. Detailed by an NYU law professor.
Title 18 USC 872 - Extortion.
Title X- 1974 Impoundment Control Act - As declared by the GAO.
Title 18 USC 2381 - Treason - Aid /Comfort to an enemy. #Trea45son

On February 4, 2020, Donald Trump said in his State of the Union Address that he would protect Social Security. On February 10, 2020, Trump submitted a budget that reduces Social Security benefits. America's seniors and their children need to be aware of Don-The-Con.

Under Trump's new 2017 tax law, the average American is turned into an economic slave paying taxes that go directly to the rich in the form of tax refunds. Learn these simple statistics and tell others.

Yet, despite these headline-grabbing travesties that would put any other President out of office, we have yet to fully assure ourselves that we have limited Trump to one term. I discuss many ways to improve our communication to the electorate and how we have not tapped into the vast reserve of celebrities who want to contribute to Trump's departure. If we fail to take the actions I list in this book we are setting up Trump to win the 2020 election.

◆ ◆ ◆

This is a booklogue. This book is designed to generate a dialogue between the reader and the author, a book-dialogue or booklogue, for short. Read the "Afterward" for more details on this.

This book is a dialogue with the media, Democrats, Republicans, and Independents. It's a communication to Democrats on how, and how not, to win the hearts and minds of Americans. It's a message to Republicans on how they have attained power, but risk it all by losing the respect of fiscal conservatives and those who believe in honesty, ethics and the rule of law.

To contribute funds, comments, and other resources (website development, for example) to the Keller Research Institute, a non-profit, or to support my next book, *20 Ways To Improve America*, please contact David King Keller, PhD. DrDavidKingKeller@gmail.com

Tom Steyer, George Soros, Mike Bloomberg, Rob Reiner, Jon Stewart, Meryl Streep, Barbra Streisand, Sally Susman, pro-Biden PACs, and other like-minded persons, please contact the author. We can turn Florida blue for $24 million if we hurry. It's a unique strategy that has never been done before and will garnish significant positive publicity. There are three TV spots that must be created to properly re-brand Trump while re-branding the Trump-enabling Republican Party. There is a way to engage voters, young and old, like never before. This is essential. Most of these tactics are revealed in "Chapter 4 - 12 Steps To

Victory." Others can only be revealed to key celebrities (you know who you are), financial decision-makers, and Biden campaign strategists.

Trump has a "Nuclear Option" guaranteeing his re-election unless we aggressively implement counter-measures starting right now.

Celebrities willing to donate a 10 second TV spot, please contact me.

Gamers and programmers who want to **#DumpTrump**, contact me.

Democratic supporting PACs, please contact me.

Tom Steyer, please contact me.

DrDavidKingKeller@gmail.com

CHAPTER 1

21 REASONS DEMOCRATS COULD LOSE

Here are 21 reasons AKA "excuses" the Democrats could lose the 2020 election.

Reason #1 - Bernie Sanders
Reason #2 - Elizabeth Warren
Reason #3 - The Electoral College
Reason #4 - AM Radio Talk Shows
Reason #5 - Radical Socialism and Welfare
Reason #6 - Open Borders
Reason #7 - Illegal Immigration
Reason #8 - Stockholm Syndrome Voters
Reason #9 - Gun Rights
Reason #10 - Misplaced American Pride
Reason #11 - Outspent
Reason #12 - Outflanked
Reason #13 - Out-Media-ed
Reason #14 - Racism and Racial Resentment
Reason #15 - Trump, the "Generous" Rebel Hero
Reason #16 - Republican Supported Third Parties
Reason #17 - The Economy
Reason #18 - Russian Assets, Hackers & Media Manipulators
Reason #19 - The Putin-Trump Partnership
Reason #20 - Voter Suppression
Reason #21 - Failure to Win A Majority of Independent Voters

These 21 challenges to a Democratic 2020 victory are covered in great detail in the companion to this book titled, *Why Trump Won The 2020 Election, 21 Reasons Democrats Lost*. That book is intended to be a shock-to-the-system-wake-up-call for the Democrats. Our Country needs the Democrats to win the White House, the Senate, and the House in 2020. That's why I spent over 3,000 hours researching and writing to reveal these challenges while developing *How Democrats Win 2020, 12 Steps To Victory*.

As I conducted research for the original manuscript, I was shocked to discover not one, not five, not ten, but over twenty federal crimes that can be alleged as having been committed by Trump. The evidence for these alleged crimes is abundant and publicly available. The statutes and the evidence for each alleged crime is detailed herein. You be the judge.

The Democrats have got to change their 2016 strategies and tactics for a new set of strategies and tactics in order to win in 2020. This book describes many that MUST be included in order to #DumpTrump.

CHAPTER 2

MESSAGING OPPORTUNITIES

The Democrats have made remarkable progress under the DNC leadership in many, many areas. True leaders will recognize their successes and ask themselves, "What were some of the missed messaging opportunities from the past that we could take some lessons from going forward?"

Naturally, we hold the good works by hard-working Democratic leadership in high regard, but even Oscar-winning stars and gold medal athletes want to know where they can improve. What follows is delivered in that spirit.

The Tweeter-In-Chief, his press and communications staff, Fox News, various right-wing internet feeds, and the extremely vast and influential neo-con AM radio talk show host network, all come together to form a formidable messaging echo-chamber that is hard to match. This vast and extremely effective Republican echo-chamber messaging apparatus is discussed in great detail in the companion book, *Why Trump Won The 2020 Election, 21 Reasons The Democrats Lost*, in Reason #13 – Outmedia-ed," and in "Reason #4 – AM Radio Talk Shows." It's no wonder that the Democratic messaging mantra has its work cut out to dominate the Republican messaging mantra echo chamber machine.

There are a number of past or current messaging challenges from which we might learn. One was the impeachment hearings.

The House impeachment of Donald J. Trump was one of the best examples of American patriotism and Constitutional governance.

First, it took an incredible amount of courage, wisdom, intelligence, and fortitude to take on the Trump messaging apparatus. One can only imagine what Trump would've done had he not been called up short while he was in the act of illegally impounding US funds for the purpose of, according to the Co-Director of the Institute of Judicial Administration at NYU School of Law Samuel Estreicher, bribing a foreign government to help him illegally, maliciously, and unethically attempt a falsely-based character assassination on his opponent, former Vice President Joseph Biden.

This author is not privy to the multitude of strategic decisions that had to be made when the impeachment trial was mounted. With the leadership's permission, I would like to examine an alternative scenario that I'm sure they considered and, for good reason, did not use. But for the sake of the reader, I would like to present the criminal statute approach. And please forgive the sarcastic remarks by my friend Frank whom I wanted to bring in for some color commentary, as it were. And because I can change the text of every book that comes out after I make a change to my Amazon-based digital manuscript, I promise to change the manuscript given any new information going forward.

I also want to say that the criminal statute approach to impeaching Donald Trump can always be taken up at any time, if not to constitutionally impeach Trump, but to further impeach his character.

During all the 24/7 coverage of the impeachment of Trump by the House of Representatives, the average citizen from Day One wanted to know just one thing, "what specific law did Trump break?"

During the weeks and weeks of the impeachment, the Democrats and their friendly media allies never *effectively* answered that question.

One option might have been to simply say, "We allege and have credible evidence that Donald Trump violated more than twenty (20) criminal codes."

The Federal statutes that we allege were violated include but are not limited to Title 52 USC 30121 (a)(2), which clearly states you cannot solicit anything of value for a U.S. election from a foreign national." This federal criminal statute is a law that Trump has allegedly violated at least three different times in a very public manner.

One, Trump allegedly admitted to violating Title 52 USC 30121 (a)(2) when he released a transcript of his July 25, 2019 call where he asked for a valuable political contribution, from a foreign national, Ukraine's President Zelensky, saying "do me a favor." He then asked the Ukrainian to announce a corruption investigation into Trump's leading 2020 election opponent, Vice President Joseph Biden. Two, when Trump gave a press conference on October 3, 2019, and asked China to investigate his political opponent, former Vice President Joseph Biden. Trump said, "China should start an investigation into the Bidens because what happened in China is just about as bad as what happened with Ukraine."[1]

And three, who can forget July 27, 2016, Trump asking Russia "if you're listening" to dig up emails on Hillary Clinton, his Presidential opponent? There appears to be nothing ambiguous about Trump's alleged breach multiple times of the Title 52 criminal code.

In fact, on October 19, 2019, the U.S. Government arrested two Ukrainians, Igor Fruman and Lev Parnas 10 for funneling "something of value," in this case foreign money from a foreign national, into a US election; and other charges, one of the statutes cited in the Department of Justice indictment was a violation of criminal code Title 52 USC 30121 (a) (2).

Title 52 USC 30121 (a)(2) is one of the serious go-to-jail laws that got Lev Parnas and Igor Fruman indicted and arrested. Both are on GPS ankle bracelets awaiting trial. Prosecutors expect convictions. A U.S. federal judge set an Oct. 5 trial date for Lev Parnas and Igor Fruman, two associates of President Donald Trump's personal lawyer Rudy Giuliani, setting the stage for more information to emerge about their

---

1. Peter Baker & Eileen Sullivan, "Trump Publicly Urges China to Investigate the Bidens," *The New York Times,* October 3, 2019, https://www.nytimes.com/2019/10/03/us/politics/trump-china-bidens.html

alleged campaign finance violations before November's presidential election.[2]

Where was the Democratic Information Machine when it came to informing the public of the laws Trump broke and the crimes Trump committed, allegedly? Was the Democratic communications team handicapped for some reason, such as not having sufficient or proper media resources, or Federal criminal code legal consulting services?

The American public kept asking what laws did Trump break? There is ample evidence that Trump may have broken more than twenty (20) laws. Yet, Trump went on Twitter and declared that he had broken no laws, and the average person on the street, it seems, currently believes that. Where was the DNC response to the question that was on everyone's mind? "What law did Trump break?"

The "DNC War Room" was always doing the best they could with the resources they had. To the outside world, the fact never fully sunk in that that the United States Government Accountability Office (GAO) declared that Trump had broken the law by violating the Impoundment Control Act, the illegal impoundment of U.S. appropriated funds by a President. Most Americans didn't read this headline in the January 16, 2020 New York Times, "Trump Administration Broke Law in Withholding Ukraine Aid."[3]

The "DNC War Room" probably did not have the information they would have needed to properly inform the public of the easily substantiated twenty-plus federal laws allegedly broken by Donald

---

2. Karen Freifeld & Jonathan Stempel, "Giuliani associates Parnas, Fruman face Oct. 5 trial, before U.S. election," *Yahoo! News,* February 3, 2020, https://news.yahoo.com/giuliani-associates-parnas-fruman-face-215000310.html
3. Emily Cochrane, Eric Lipton and Chris Cameron, "G.A.O. Report Says Trump Administration Broke Law in Withholding Ukraine Aid," *New York Times*, January 16, 2020, https://www.nytimes.com/2020/01/16/us/politics/gao-trump-ukraine.html

Trump. It's not the DNC's fault if no one had pulled in Federal criminal prosecutors to give them criminal statute advice.

<u>Summary List of Trump's 25 alleged Federal Crimes</u>

All of the following alleged crimes are supported by publicly available evidence.

For more than a summary of Trump's alleged crimes, go to "Chapter 3 - Trump's 25 Alleged Federal Crimes" for a description of the criminal codes and the evidence proving the alleged violations.

In that section, you will find, for example, a leading law professor at NYU Law School who lays out the case that, in his opinion, Trump violated Title 18 USC 201, the federal criminal statute on bribery. He describes the criminal code criteria, the evidence, and the associated case law, which demonstrates beyond any legal doubt in his mind that Trump violated the federal criminal code on bribery.

25 Criminal Codes Allegedly Violated by Trump

#1: Title 52 USC 30121 (a) (2), Solicitating a foreign national to contribute to a US election violates the FEC Act of 1974.

#2: Title X - Impoundment Control Act of 1974. Illegal impoundment of US funds.

#3. Title 18 USC 872, Extortion. Trump withheld $371 million in aid and a White House meeting to extort "a favor."

#4. Title 18 USC 201, Bribery, offering U.S. official acts (money and meetings) in exchange for attacking a political foe.

#5. Title 18 USC 1503, Obstruction of Justice. Trump ordered all US Government employees to ignore subpoenas.

#6. Title 18 USC 1505 - Obstruction of Congress. Refused to provide subpoenaed witnesses and documents.

#7. **Title 18 USC 2381 – Treason:** Aid /Comfort to an Enemy, Russia. At Helsinki 7/16/18. At White House on 5/3/19 and 7/25/19.

#8. Article I, Section 9, Clause 8 U.S. Constitution: **Emoluments Clause.** Millions received from foreign governments going into his business.

#9. Title 18 U.S. Code § 2101. Incite to violence. Trump incites devotee to threaten murder against whistleblower attorney.

Four Whistleblower Laws: Thanks to attorney David K. Colapinto https://www.kkc.com. More info on Colapinto and the Nat'l Whistleblower Center in "Chapter 3 - Trump's 25 Alleged Federal Crimes."

#10. The Inspector General Act of 1978– Section 7 (a), (b), and (c): Violated by revealing confidential whistleblower information.

#11. Title 5 USC §552a. - The Privacy Act of 1974: Violated by revealing confidential whistleblower information taken from a secret US government form.

#12. Title 50 USC §3234 - Prohibited Personnel Practices In The Intelligence Community. Violated his Executive intel duties.

#13. Title 18 U.S. Code § 1513. Retaliating Against A Witness, Victim, or An Informant. Vicious verbal attacks /tweets.

More alleged crimes:

#14. Vicarious Liability under Common Law. Asking Russia to interfere in the US election on July 27, 2016, and they did.

#15. Title 18 U.S.C. § 1001 (a) (1) (2) (3)– Making False Statements. In the hundreds. Some very egregious.

#16. Title 18 U.S. Code § 1512 - Witness Intimidation

#17. Title 2 U.S. Code § 192, "Refusal To Produce Documents

#18. Title 44 U.S.C. §§ 2201–2207, The Presidential Records Act- Destruction

#19. 18 U.S. Code Chapter 31 - Embezzlement and Theft - Derivative of violating the Impoundment Control Act (ICA).

#20. 18 U.S. Code § 641 - Converting Public Money for Personal Gain is a derivative crime when the ICA was violated.

#21. 18 U.S. Code § 648 - Custodian Misusing Public Funds was a derivative crime when violating the ICA.

#22. Title 38 U.S. Code § 6101 - Misappropriation by Fiduciaries was a derivative crime when violating the ICA.

#23. 10 U.S. Code § 921 - Art. 121. Larceny and Wrongful Appropriation was a derivative crime when violating the ICA.

#24. 18 U.S. Code § 666 - Theft or Bribery Concerning Programs was a derivative crime when violating the ICA.

#25. Title 18 U.S. Code § 912. Impersonating the Census Department / a Census Officer in a fraudulent Facebook ad.

The above 25 crimes are easily substantiated and easily alleged.

All of the above alleged criminal violations are described in much greater detail in "Chapter 3 - Trump's 25 Alleged Federal Crimes."

In "Trump's 25 Alleged Federal Crimes" you will find descriptions of the specific criminal codes and URL links to evidence.

Dear readers and former federal prosecutors: Please contact me with more criminal code violations and more evidence of the violations listed. Your contribution could appear in version 2.0 of this book with credit to you unless you wish anonymity. Attorneys and federal prosecutors are invited to be co-authors on a separate book on this topic, *Trump's Alleged Federal Crimes: The Statutes and Evidence*. Contact DrDavidKingKeller@gmail.com

34 DNC Communication Opportunities:

1. Mueller Report: Much damning evidence went unused. Mueller's report "indicted, convicted or gotten guilty pleas from 34 people and three companies, including top advisers to President Trump, Russian spies, and hackers with ties to the Kremlin."[4]

> Yet, many Americans believe the Mueller investigation "exonerated Trump" and was a waste of taxpayer money. Who allowed that perception? The DNC convicted or gotten guilty pleas from 34 people and three companies, including top advisers to President Donald Trump, Russian spies, and hackers with ties

---

4. Ryan Teague Beckwith, "Here Are All of the Indictments, Guilty Pleas and Convictions From Robert Mueller's Investigation," *Time*, November 15, 2019, https://time.com/5556331/mueller-investigation-indictments-guilty-pleas/

to the Kremlin. The charges range from interfering with the 2016 election and hacking emails to lying to investigators and tampering with witnesses.

Time article, published on March 22, 2019, titled, "Here Are All of the Indictments, Guilty Pleas and Convictions From Robert Mueller's Investigation," outlines details.[5]

Mueller's team exposed at least 140 contacts between the Kremlin and the Trump team, netted 199 criminal charges, 37 indictments or guilty pleas, and five prison sentences.[6]

The indictments named two shell companies and 13 Russian nationals, including Yevgeniy Prigozhin, who is nicknamed "Putin's chef" and 12 Russian military intelligence officers.

On March 16, 2020, the Trump administration took advantage of the "six headlines strategy."

The "six headlines strategy" is a technique to bury a story you want as few of the public to hear about as possible.

You incorporate this strategy when there are numerous other competing headlines created by other circumstances, or you, yourself, create them as a method to bury your super-negative story. This technique will push your story on to the back pages or not get covered at all. When incorporating this art of diversion, you either create the competing headlines, or you wait till they occur, and then you release the "news" that you don't want to be covered. In cases where you are caught off guard with some negative news, you create the competing headlines

---

5. Ryan Beckwith, "Here Are All of the Indictments, Guilty and Convictions From Robert Mueller's Investigation," *Time,* November 15, 2019, https://time.com/5556331/mueller-investigation-indictments-guilty-pleas/
6. Tom Steyer, "Democratic leaders, stop dragging your feet and impeach Trump now," *NBC News,* September 12, 2019, https://www.nbcnews.com/think/opinion/democratic-leaders-stop-dragging-your-feet-impeach-trump-now-ncna1052171?cid=public-rss_20190912

with stories that you had "sitting on the shelf" for moments like this. Or you scramble to quickly create a diversion so great that your negative news doesn't get the air time or print space that it normally would have.

Using a version of the six-headlines strategy to "bury" a story, on

On March 16, 2020, The charges against Concord Management and Consulting are dismissed with prejudice.

> "With jury selection set to begin in just over two weeks, prosecutors asked a federal judge to permanently dismiss the charges special counsel Robert Mueller brought two years ago against two Russian firms linked to a St. Petersburg businessman known as Putin's chef, Yevgeny Prigozhin."[7]

March 16, 2020, the DOJ dropped its 2016 election interference case against Oleg Deripaska, "Putin's Chef." The case was dropped less than 30 days before Yevgeniy Prigozhin's trial was to begin, on April 6, 2019. It was dropped in the media version of the "dead of night," in an after-hours filing on a Friday pushing the news onto the more limited weekend news teams who were struggling to keep up with hundreds of other developments. The announcement came during the height of the multiple headlines being written and aired about the coronavirus pandemic. There were many more than six headlines about all of the deaths, and global economic havoc. The announcement occurred at the same time as the headline-grabbing news of the worst US stock market

---

7. Gerstein, Josh *"Justice Department drops plans for trial over Russian interference in 2016 U.S. election,"* *Politico,* March 16, 2020, https://www.politico.com/news/2020/03/16/russia-election-justice-department-132875

drop in history. All of these headlines effectively "buried" coverage of this potentially treasonous news. In this morass of competing headlines, the Trump DOJ dropped all charges against Putin's Chef and his companies for interfering in the 2016 election. Why? Incredulously, the DOJ said one reason was, "Prosecutors also cited the failure of the company, Concord Management and Consulting, to comply with trial subpoenas and the submission of a 'misleading, at best' affidavit by Yevgeniy Prigozhin, a co-defendant and the company's founder. Prigozhin is a catering magnate and military contractor known as "Putin's chef" because of his ties to Russian President Vladimir Putin." An uncooperative defendant. Well, that's so unfair the prosecutors had no choice but to drop their case, right? It wasn't by any chance related to the fact the trial hearings, which would be detailing Russia helping Trump get elected in 2016, would coincide with Trump's 2020 bid for re-election, would it?[8]

A day after this incredible and highly suspicious development, I heard nothing from the DNC, but I may have missed it. I'm on multiple DNC text, and email feeds. Yet, I did get my daily donation request via text from the DNC.

2. TCJA tax theft by Trump. The largest theft of Treasury in U.S. history. Where are the billboards in the swing states? Where is the dedicated Democratic website link on this issue?

See Cartoons in "Chapter 6" on this TCJA tax heist and descriptions of the damage to the average American in *Appendices 5, 6, 7, and 10.* There are 22 references to the disastrous TCJA in the companion book,

---

8. Spencer S. Hsu, "Justice Dept. Abandons prosecution of Russian firm indicted in Mueller election interference probe," *The Washington Post*, March 16, 2020. https://www.washingtonpost.com/local/legal-issues/us-justice-dept-abandons-prosecution-of-russian-firm-indicted-in-mueller-election-interference-probe/2020/03/16/5f7c3fd6-64a9-11ea-912d-d98032ec8e25_story.html

Why Trump Won The 2020 Election, 21 Reasons The Democrats Lost, along with a scathing denunciation by US Senator Bernie Sanders.

3. Is Trump a Russian asset: unexplored, unexplained, and unexploited. Where is the Dem website on this issue?

See "Reason #19 – The Russia-Trump Partnership" in *Why Trump Won The 2020 Election, 21 Reasons Democrats Lost*. See Russian elements discussed in Trump's alleged federal crime of treason in "Chapter 3- Trump's 25 Alleged Federal Crimes. "

1. Tariffs damaging farmers, consumers, and taxpayers not being fully highlighted. Why is this not featured on the Dem website?

   The ill-conceived Chinese tariffs damaged Americans. To mention just two examples: farmers with lost income and American taxpayers saddled with a $12 Billion (yep, that's a "B") bailout to the farmers when Trump gave farmers Billions in taxpayer dollars in bailout money.[9]

   Tariffs to cost average American household $2,000! WTF! Where was (is) the 24-hour outrage by the DNC? Where were the texts? The blogs? The press conferences? The sandwich boards in front of the White House? When the average American doesn't have $500 in savings, $2,000 is a crushing blow.[10] [11]

---

9. Jacqueline Alemany, Jennifer Janisch, and Katiana Krawchenko "Trump administration announces $12 billion "bailout" for farmers hit by tariffs," *CBS News*, July 24, 2018, https://www.cbsnews.com/news/trump-administration-to-announce-12-billion-in-aid-to-farmers-affected-by-tariffs/

10. Aarthi Swaminathan, "Trump tariffs are set to cost U.S. households $2,000 in 2020, research group finds," *Yahoo! Finance*, September 7, 2019, https://finance.yahoo.com/news/trump-tariffs-cost-2020-research-151755274.html

11. Kathryn Vasel, "6 in 10 Americans don't have $500 in savings," *CNN*, January 12, 2017, https://money.cnn.com/2017/01/12/pf/americans-lack-of-savings/index.html

2. Dems are not currently providing key messaging visuals. Where are the visual props on the DNC website that would quickly and effectively tell the story of Trump's travesties? Some examples follow.

3. Where is the digital counter counting all the Trump lies? Where is the Dem website on this?

4. Where is the digital counter on the Dems website counting all the Trump- Russian connections as they were discovered and made public? Each connection listed is hyperlinked to a URL providing all the details.

5. Where is the continually changing digital display that shows all the money Trump is making at his hotels and his golf resorts while U.S. taxpayer money is used to wine and dine international visitors at these Trump properties?

6. Where is the digital display counting U.S. tax dollars spent on Trump's golfing … now headed to exceed $250 million? (¼ $Billion)?[12]

7. Where is the daily Smithsonian-based "life expectancy of certain species" clock ticking backward given unchecked climate change?[13]

8. Where is "The Best of" lists and links on the DNC website? Where is Best Music Video featuring Ron Zimmerman and his

---

12. Justin Rohrlich, "Trump golf cart rentals have now cost US taxpayers more than half a million dollars," *QZ.com*, November 21, 2019, https://qz.com/1753518/trump-golf-cart-rentals-have-now-cost-us-taxpayers-550000/
13. Sarah Zielinski, "Climate Change Will Accelerate Earth's Sixth Mass Extinction," *Smithsonian Magazine*," April 30, 2015, https://www.smithsonianmag.com/science-nature/climate-change-will-accelerate-earths-sixth-mass-extinction-180955138/

brilliant, "The Liar Tweets Tonight" sung to the tune of "The Lion Sleeps Tonight?"[14]

9. Where is YouTube singing Founders music video, "The Day Democracy Died," sung to the tune of the "The Day The Music Died."[15] It's an excellent musical condemnation of Trump.

10. Where's "Today's Best Political Cartoon?" on the DNC website?" Vote for your "Best Cartoon of the Week."

11. Where's "Best Tweet"? Like the parody of Trump's disinfectant statements mouthed and acted beautifully.[16]

12. Where's "Best News Clip," (Rachel Maddow, Anderson Cooper, Morning Joe, etc.), "BEST SNL Clips," "Best Late Night Comic jokes." Stephen Colbert, Jimmy Fallon, Jimmy Kimmel, Trevor Noah, John Oliver, Bill and would love to provide the support. Etc.?

Where are the best quotes and soundbites from the Trump administration? Like Stephen Miller, senior advisor for policy to President Donald Trump, advocating a student smoking lounge on Duke University campus in 2006.[17]

13. Dear DNC Website: Please, Engage! Entertain! Drive millions to your DNC website who would not have otherwise ever gone there.

53 million people go to the New York Times website. How many million people a week would be clicking on the DNC website for a few laughs. From late night comics. From humorous political

---

14. YouTube, https://www.youtube.com/watch?v=TkU1ob_lHCw
15. YouTube, https://www.youtube.com/watch?v=-Ue5F57dZMU
16. Twitter, https://twitter.com/sarahcpr/status/1253474772702429189
17. Stephen Miller, "Making Duke perfect: Part II," October 23, 2006, *Duke Chronicle*, https://www.dukechronicle.com/article/2006/10/making-duke-perfect-part-ii

cartoons. Short stand-up comic clips. I know I would be clicking on DNC every day for 3 new laughs a day. Second only to my email feed. Far more often than I would the NYTimes.com. Please give us a chance for some daily political humor. How many would linger and visit other pages on the DNC website once there? How many would donate? How many would volunteer?

14. Failure to learn from Trump that 2-word memes work. Duh!

Two-word meme's work. Lyin' Ted. Crooked Hillary. They become earworms that stick and can help lay to waste the victim of the meme. So, where were the Dems two-word memes for Trump? Don-the-Con. Traitor Trump. Lyin' Don. Criminal Don. Stealin' Don. Putin's Puppet. Toxic Trump. Social Security Killer Trump. This last four-word meme might help deliver Florida, and squeaky tight swing states. People over 65 vote.

Using memes in a very focused multi-media campaign could make Florida blue in 2020 for under $40 million. Ten PACs each contribute $10 million. See my private memo for details.

Come on Dems. Let's learn from Don-the-Con, the pro of demonization? People vote their pocketbook first. There were about 75 million Americans over 65 in 2020.[18] "Social Security Killer Trump" would get their attention.

75 million. That's a lot of people dependent on Social Security. How many of them would have voted for "Trump-the-Social-Security-Killer"? Trump and Republicans want to reduce Social Security to pay for tax cuts for the wealthy. See the companion book, *Why Trump Won The 2020 Election 21 Reasons The Democrats Lost,* for details on the Trump-Republican attacks on

---

18. PopulationPyramid.net, "United States of America Population Pyramid," *PopulationPyramid.net*, December 2019,
,https://www.populationpyramid.net/united-states-of-america/2020/

Social Security. In that book you will excerpts like, "in Trump's latest budget, he cuts trillions of dollars from Medicare, Social Security, education, and more."[19]

15. Where is the swamp bulletin board placing swamp monsters into the DC swamp image with every swamp monster action? For example, the EPA appointee is a lobbyist for the fossil fuel industry, and an executive order dismantling Wall Street oversight, etc.[20]

16. Why are the four swing states of Florida, Wisconsin, Michigan, and Pennsylvania being administered by hard-working, but poorly paid State Directors and unpaid city and county Democratic leaders having to work almost full time as free volunteers? Dems spent nearly a billion dollars in 2016 and lost. Where is the money for day-to-day Dem infrastructure following that bitter lesson in these four must-win states?

17. Where is the "Trump's Travesties" website or its tab on the DNC website?

18. Where is the daily drumbeat about the corporations that have paid no taxes; and the visuals of potholes caused by their 18-wheelers but repaired using our hard-earned tax dollars, not theirs.

19. Where is the photo of 48,000 people who worked all year, so their hard-earned Federal tax dollars could be used to give Jeff Bezos' Amazon a $129 million tax refund on his $10 Billion profit? A football stadium full of 48,000 people can provide one example

---

19. Ron Bieber, "Opinion: Trump's tax cuts benefit top 1%, hurt working class," *Detroit News*, December 10, 2019,
https://www.detroitnews.com/story/opinion/columnists/labor-voices/2019/12/11/opinion-trump-tax-cuts-benefit-one-percent-hurt-working-class/2631031001/
20. Marik V. Rennenkampff, "Trump is flooding the swamp that Obama drained," *The Hill*, February 4, 2020, https://thehill.com/opinion/white-house/481407-trump-is-flooding-the-swamp-that-obama-drained

of the number of economic slaves created by TCJA. There's your photo. Hello? See *Appendices 5, 6, 7, and 10* for stats and reference sources.

20. Where is the link to the YouTube video of President Jimmy Carter stating, Trump is an illegitimate President put in office by Russia?[21] Why isn't that YouTube link on the Dem website? After all, Jimmy Carter is a living past-President. Carter is respected by the key demographic of evangelicals. Carter is highly regarded by most Americans who know about his Habitat For Humanity.

21. Where is the "legitimate" Democratic shadow government complete with "Cabinet-level advisors" commenting every day for the media on Trump administration errors?

22. Where is the roll of paper, hanging out of a building's 10th-floor window dropping all the way to the ground, listing Trump's Russian connections? That would have been a visual meme. A visual "earworm." Once seen, never forgotten.

23. Where is the 20-story high roll of paper hanging out of an office building's 20th-floor window listing Trump's lies? Once seen, never forgotten.

24. Where is the daily tweet asking, "where's the promised Mexico money to build the wall?" Where is the Dem website page on this? Where were the multiple video clips showing Trump's multiple promises to get money for a border wall from Mexico contrasted with multiple video clips of Trump shutting down the US Government demanding taxpayer dollars in the budget for the wall, and Trump demanding money from US military budget for

---

21. NBC News, "Jimmy Carter Suggests Trump Is Illegitimate President Because Of Russian Interference," *NBC News*, June 28, 2019, https://youtu.be/oHB3xRj47bY

the border wall? Jon Stewart's team could have put this together in an afternoon.

25. Where is the digital clock listing the days since Trump said Mexico would build the wall? Or, the Live YouTube feed of the clicking "Wall" clock under "Two-Faced Liar Trump" who shut Government down demanding U.S. taxpayers pay for the Wall?

26. Where is the LIST of legislation on key issues vital to American life being passed by the House, but blocked by Moscow Mitch and the Republican extreme radical Socialists, e.g., bi-partisan HR-8 firearm safety bill? Where's the Times Square billboard listing the number of bills to help Americans but blocked by nuclear and Senate Republicans?

27. Where is the fast-moving digital counter listing the U.S. Treasury dollars per minute given by the extreme radical Republican Socialists to their elite, rich friends? About $268 Billion per year equals $509,893 per minute or $8,498 per second. A fast-moving digital counter tells the story! See *Appendices 6 and 7* for more details and reference sources.

28. Where is the fast-moving digital counter that lists how many minutes a day, the average American is working, so their Federal tax dollars can be given to the rich corporations who pay no taxes and get refunds? 51.6 minutes of every hour worked goes to benefit the rich elite under Trump's new tax heist legislation. See *Appendices 5, 6, 7 and 10* for more details on this.

29. Where is the fast-moving digital counter that listed how many days a year average Americans worked so that $4.3 Billion of their Federal tax dollars could be given as TAX REFUNDS to 55 Corporations that made over $79 Billion in profits? See Appendix 5a, 5b, and 5c for a list of those 55 corporations. 589 million workdays a year are worked by average Americans to pay that $4.3 Billion in 2018 TAX REFUNDS to those super-rich

corporations and to the richest man on the planet, Jeff Bezos' company, Amazon. (Multiple reference sources follow.)

To repeat, those Corps made $79 B in profits in 2018. References: U.S. Median income = $36,000; Federal tax on $36,000 = $2,662. So, $4.3 Billion tax refund in 1 yr. / $2,662 per year in Fed Taxes paid in = 1,615,000 years. 1,615,000 years x $2,662 = $4.3B. Or, you could say 1,615,000 taxpayers worked all year to pay in their $2,262 in taxes so that their $4.3 Billion in taxes could be given as a cashback refund to those 55 super-profitable corporations who paid no taxes. Or, you could say 1, 615,000 taxpayers worked 5 days a week x 50 weeks = 250 days x 1,615,000 people = 403 million days worked to pay that $4.3 Billion in taxes so that 100% of their tax dollars could be given as a cashback tax refund to those 55 corporations who make Billions in profit and pay ZERO taxes.[22] [23]

Per CBS News,

> …60 profitable Fortune 500 companies paid no taxes on a total of $79 billion of profits earned in 2018…these corporations received a net tax rebate of $4.3 billion. The analysis is based on the corporations' annual financial reports, which were filed earlier this year to report their 2018 results.[24]

30. Where is TrumpsTravesties.com listing all of the devastation wrought by Trump cross-referenced by topic and by date with a proof source cited?

---

22.   Wikipedia,   "Median   income,"   *Wikipedia*,   June   12,2020, https://en.wikipedia.org/wiki/Median_income

23. Smart Asset, Federal Income Tax Calculator," *Smart Asset*, Retrieved June 16, 2020, https://smartasset.com/taxes/income-taxes#bAETUfiszP

24. Megan Cerullo, "60 of America's biggest companies paid no federal income tax in 2018," *CBS News*, April 12, 2019, https://www.cbsnews.com/news/2018-taxes-some-of-americas-biggest-companies-paid-little-to-no-federal-income-tax-last-year/

Gutting environmental protection laws. Putting CEO of fossil fuel company in charge of EPA. Quitting Paris Climate Agreement. Putting the swamp monsters in charge of various administrative agencies. Putting a person with ZERO experience in intel in charge of the entire US intel network, etc.

Thousands of politicians and journalists need a Wikipedia of Trump's atrocities7. Give it to them, DNC! With tons of references.

31. Where are the TOP TEN Dem responses to the TOP TEN reasons why people say they are voting for Trump?

    Americans all over the Country need their cocktail hour of sound bites to compete with the well-rehearsed Trump-lover mantras.

    See *Appendix 8* in the companion book, *Why Trump Won The 2020 Election, 21 Reasons The Democrats Lost,* for 150 reasons eight people love Trump. These are real average Americans from around the Country who sought a part-time $15 an hour Internet research job.

32. Where is the non-existent rapid response team to refute all the lies being put forth on A.M. radio talk shows? Why weren't 100 volunteers in each State given multiple burner phones to call the lying con-serving talk show hosts like Mark Levin who make bizarre blanket statements such as, "The Democrats hate America and they hate the Constitution." What?! Three people need to immediately call in and say,

    > Wait a minute. I'm a proud Democrat, and I love America, and I love the Constitution, and so do all of my Democratic friends. I think some of what you say is valuable, and I support many of your sponsors, so please don't devalue those good statements with statements that are provably false. Thank you and God Bless America,

and God bless the American Flag and all our Veterans who have sacrificed so much for all of us.

33. The classic neo-con AM radio talk show's typical lie in September 2019, and October 2019 is that the Democratic impeachment meetings excluded all Republicans and that Republicans were given no access to the witnesses or the documents. Total lies. As USA Today pointed out that there were 47 Republicans in attendance to those hearings, and they were allowed to ask questions of witnesses and view all documents.[25] But the fact that round one of the impeachment investigation interviews were fully open to Republican attendance and participation was not what average Americans trying to get a little news from their local AM talk radio were told. Where was the immediate response to counter those lies by another caller in the area? It would be so easy to set up a website for volunteers and have Soros, or Steyer, or Bloomberg, or you chip in some small change to subsidize burner phones from Wal-Mart. You need a phone that's not your personal phone because the phone numbers are grabbed by the station and sold and spammed. At least mine was. (I made one call providing an alternative view and got 10 spam calls later that day, and ongoing spam calls to the point I had to purchase a special spam filter from my phone company. Maybe they only "spam" callers they don't like. I don't know.)

34. Where is the Democratic Information Machine?.

The Democratic Messaging Machine needs more support. More funds. More staff. Where is the Democrat's mirror image of all the press support the President has at his disposal?

---

25. Nicholas Wu, "Republicans say Trump impeachment probe is happening in 'secret,' but 47 GOP lawmakers have access," *USA TODAY*, October 24, 2019, https://www.usatoday.com/story/news/politics/2019/10/24/trump-impeachment-gop-lawmakers-who-have-access-inquiry/4083246002

In 2019 and in 2020, during the impeachment hearings, Democrats Dems relied virtually 90% of the time on Nancy Pelosi and to a much lesser degree on Chuck Schumer for their primary announcements. Also Adam Schiff, and few cameos by oothers. Where was the daily appearance of the Dem version of Kellyanne Conway, Sarah Sanders, and Kayleigh McEnany? It's not fair to ask Xochitl Hinojosa, the DNC Comm Director, to compete with half a dozen Trump press staffers. Give the voracious 24/7 news networks more people with various personalities to interact with just like Trump does.

Both Parties have their two leaders in Congress. But on top of their Congressional mouthpieces, the Republican communication machine had Trump, Conway, and Harvard Law grad Kayleigh McEnany, along with Deputy Press Directors who were always all over the media. Where are the Democratic counterparts?

The Republicans know that the media likes multiple voices from multiple personalities.

How hard would it be to hire a Democratic version of Kellyanne Conway and Kayleigh McEnany? The media would have loved it. Dueling Communication Directors. What could be better? Dueling Press Secretaries would be great sound bite material for any news director. And a LOT MORE press for the Democratic message.

Are the Republicans playing at the NFL pro-level to the Dems high school JV?

35. Did Democrats flub the Mueller investigation communication?

"Totally exonerated," is the message many Americans got from the Mueller investigation.

The take-away soundbite is so bad that Keller Research Institute surveys reported people out in the public were saying what many in the media were also saying, "The Mueller report completely exonerated President Trump."

My question to fellow Dems. Seriously? Tis that the message we want the public to receive on the Mueller Report?

The Democrats and the fans of Rachel Maddow were so convinced of a full-on collusion conviction of Trump by the Mueller team that the Democratic communication machine seemed to have sat on their hands, messaging-wise. Which seemed to make sense, right? Why spoil the punch line? All the while Mueller was spoon-feeding conviction after conviction of Trump's associates and Russian Government officers who helped elect Trump. Mueller went so far as to blatantly describe Trump as "Co-Conspirator #1," more than once, whom everybody knew meant Donald J. Trump.

But instead of messaging out and billboarding all of these convictions as they came out as absolute proof of an obvious connection between the 2016 Trump For President campaign and Russian interference, and obstruction of justice, everyone seemed to be waiting for the "collusion" shoe to drop, the smoking gun in the final report.

The Mueller Report, officially titled, "Report on the Investigation into Russian Interference in the 2016 Presidential Election," was completed and released to Mueller's ultimate boss for this role, the Attorney General William P. Barr.

Trump's fingerprints on the collusion "smoking gun" didn't come on March 22, 2019, when Special Investigator Robert Mueller gave his final report to Attorney General William Barr, nor on April 18, 2019, when the report was released, heavily redacted, to the public.

Mueller to the rescue.

Mueller had to connect the dots for the botched Democratic messaging with two public statements. In the first instance, Mueller said, in essence, if we had evidence of the President's innocence, we would have said so.

 Wow! Anybody beyond high school knows what that means.

Specifically, as reported in the Washington Post on May 29, 2019, Mueller's statement, annotated: 'If we had had confidence that the president clearly did not commit a crime, we would have said so.'[26]

And, in the second instance, on May 29, 2019, Mueller stated, in essence, the reason our DOJ special investigative commission did not indict Donald Trump for obstruction of justice is that the Department of Justice has a policy of not indicting a sitting President, that would be the duty of Congress. Wow, again! Mueller, who had been FBI Director for thirteen years, just said, but for a DOJ Office of Legal Counsel guideline opinion, the President would have been criminally indicted!

Hello! DNC communication machine, where were you? Where was the headline, "Trump might be in jail right now, except for a DOJ opinion memo?"

By then, for nearly half the Country it seems, it was basically too late. The "witch hunt" mantra won the day, and all those who wanted to love President Trump found comfort and proof within the messaging that initially came out when the Mueller Report was released to the DOJ' AG, the Trump-appointed AG Barr.

Now the Democrats with considerable help from Mueller's public statements are playing catch-up.

---

26. Amber Phillips, "Mueller's statement annotated: 'If we had had confidence that the president clearly did not commit a crime, we would have said so'," *Washington Post,* May 29, 2019, https://www.washingtonpost.com/politics/2019/05/29/muellers-statement-annotated-if-we-had-confidence-that-president-clearly-did-not-commit-crime-we-would-have-said-so/

36. TCJA, The Largest Theft of U.S. Treasury Funds In American History, Virtually Ignored Media-Wise.

It was a daylight robbery in full view of all the cameras.

A group of people, Republicans, who had third world-like dictator control of the United States legislative branch and the executive branch in 2017 (having a Republican President and a Republican voting majority in both the Senate and the House) planned a $2.6 Trillion heist of the U.S. Treasury.

Without any regard for the devastating bankruptcy-tilting fiscal impact of "stealing" $2.6 Trillion from the U.S. Treasury Credit Card, the Republican Congressional majority, on a solely partisan vote, passed TCJA.

Now, we will have to borrow even more from China. This makes China stronger and the U.S. weaker.

The Republicans have abandoned their fiscal conservative image and shown themselves to be radical socialists providing government welfare for the rich saying to the average taxpayer, "let'em eat cake."

This was basically done in the dark of night, examination-wise.

The standard procedure when Congress contemplates a change in tax law is that it must first go to the Joint Committee on Taxation (JCT) for an independent review on the impact of the changes being considered.

The TCJA tax heist is taxation without representation.

Every citizen will bear the burden for generations.

JCT was not given time to conduct their analysis.

More precisely, the Republican socialists, knowing what they were doing, was fiscal suicide in the long run, did not want to wait for the JCT to weigh in.

So, they rushed through the new tax law in record time, just 51 days. The last major tax restructure in 1986 was done over a 324-day period. The tax structure, the 1040 filing form, and other fundamental tax issues had remained unchanged for 31 years. Now in the governmental equivalent of a "blink of an eye," it is changed with Senator Bernie Sanders publicly stating that the bill was being changed by lobbyists at the same time it was coming up for a vote. Here is a link to the video of that statement courtesy of RealClear Politics on December 1, 2017, as part of an article by Tim Haines:[27]

Trump signed the tax bill on the same day the Joint Committee on Taxation (JCT) analysis came out. That JCT report proved all the hype about tax cuts for the middle class and thousands of new jobs with each worker receiving a $4,000 a year pay increase was smoke and mirrors behind the largest criminal theft of US treasury funds in US history.[28]

The Trump Socialist Republican-Government-welfare-for-the-rich-Party may have justified their multi-trillion-dollar withdrawal on the United States Treasury credit card, in part, on the gratitude they expected to receive from the wealthy beneficiaries. It was a simple calculation for Republicans to know that those elite beneficiaries might show their appreciation by giving a percentage of that money back in the form of a campaign contribution to reward those that gave them their newfound money. Call it a tip, a gratuity. In the criminal world, it's called a VIG. The Republicans who perpetrated this Treasury heist stand to receive billions in "campaign" donations, much less than a 10% tip, which would amount to about $28 Billion. Remember where the

---

27. Tim Haines, "Sanders: This Tax Bill Will Be Remembered As One Of The Greatest Robberies In American History," *RealClear Politics*, December 1, 2017, https://www.realclearpolitics.com/video/2017/12/01/sanders_this_tax_bill_will_be_r emembered_as_one_of_the_great_robberies_in_history.html

28. Galen Hendricks & Seth Hanlon, "The TCJA 2 Years Later: Corporations, Not Workers, Are the Big Winners," *Center For American Progress,* December 19, 2019, https://www.americanprogress.org/issues/economy/news/2019/12/19/478924/tcja-2-years-later-corporations-not-workers-big-winners/

Socialist Republicans got this money, they used our good faith and credit to borrow it from the Bank of China. Now, we, the citizens who actually pay taxes, have to pay off that credit card debt. See *Appendices 5, 6, 7, and 10* for the data sources on the enormous TCJA benefits received by corporations and wealthy Americans, and the enormous burden TCJA placed on the average American.

After TCJA, there's no such thing as a "conservative" Republican, only fiscally irresponsible socialists providing government welfare for the rich, creating a national debt disaster. "Conservative" is a public relations scam that the asleep-at-the-switch Democrats let them get away with. Where was the Democratic press conference officially removing the term "conservative" from any and all Republicans?

Had we been attacked by a foreign country or invaded by aliens from outer space, the Socialist Republicans may have had an excuse to tap our credit for trillions. Instead, they gave hard-earned tax dollars not to the poor and struggling middle class but to those who have the least need for government largesse, the wealthiest of the wealthy. See *Appendices 5a, 5b, and 5c* for a list of 55 corporations who made over $100 Million in net profit and paid zero taxes on their $79 Billion in total net profits.

These rich folks will simply add a 2nd yacht next to their 4th home. Forty-eight thousand working women and men spent part of their 2018 workweek paying Federal taxes so that the Trump-Republican Socialist Party Dedicated to the Rich could give $129 million in tax refunds to Jeff Bezos. Bezos, the richest man on the planet, and his Corporation made $10 Billion in net profit, paid no taxes and received a $129 million tax refund. See *Appendix 12* for reference sources on these statistics.

This Republican Socialist government welfare for the rich is far more expensive and infinitely more perverse than any welfare program for the poor, disabled, and unemployed ever offered by the Democrats.

Remember, poor people spend 99.9% of their available funds on goods and services, which grows the GDP. What do you think the richest man on the planet is going to do with his extra $129 Million? You can bet Jeff Bezos won't be buying goods at Wal-Mart, helping to employ people there.

However, the TCJA tax heist was smart, in an evil kind of way, if POWER through money is your primary motivation. Now, all those corporations and elite rich all have their hands dirty by accepting all that "free" credit card Bank of China loan money stolen from the U.S. Treasury. Well played, Machiavelli!

Taxpayers for Common Sense, a non-profit that works to ensure that taxpayer dollars are spent responsibly, and that government operates within its means referred to the 2017 Republican Congressional handling of taxpayer dollars as "the Art of The Steal from future generations."[29]

Where was a similar message from the Democrats about Republicans using TCJA to steal our tax dollars? Where was the presentation of the damaging TCJA facts on the DNC website? Nowhere.

37. Iowa. Need I say more? How embarrassing to watch the DNC make their great comeback after waiting three years since Trump's inauguration only to demonstrate an inability to master third-grade level math. The caucus was on February 3, 2020, the final count, after recounts, came on February 27, 2020. 24 days! The Republicans had their results the night of February 3. 2020. America was watching and judging which Party had the skills to run the US Government. As to the amount of energy and money spent in Iowa, the Reid J. Epstein New York times April 9, 2020

---

29. Taxpayer Staff, "#BBA2019 – The Art of the Steal, from future generations," *Taxpayer.net*, July 23, 2019, https://www.taxpayer.net/budget-appropriations-tax/art-of-the-steal-from-future-generations/

article headline sums it up, "Iowa Was Meaningless."[30] How do we avoid another "Iowa"?

38. Was The Impeachment Messaging Botched?

With all due respect to the American patriots that sought to prosecute the impeachment of Donald J. Trump, their central tactic was flawed. The House impeachment prosecutors did not present what might have been a successful case.

The best message that the House impeachment prosecutors could come up with when they summarized their case against President Donald Trump was that, "He tried to cheat on the election, and he'll probably try to cheat again."

Specifically, United States Representative Hakeem Jeffries (New York -D), House Impeachment Manager, provided this summary of the impeachment case on the floor of the Senate, "The president tried to cheat. He got caught."[31]

Upon hearing that, my friend Frank said to me, "Are you kidding me?"

Donald Trump allegedly committed over twenty federal crimes with extensive publicly available evidence that could have been used to substantiate those crimes.

These twenty-plus federal crimes are clearly described in this book in "Chapter 3 - Trump's 25 Alleged Federal Crimes."

---

30. Reid J. Epstein, "Iowa Was Meaningless," *New York Times*, April 9, 2020, https://www.nytimes.com/2020/04/09/us/politics/iowa-caucuses-meaning.html
31. John Bennett, "Trump impeachment trial: Democrats say president 'cheated but got caught' as defence team readies 'robust' case," *Independent*, January 24, 2020, https://www.independent.co.uk/news/world/americas/us-politics/trump-impeachment-trial-mulvaney-senate-ukraine-military-a9301066.html

Instead of pointing out blatantly obvious and easily provable criminal behavior, the message the House prosecution team left with the Average American was, "He tried to cheat on the election."

And the average American response was a big yawn the same as that of people I heard on National Public Radio, which was, "Yeah, but he didn't break any laws."

What? Multiple laws were broken by Trump (allegedly). Multiple crimes were committed by Trump (allegedly). But you wouldn't know it, even after what felt like a thousand hours of day and night hearings.

With all due respect to the hard-working defenders of American democracy on the prosecutorial team for the House of Representatives, they should forever fire whoever "workshopped" their selected sound bite.

Again, old friend Frank said, "Somebody did some horrific research and followed deeply flawed logic because the sound bite that we kept hearing was, 'Donald Trump tried to cheat on the election, and he might do it again.'" Frank's response, "Give me a break!"

The average American doesn't have a lot of appreciation for the political process. A 2019 Gallup poll reported that only 32% of Americans hold the US political system in high regard.[32]

 So, when someone tells them that one of the politicians "tried to cheat," their brain goes, "What does that even mean?"

Do you think the phrase, "He tried to cheat on the election," had any visceral impact on the gut of the average listener? People I spoke with said, "No."

---

32. Megan Brenan, "American Pride Hits New Low; Few Proud of Political System," *Gallup*, July 2, 2019, https://news.gallup.com/poll/259841/american-pride-hits-new-low-few-proud-political-system.aspx

On the other hand, if Donald Trump were being impeached because he allegedly committed more than a dozen crimes against the United States, now you have the average American's attention.

Dear DNC leadership, do you get the difference: cheater vs. criminal?

In fact, you were only saying, "Attempted cheater." Compare that sound bite to "Criminally accused."

"Criminal?" Did you say, "criminal?" Now, the American public sits up and says, "All right, let's hear the details. Is he really a criminal? Tell me everything. You have my complete and undivided attention."

But the foundation for your case was he "tried" to "cheat." This sounds like he didn't actually "do" anything wrong, but he was trying to, but got caught and stopped. Oh, and he "may try again." And for this attempted cheating, he should not be allowed to be President. Frank's response, "Boring!"

Frank said he wanted to scream, "Are you kidding me?" every time he heard one of the House prosecutors say, "He tried to cheat in the election."

Heck, Trump didn't just try to "cheat," there was abundant public evidence that Trump could have been accused of committing more than a dozen federal crimes.

Trump allegedly committed three federal crimes just in that July 25, 2019, phone call with Ukraine's President: one, soliciting a contribution to a US election from a foreigner, two, bribery, and three, extortion. All are serious federal crimes punishable with fines and prison terms. The actual criminal codes that were violated along with the factual evidence are detailed in "Chapter 3 –Trump's 25 Alleged Federal Crimes."

In "Chapter 3" you will read Law Professor and Co-Director of the Institute of Judicial Administration at NYU School of Law Samuel

Estreicher's detailed analysis of Trump's actions as definitely meeting the criteria for the federal crime of bribery.

According to the U.S. Government Accountability Office, a week before that July 25th call, Trump had already broken the federal law by illegally impounding Congressionally appropriated funds. These were funds earmarked to aid Ukraine in their hot war trying to fight off a Russian invasion of their sovereign territory, where 14,000 Ukrainians defending their new democracy had already lost their lives.[33] [34]

We may not be able to send Trump to prison if found guilty for having committed multiple federal crimes, if we follow the guidance of a Department of Justice (DOJ) Office of Legal Counsel (OLC) guidance memo. That memo merely establishes a "guideline" that the DOJ does not indict a sitting President. (Remember that's just a guideline, not the law.) But we can legally remove him from office if we believe he broke one or more federal laws. In this case, more than 20 federal laws.

The House Prosecution could have said,

> We are not asking you to put Donald Trump in prison for allegedly committing 20 criminal acts in violation of United States federal criminal laws. What we are saying is that if you decide that Trump did, in fact, commit any one of these 20-plus federal crimes, then you must hold him accountable and remove him from office. If Trump, in your opinion, did break one or

---

33. Karoun Demirjian, Josh Dawsey, Ellen Nakashima, and Carol D. Leonnig, "Trump ordered hold on military aid days before calling Ukrainian president, officials say," *Washington Post*, September 23, 2019, https://www.washingtonpost.com/national-security/trump-ordered-hold-on-military-aid-days-before-calling-ukrainian-president-officials-say/2019/09/23/df93a6ca-de38-11e9-8dc8-498eabc129a0_story.html

34. Courtney Bublé, "GAO: Trump Administration Violated the Law by Withholding Ukraine Aid," *Government Executive,* January 16, 2020, https://www.govexec.com/oversight/2020/01/gao-trump-administration-violated-law-withholding-ukraine-aid/162485/

more federal laws, then that meets the standards for impeachment as set down by the U.S. Constitution.

Now, we are speaking about matters of great substance, federal crimes.

Now, we have a Law and Order, NCIS, Forensic Files, Cold Case Files, and Unsolved Mysteries TV show all rolled into one with the rapt attention of all of America. Everybody wants to know, "Is our President a criminal?" "Did Trump commit any of those crimes?" Hundreds of talking heads and criminal legal experts all expounding with phrases like, "Based on what I've heard and read, my opinion on "X" alleged crime is ______." "Will the Senate Jury find Trump guilty of a crime? Multiple crimes?" Frank's response? "Now that would have been exciting TV."

The number of present and former Federal criminal prosecutors interviewed day and night 24/7 by the hungry news networks, each network interviewer vying to one-up their competitors with the most sensational criminal accusation, would have made the House's case for them. And this long line of Federal prosecutors would have done the House's most important job, convince the jury of public opinion.

When Democratic Congressional leaders review the 20-plus federal crimes presented in "Chapter 3," they may decide, "that approach probably would have generated a better result than the one we got."

If I am missing something, please tell me because, if convinced, I can change the digital file at Amazon's publishing division that is used to print this book within minutes. And with Amazon's print-only-when-ordered technology, the very next new book ordered (or downloaded) will reflect those changes. This is part of my "booklogue" promise. This is a book-dialogue with you, the reader. Just email me at DrDavidKingKeller@gmail.com

Again, I say this with respect for the House leadership and Prosecution Team, that I know you are dedicated patriots who wanted to serve

America, but, in fact, you set America back by allowing Trump supporters and enablers to say, "Trump was completely exonerated, again. It was just another witch hunt."

The majority of Americans polls indicated, wanted Trump to be removed from office.[35]

That American majority might believe that the House impeachment team denied them the justice they were seeking. I say this because at least 20 crimes were allegedly committed by Trump. Yet, all we heard was that all the evidence led to some vague conclusion about cheating in politics. Wrong. The evidence overwhelmingly pointed to criminal behavior with multiple federal laws broken (allegedly) with potential jail time, if convicted, exceeding 100 years.

Dear Democratic leadership, with all due respect for you and your colleagues, please review the 25 alleged federal crimes committed by Trump and the publicly available evidence proving the allegation. These alleged crimes are detailed in Chapter 3 titled, "Trump's 25 Alleged Federal Crimes." In that Chapter, please read a brief excerpt of what Law Professor and Co-Director of the Institute of Judicial Administration at NYU School of Law Samuel Estreicher and his associate Christopher Owen said. They state in their highly detailed presentation on the charge of bribery against Trump where they conclude Trump did indeed commit the federal criminal act of bribery.

After reviewing these 25 alleged crimes by Trump, the House prosecution team will, I believe, conclude that highlighting Trump's alleged criminal acts may have been a better approach. Here is the URL to a convincing legal argument for bribery:[36]

---

35. Steve Benen, "National poll: US majority wants to see Trump removed from office," *MSNBC*, January 21, 2020, https://www.msnbc.com/rachel-maddow-show/national-poll-us-majority-wants-see-trump-removed-office-n1120961
36. Samuel Estreicher and Christopher Owens, "Did President Trump Commit the Federal Crime of Bribery?," *Verdict Justia,__*December 3 __2019,

All of Trump's 20 plus alleged federal crimes are described in "Chapter 3 - Trump's 25 Alleged Crimes." All the crimes are tied to their specific federal criminal statute and the abundance of available public evidence. None of the crimes are described in more detail than the alleged crime of bribery, which is presented in microscopic legal detail by a highly accredited law professor at NYU Law School.

Looking back, on December 13, 2019, at 2 pm Eastern, when the gentleman that first came out of the House Judiciary and stood in front of the cameras and said words to the effect, that they had adopted articles of impeachment and we are going to prosecute Donald Trump because he "cheated on the election" and if he is allowed to remain in office as President, and if he is not impeached, he'll "probably cheat again."

Again, Frank asked, "What do those words even mean? It has no intellectual impact whatsoever! It was the biggest screw up of any multimillion-dollar campaign designed to besmirch, much less remove from office, someone for committing high crimes and abuse of power."

Every American wanted to know what was the high "crime?" Yet, the prosecutorial team tiptoed around the word "crime." In fact, they seemed to avoid it like the plague for some reason that boggles the mind.

What the prosecutorial team never said or explained to the American public was that, in fact, there were no criminal codes in 1787 when the Articles of Impeachment were adopted into the Constitution. Therefore, no language involving federal criminal statutes could have been mentioned in the Articles of Impeachment because none existed. Federal criminal codes were created years after the Articles of Impeachment were added to the Constitution. That's why the

---

https://verdict.justia.com/amp/2019/12/03/did-president-trump-commit-the-federal-crime-of-bribery

Constitution used a term that was well understood in those days, "high crimes and misdemeanors."

But the average American doesn't have a clue what that "high crimes and misdemeanors" means. The average American, on the other hand, does understand that we are a land of laws and criminal codes. And if you break the law, there are consequences. And those consequences are clearly spelled out in the criminal code.

But who would understand the nebulous terms of "cheating in an election" unless that activity is tied to a specific criminal code? It could have been, but it was wasn't, and so, the central theme of the House's prosecution was left as vague and ambiguous in the mind of the average American, I believe. And the Republicans pounced on the ambiguity and yelled from the rooftop that no laws were broken. Worse, the Republicans were able to say that there were not even any allegations of any laws broken. "Therefore," they said, "the House's case had no merit and was base-less."

On January 26, 2020, speaking from the White House, "Lawyer Alan Dershowitz said Sunday that he believes President Donald Trump must be charged with a crime to be removed from office …"[37]

The House prosecution team had a failed strategy because they chose not to mention any of the twenty-plus alleged criminal acts of Donald Trump. Trump's attorneys pounced on this error, and it also left many to believe that "Trump must be innocent because he was not convicted in the Senate jury trial."

The House prosecutors thought they could speak in highly nuanced terms about "abuse of power" with no reference to any criminal codes.

---

37. Daniel Uria, "Dershowitz: Democrats' case meritless because no crime committed," *UPI,* January 26, 2020,
https://www.upi.com/Top_News/US/2020/01/26/Dershowitz-Democrats-case-meritless-because-no-crime-committed/2921580058954/

Dear House prosecutors, that may have worked in a law school's moot court where nuance was expected and appreciated.

Unfortunately, the Democrats apparently didn't realize their audience was not made up of law school professors attending moot court. Their actual audience was the court of public opinion. More specifically, the House prosecution team needed 67 Senators to agree with them in order to impeach the President, but they started with only 47 Democratic Senators. This meant they had to convince 20 Republican Senators who did not want to agree with them, but would have been forced to agree had the case been an overwhelming and convincing presentation of criminal behavior. A criminal case so well presented that the constituents of 20 Republican senators would have insisted that their Senate representatives agree with the overwhelming criminal evidence and, therefore, had to vote to remove the criminal.

In fact, all the House prosecution had to do was bring to reality what the polls showed a majority of Americans already wanted even before the House began their formal impeachment prosecution case in the Senate chambers, removal of Trump from office.[38]

When you read "Chapter 3," the alleged criminal violations of four whistleblower laws by Trump are so clear and so present that there would have been no defense. Specifically, when Donald Trump tweeted out the name of the Whistleblower to his 75 million followers on his Twitter account, he allegedly violated multiple Federal Whistleblower laws.

The defense against those criminal accusations would've been baseless. Why?

---

38. Steve Benen, "National poll: US majority wants to see Trump removed from office," *MSNBC*, January 21, 2020, https://www.msnbc.com/rachel-maddow-show/national-poll-us-majority-wants-see-trump-removed-office-n1120961

The simple answer is, the act of revealing the Whistleblower's name, in and of itself, violated his oath as an executive officer in charge of the Intelligence community.

Trump also violated the secrecy acts surrounding certain confidential government documents.

Trump violated the Whistleblower Act itself because it statutorily requires that the name of the Whistleblower be held in confidence. Releasing the name of the whistleblower is a violation of Federal criminal code. See "Chapter 3" for more details.

In summary, the House prosecution team had more than 20 federal laws that had been allegedly violated, and there was plenty of publicly available evidence to prove each and every one of those crimes. This approach would have satisfied the court of public opinion that the evidence was so overwhelming in each of these criminal acts that there really was no defense. The conviction of the majority of the American public beyond a reasonable doubt that multiple criminal laws were violated should have been easy to accomplish.

But for reasons that boggle the mind, the House prosecution team decided to assiduously avoid the term "crime." This was a tactical and strategic error that should bewilder anybody who examines these 20-plus criminal codes because of the overwhelming evidence that they were violated by the President (allegedly).

In order to win the 2020 election, the Democrats have to compensate for their wide range of past messaging failures.

CHAPTER 3

TRUMP'S 25 ALLEGED FEDERAL CRIMES

The Evidence

Another reason the Democrats risk losing the 2020 election is that they, so far, have failed to publicize Trump's alleged crimes.

My question to the Democratic leadership communication apparatus and its friendly media in April 2019 is the same one I have today.

"Why haven't you been publicizing the many evidence-based crimes allegedly committed by Trump?"

I know you have at times, but where is "The List?" Where is the "Trump List of Alleged Crimes?" Where is the website tab titled, "Trump's Alleged Federal Crimes" on the DNC website? Where is the separate website titled www.TrumpsAllegedCrimes.com sponsored by donors and PACs?

Rachel, Mika, Alex, Andrea, Chris, Joe, Ari, Melvin, Richard, Touré, Al, Lawrence, Don, Jake, Wolf, Brooke, Jim, John, Anderson, Fareed, Kate, Zain, and many other wonderful journalists, too many to list, you are the best. Can you please help promulgate this list?

Why don't polls show that 85% of Americans believe Trump has broken the law on at least one occasion?

The laws are clear, and the publicly available evidence makes the criminal violations abundantly obvious.

This "crimes list" should have been a daily drumbeat until every American got the message that, "The evidence is overwhelming that indicates Trump could be accused of violating multiple federal criminal statutes."

Where is the daily ad on Fox News that provides a scrolling list of Trump's Alleged crimes? Where is the YouTube video?

Where is the weekly ad in the Wall Street Journal?

"Trump Broke The Law …" was the NPR headline on January 16, 2020.[39]

The full headline read, "Trump Broke The Law In Freezing Ukraine Funds, Watchdog Report Concludes." The "watchdog" was the non-partisan US Government Accountability Office (GAO).

Let's repeat that headline in all caps for reasons that will be obvious in a moment. "TRUMP BROKE THE LAW." A branch of the United States Government, the non-partisan Government Accountability Office, the GAO, said in a public press release on January 16, 2020, "TRUMP BROKE THE LAW." For some reason, the Democrats did not pound this headline into the brain of the average American. We know of that failure by the Democrats because two months later, a March 2020 survey by Pew Research showed that 25% of those polled believe that Trump did nothing wrong.[40]

---

39. Ayesha Rascoe, "Trump Broke The Law In Freezing Ukraine Funds, Watchdog Report Concludes," *NPR*, January 16, 2020, https://www.npr.org/2020/01/16/796806517/trump-broke-the-law-in-freezing-ukraine-funds-watchdog-report-concludes
40. John Gramlich, "Looking back on impeachment, a quarter of Americans say Trump did nothing wrong," *PEW Research,* March 17, 2020, https://www.pewresearch.org/fact-tank/2020/03/17/looking-back-on-impeachment-a-quarter-of-americans-say-trump-did-nothing-wrong/

How is that statistic possible when the evidence that follows indicates Trump probably broke more than 20 laws?

Examine the law, then examine the evidence.

I invite you, the readers, to read the criminal codes listed below that allegedly apply to President Trump's actions, and then decide for yourself.

Remember, after the July 25, 2019 phone call transcript between President Trump and President Zelensky was released by Trump (a redacted version, according to many.) Donald Trump kept calling it a "perfect" transcript. Trump, at one point, had people at a rally wearing T-shirts that said, "Read the transcript." Well, I respectfully suggest that you, "Read the code." Read the criminal code. Read the wording of these criminal codes below, along with the publicly available evidence that demonstrates rather clearly that Trump allegedly violated those criminal codes and decide for yourself.

The DNC War Room, it seems to this researcher, never promulgated the easily substantiated laws that Trump allegedly broke. Here's a list with the criminal code described and the evidence allegedly proving the violation.

I am asking you the reader, other attorneys, and legal researchers to help this author refine and augment this list of alleged criminal violations.

Unless in direct quotes, the words describing the alleged crimes listed above and below are my own and not those of an attorney.

These legal statutes, above and below, are meant to serve as a place to start to understand the possible one-man "crime wave" centered in the White House with a partial list of the alleged crimes committed by Donald Trump.

Dear reader, if you know of other criminal and civil statutes allegedly violated by Donald Trump, please send them to this author at DrDavidKingKeller@gmail.com.

Remember this is a man, Trump, who told a U.S. Federal Judge in the Second Circuit Court of Appeals through his attorney on October 23, 2019, that he was above all laws of the United States of America and he could not be held liable for anything even cold-blooded murder as long as he was President. Here's a URL link of his live audio statement through his attorney (Find the video arrow and press it.):[41]

That statement by Trump through his representative means, for example, that he could tie you up in your house along with your children and pets, set your house on fire, and watch all of you including your pets burn alive screaming until you died, and he would be guilt-less and could not be held liable, and he could walk away a free man even while he held the gas can and matches in his hand with the police standing by helpless to stop him, as long as he was President. That's what, in essence, Trump told a Federal Judge through his attorney on October 23, 2019. This is Trump's alleged criminal mind broadcast live for all to hear on audiotape: (Find the audio white arrow and press it.):[42]

Keep Trump's claim that he can legally murder without penalty in mind as you review the evidenced-based alleged crimes.

Trump's Alleged Federal Crimes:

#1: Title 52 USC 30121(a)(2)

---

41. Ian Millhiser, "Trump's lawyer: If Trump shoots someone on 5th Avenue, nothing could be done," *Vox*, October 23, 2019, https://www.vox.com/2019/10/23/20928680/nothing-could-be-done-trump-fifth-avenue-immunity-mazars-vance

42. Ian Millhiser, "Trump's lawyer: If Trump shoots someone on 5th Avenue, nothing could be done," *Vox*, October 23, 2019, https://www.vox.com/2019/10/23/20928680/nothing-could-be-done-trump-fifth-avenue-immunity-mazars-vance

Asking a foreign national to contribute to a U.S. election is against the law.

The specific criminal statute:[43]

Trump allegedly broke this law at least three times:

> 1. July 27, 2016: "Russia, if you're listening…"
>
> 2. July 25, 2019: "Do me a favor" Ukraine Pres.
>
> 3. October 3, 2019: "China" investigate Bidens.

See January 2, 2019, *USA Today* article titled, "Trump Illegally Asked Russia To Help Him Win In 2016. He Shouldn't Get Away With It." It explains that a public request for Russian help in finding Hillary Clinton's emails was a violation of US law.[44]

Brendan Fischer, an attorney with the Campaign Legal Center, believes there was a violation of the law.[45]

FEC Chair Ellen Weintraub declined to talk about the specifics of Trump's case but noted that "The law is pretty clear. ... It is absolutely illegal for anyone to solicit, accept, or receive anything of value from a foreign national in connection with any election in the United States."

---

43. Legal Information Institute, "52 U.S. Code § 30121.Contributions and donations by foreign nationals," *Cornell law school*, 20 March 2020, https://www.law.cornell.edu/uscode/text/52/30121

44. Fred Wertheimer & Norman Eisen, "Trump Illegally Asked Russia To Help Him Win In 2016. He Shouldn't Get Away With It," *USA TODAY,* January 2, 2019, https://www.usatoday.com/story/opinion/2019/01/02/trump-broke-law-russia-clinton-emails-hold-him-accountable-column/2449564002/

45. Brian Naylor, "Trump's Ukraine Call Might Violate Election Laws, But No One's Enforcing Them," *NPR,* October 5, 2019, https://www.npr.org/2019/10/05/767261398/trumps-ukraine-call-might-violate-election-laws-but-no-one-s-enforcing-them

FEC Chairwoman Ellen Weintraub stated in a TV interview that, "Soliciting foreign interference doesn't just violate norms. It also violates the law."[46]

Who can forget, July 27, 2016, Trump asked Russia, "If you're listening," to dig up dirt on Hillary Clinton, his Presidential opponent?

Per the FEC Chair, it can be alleged that Trump broke the FEC Act law with that statement. With the release of the transcript on July 25, 2019, it's clear, Trump asked for a valuable political contribution from a foreign national, Ukraine's President Zelensky, by saying, "Do me a favor." He then asked the Ukrainian President to announce a criminal investigation in regards to Trump's leading 2020 election opponent, former Vice President Joseph Biden.

Then Trump gave a White House press conference on October 3, 2019, and asked China to investigate his political opponent, former Vice President Joseph Biden. Trump said, "China should start an investigation into the Bidens because what happened in China is just about as bad as what happened with Ukraine."[47]

There appears to be nothing ambiguous about Trump's alleged breach of the Title 52 criminal code.

In fact, on October 19, 2019 the U.S. Government arrested two Ukrainians, Igor Fruman and Lev Parnas for funneling "something of value," in this case, foreign money from a foreign national into a US election, and other charges; and one of the statutes cited by the

46. Aaron Rupar, "America's top election official explains why Trump may be committing crimes," *Vox*, October 4, 2019, https://www.vox.com/2019/10/4/20898491/trump-foreign-solicitation-ukraine-china-fec-ellen-weintraub

47. Peter Baker & Eileen Sullivan, "Trump Publicly Urges China to Investigate the Bidens," *The New York Times*, October 3, 2019, https://www.nytimes.com/2019/10/03/us/politics/trump-china-bidens.html

Department of Justice indictment is the violation of criminal code Title 52 USC 30121 (a) (2).

Title 52 USC 30121 (a)(2) is one of the serious go-to-jail laws that got Lev Parnas and Igor Fruman indicted and arrested. Both are currently on GPS ankle bracelets awaiting trial. Prosecutors expect convictions. A U.S. federal judge set an Oct. 5, 2020 trial date for Lev Parnas and Igor Fruman, two associates of President Donald Trump's personal lawyer Rudy Giuliani, setting the stage for more information to emerge about their alleged campaign finance violations before November's presidential election.[48]

Violating FEC laws is very serious. As we know, people have been arrested at the airport as they were about to leave the Country for violating said laws. Just ask Lev Parnas and Igor Fruman, who were arrested for violating Title 52 USC 30121 (a) (2) amongst other statutes. The actual Federal complaint is online. To read it, go to this URL:[49]USA Today ran this headline on January 2, 2019, "Trump illegally asked Russia to help him win in 2016. He shouldn't get away with it." The byline stated, "Trump's public request for Russian help in finding Hillary Clinton's emails was a violation of US law. There are ways to hold him accountable. Federal campaign finance law prohibits any person from soliciting campaign contributions, defined as anything of value to be given to influence an election, from a foreign national, including a foreign government."[50]

---

48. Karen Freifeld & Jonathan Stempel, "Giuliani associates Parnas, Fruman face Oct. 5 trial, before U.S. election," *Yahoo! News,* February 3, 2020, https://news.yahoo.com/giuliani-associates-parnas-fruman-face-215000310.html

49. The United States Attorney's Office Southern District of New York, "Lev Parnas And Igor Fruman Charged With Conspiring To Violate Straw And Foreign Donor Bans," *US Department of Justice,* October 10, 2019, https://www.justice.gov/usao-sdny/pr/lev-parnas-and-igor-fruman-charged-conspiring-violate-straw-and-foreign-donor-bans

50. Fred Wertheimer & Norman Eisen, "Trump illegally asked Russia to help him win in 2016. He shouldn't get away with it," *USA TODAY,* January 2, 2019,

#2: Title X - Impoundment Control Act of 1974. Illegal impoundment of US funds by the President.

Open this URL for details on the actual code / law:[51]

Even the non-partisan Government Accountability Office (GAO) has publicly stated that Trump broke this law.

"White House violated the law by freezing Ukraine aid, GAO says," was Politico.com headline story written on January 16, 2020, by reporters Andrew Desiderio, Kyle Cheney, and Caitlin Emma.[52][53]

Title 2 USC 601, Title X of the Act, The Impoundment Control Act (ICA) of 1974 established procedures to prevent the President and other government officials from unilaterally substituting their own funding decisions for those of the Congress. The Act also created the House and Senate Budget Committees and the Congressional Budget Office.

Trump, per the GAO, violated the Impoundment Control Act (ICA). Here are the details: On Jan. 15, 2020, the day House managers transmitted two articles of impeachment to the Senate, the Government Accountability Office, a nonpartisan public auditor, reported that President Trump violated the Impoundment Control Act by unilaterally withholding $214 million of legislatively appropriated Defense Department aid for Ukraine without obtaining authorization from Congress. Allan Lichtman writing for *The Hill* reported,

---

https://www.usatoday.com/story/opinion/2019/01/02/trump-broke-law-russia-clinton-emails-hold-him-accountable-column/2449564002/

51. Legal Information Institute, "2 U.S. Code § 601.Establishment," *Cornell law school*, March 20, 2020, https://www.law.cornell.edu/uscode/text/2/601

52. Emily Cochrane, Eric Lipton and Chris Cameron, "G.A.O. Report Says Trump Administration Broke Law in Withholding Ukraine Aid," *New York Times*, January 16, 2020, https://www.nytimes.com/2020/01/16/us/politics/gao-trump-ukraine.html

53. Andrew Desiderio, Kyle Cheney and Caitlin Emma, "White House violated the law by freezing Ukraine aid, GAO says," *Politico,* January 16, 2020, https://www.politico.com/news/2020/01/16/white-house-violated-the-law-by-freezing-ukraine-aid-gao-says-099682

> Faithful execution of the law does not permit the President to substitute his own policy priorities for those that Congress has enacted into law," the Government Accountability Office concluded. A violation of the Impoundment Control Act is not a minor technicality. At the height of the Watergate scandal in 1974, Congress passed the law to prevent a rogue president like Richard Nixon from withholding lawfully appropriated funds. A president who seeks to put a hold on such funds for policy purposes must transmit to both the House and Senate "a special message" specifying "the amount of budget authority which he proposes to be rescinded or which is to be so reserved" and "the reasons why the budget authority should be rescinded or is to be so reserved.

Trump disputed the conclusion of the Government Accountability Office, saying that he acted lawfully under his authority to carry out American foreign policy.[54]

In a rebuke to Trump's "policy" defense, Thomas Armstrong, general counsel for the watchdog Government Accountability Office stated that the 1974 ICA law that governs budget procedure within the government "does not permit OMB to withhold funds for policy reasons," as reported by Ayesha Rascoe of NPR on January 16, 2020.[55]

ICA violation: In another blow to Trump's "policy" defense, in an article titled, "Unredacted documents show Trump explicitly broke the

---

54. Allan Lichtman, "What law did Donald Trump break?," *The Hill*, January 23, 2020, https://thehill.com/opinion/white-house/479547-what-law-did-donald-trump-break

55. Ayesha Rascoe, "Trump Broke The Law In Freezing Ukraine Funds, Watchdog Report Concludes," *NPR*, January 16, 2020, https://www.npr.org/2020/01/16/796806517/trump-broke-the-law-in-freezing-ukraine-funds-watchdog-report-concludes

law", Quin Hillyer on January 2, 2020, in the *Washington Examiner* reported,

> Unredacted documents acquired through FOIA court filing show repeated warnings from Defense Department officials to White House personnel that Trump's delay in releasing legally mandated aid to Ukraine was unlawful. Hillyer also noted that "While the Impoundment Control Act makes these requirements explicit on statutory grounds, Supreme Court precedent implies (but does not explicitly say) that presidential impoundment of duly appropriated funds is also unconstitutional.[56]

GAO website describes ICA at this URL:[57]

#3. Title 18 USC 872, Extortion. Trump ordering the withholding on July 25, 2019, of $371 million in Congressionally approved military aid needed to protect Ukraine from its Russian invasion that had already killed 14,000 Ukrainians, that Trump ordered held until President Zelensky committed to publicly announce an investigation into Joseph Biden, Trump's 2020 political opponent. See[58]

Extortion by officers or employees of the United States violates U.S. Federal Law 18 U.S. Code § 872, Extortion.

Did Trump use criminal extortion in his dealings with Ukraine by:

1.   Stopping nearly $400 million of vitally needed, Congressionally-mandated, U.S. military aid to Ukraine. Ukraine was, and is, in a hot

---

56. Quinn Hillyer, "Unredacted documents show Trump explicitly broke the law," *Washington Examiner,* January 2, 2020, https://www.washingtonexaminer.com/opinion/unredacted-documents-show-trump-explicitly-broke-the-law

57. U.S. Government Accountability office, "Impoundment Control Act of 1974," *GAO*, Jun 29, 1978, https://www.gao.gov/products/106251

58. Legal Information Institute, "Extortion by officers or employees of the United States. 18 U.S.C.§ 872," *Cornell law school*, March 20, 2020, https://www.law.cornell.edu/uscode/text/18/872

war with Russia with Ukrainians dying nearly every day defending Ukraine against Russia's invasion of Ukraine. At this same time Trump, and his attorney, presumably sought evidence of support from Ukraine's new President that he was "playing ball" and producing "dirt" on Joe and Hunter Biden, and

2. By withholding promised prominent U.S. visual support of new Ukrainian President by abruptly canceling attendance of President Zelensky's inauguration by Vice President Mike Pence which had long been planned and expected; and, instead, sent Energy Department Secretary Rick Perry; and

3. By withholding a White House visit, sought by Ukraine's President, to have an official welcoming into the democratic world of one of the worlds' newest democracies by one of the world's oldest and most powerful democracies.

The 2nd request had already been denied as part of Trump's alleged power play extortion plan. The remaining two requests of Ukraine were being withheld in a quid pro quo demand by Trump. You give me dirt on my political opponent by simply declaring an investigation into Joseph Biden and his son, and I will give you the things you are seeking (the quid) for the thing I want (the quo.)

One of the central defenses of President Trump's actions regarding Ukraine is that he's really just interested in rooting out corruption. Ukraine is a corrupt country the argument goes, so why shouldn't U.S. aid and other things be conditioned on that? That argument, of course, ignores how seldom Trump has shown concerns about global corruption in the past. It also ignores the self-serving nature of the two specific investigations he has sought.

The two investigations Trump wanted Ukraine to announce were: one, an investigation into Biden, and two, an investigation into a non-existent Ukrainian DNC server hypothetically used in the 2016 election, which was a hoax developed by Russia to distract from Russia's own interference in the 2016 US election. The "excuse" that Trump was only interested in curbing alleged corruption in Ukraine ignores the fact that Trump released the appropriated aid to Ukraine in 2017 and in 2018 without any strings or discussions about corruption. But "out of the blue" strings got attached as soon as Trump was entering the 2020 election cycle and wanted help in smearing his presumed 2020 opponent, Vice President Joseph Biden. And scarily, Trump unilaterally, with no support from anyone else in the entire Administration or State Department, wanted to create a false distraction from Russia's interference in the 2016 US election by promoting a hoax invented by Putin that it was not Russia, but it was Ukraine.[59]

Trump's intermediary to Ukraine, Richard Sondland, the US Ambassador to the European Union, stated in a Congressional hearing that Trump wasn't really interested in an actual investigation, just the "announcement" of an investigation.[60]

On November 10, 2019, CBS News reported,

> California Congressman Eric Swalwell, a Democrat on the House Intelligence Committee, said the lawmakers had amassed enough evidence through hours of testimony from current and former administration officials to prove President Trump participated in an "extortion scheme" to pressure the Ukrainian government.

On "Face the Nation" Swalwell said,

---

59. Annieli, "Guilty Trump: conspiracy to commit Bribery and Extortion because he believes nonsense," *DailyKos.com*, November 09, 2019, https://m.dailykos.com/stories/2019/11/9/1898190/-Guilty-Trump-conspiracy-to-commit-Bribery-and-Extortion-because-he-believes-nonsense

60. David A. Graham, "Trump Wanted an Announcement — Not an Actual Investigation," *MSN*, November 20, 2019, https://www.msn.com/en-ca/news/newspolitics/trump-wanted-an-announcement-----not-an-actual-investigation/ar-BBX3imw

> We have enough evidence from the depositions that we've done to warrant bringing this forward, evidence of an extortion scheme, using taxpayer dollars to ask a foreign government to investigate the president's opponent.[61]

Trump allegedly committed extortion. In an article on October 10, 2019, in The Intercept, titled "The Actual Laws Trump Has Broken, Just With the Ukraine and China Affairs, Could Land Him 10 Years in Prison." Ryan Grim, the article's author, quotes writers Tucker Carlson and Neil Patel for the Daily Caller as saying, "Donald Trump should not have been on the phone with a foreign head of state encouraging another country to investigate his political opponent, Joe Biden."[62]

Extortion: Max Boot, the well-known journalist and Senior Fellow in National Security Studies at the Council on Foreign Relations, penned an op-ed for the Washington Post on September 22, 2019, titled, "This may be the worst Trump scandal yet." Speaking of the intimidation Trump was using against Ukraine's President to extract personal political favors, Boot writes,

> A mob enforcer doesn't have to say, "pay up, or we will destroy your store" to be guilty of extortion. The message is conveyed clearly enough if he says, "nice store, shame if anything happened to it," combined with the storekeeper's knowledge of what the mafia has done to those who didn't pay up.[63]

---

61. Camilo Montoya-Galvez, "Swalwell says Trump's "extortion scheme" on Ukraine at center of impeachment inquiry," *CBS News,* November 10, 2019, https://www.cbsnews.com/amp/news/trump-impeachment-inquiry-latest-rep-eric-swalwell-says-trump-extortion-scheme-at-center-of-inquiry-on-face-the-nation
62. Ryan Grim, "The Actual Laws Trump Has Broken, Just With the Ukraine and China Affairs, Could Land Him 10 Years in Prison," *The Intercept*, October 10, 2019, https://theintercept.com/2019/10/10/trump-crimes-law
63. Max Boot, "This may be the worst Trump scandal yet," *Washington Post,* September 22, 2019, https://www.washingtonpost.com/opinions/2019/09/22/trumps-ukraine-gate-extortion

#4. Title 18 USC 201 Bribery

NYU Law Professor Samuel Estreicher states,

> Per the text of § 201 and Department of Justice (DOJ)'s Criminal Resource Manual, § 2041, Bribery of Public Officials, § 201 contains two sets of crimes: the giving and accepting of a bribe (§ 201(b)(1)-(2)) and the lesser offenses of giving and accepting a gratuity (§ 201(c)(1)-(2)).

Professor Estreicher, Co-Director, Institute of Judicial Administration, at NYU School of Law, co-wrote an article in *Justia* on December 3, 2019 with Christopher Owens titled, "Did President Trump Commit the Federal Crime of Bribery?" He states,

> The federal offense of bribery thus contains five elements: (1) a public official (2) who demands, accepts, promises, etc. (3) "anything of value" (4) corruptly and with the intent to influence or be influenced in the performance of (5) an "official act.

Law Professor Estreicher concludes Trump's conduct satisfies all five criteria, and, thus, committed the crime of bribery. Law Professor Samuel Estreicher's entire analysis is here:[64]

From the above analysis, we also learn from Professor Estreicher one might also conclude that Trump was also guilty of the "lesser" Federal crime of giving and accepting a gratuity in violation of Title 18 USC § 201(c)(1)-(2).

Jacob Sullum in Reason.Com tells us in an article titled "Far From Avoiding 'Quid Pro Quo' Talk, Calling Trump's Conduct Bribery Requires It." And Sullum adds, "Whether you think of his pressure on Ukraine as bribery, extortion, or simply an abuse of power, the link

---

64. Samuel Estreicher and Christopher Owens, "Did President Trump Commit the Federal Crime of Bribery?," *Verdict Justia,* December 3, 2019, https://verdict.justia.com/amp/2019/12/03/did-president-trump-commit-the-federal-crime-of-bribery

between military aid and politically beneficial investigations is crucial."[65]

Reason.com reported on November 15, 2019, Napolitano told Cavuto that,

> Fox News Judge **Andrew Napolitano, who was a** New Jersey Superior Court judge from 1987 to 1995, thinks Trump "pretty clearly" violated criminal bribery laws. And **Reason goes on to report,** "The bribe is to grant or withhold military assistance in return for a public statement of a fake investigation into the elections," said House Speaker Rep. Nancy Pelosi (D–Calif.) at a press conference on Thursday. "That's bribery." Weighing in on Neil Cavuto's Fox News program, Judge Andrew Napolitano <u>explained</u> that "it wouldn't matter if it was Joe Biden or Joe Blow" who was at the center of the investigations sought by Trump. It's also inconsequential. Judge Andrew Napolitano said, "whether the favor comes or not. I think that the argument that asking for a favor in return for doing a legal obligation—releasing the [security] funds—is pretty clearly a violation of criminal bribery laws.[66]

In November of 2019, Jeffrey Toobin of the New Yorker writes,

> …a relevant criminal statute is a familiar one in the federal courts, called the Hobbs Act... It prohibits what's known as "extortion under color of official right." Samuel W. Buell, a professor at Duke Law School who is a former federal prosecutor, said, "The traditional way the Hobbs Act is used is

65. Jacob Sullum, "Far From Avoiding 'Quid Pro Quo' Talk, Calling Trump's Conduct Bribery Requires It," *Reason,* November 15, 2019, https://reason.com/2019/11/15/far-from-avoiding-quid-pro-quo-talk-calling-trumps-conduct-bribery-requires-it/?amp

66. Billy Binion, "Justin Amash to Trump: Let Bolton, Giuliani, and Mulvaney Testify," *Reason,* November 15, 2019, https://reason.com/2019/11/15/JUSTIN-AMASH-TO-TRUMP-LET-BOLTON-GIULIANI-AND-MULVANEY-TESTIFY/?AMP

when public officials solicit bribes. The idea is that there is an inherent power relationship between a public official and people who need things from that official. If the public official demands money, that's seen as extortion, and thus a violation of the Hobbs Act." "The idea behind the case would be Trump conditioned the release of military aid to Ukraine on the President of Ukraine coming across with the dirt on the Biden family," Buell said, adding, "He's misusing official power to obtain things of value to him. That's the heart of what the Hobbs Act is supposed to prohibit. With Trump, the quid pro quo is taxpayer money in return for political dirt. The President and his supporters made the argument that he should not be impeached because there is no proof of any underlying crime. The provisions of the Hobbs Act show that Trump and his supporters may be wrong about that.[67]

On November 4, 2019, in the Huff Post S.A. Date penned an article titled, "Another Term For Trump's Quid Pro Quo? Extortion."

Journalist Date states that,

> Former federal prosecutors say the president's interactions with Ukraine also amount to extortion, as defined by the Hobbs Act.

> The relevant law is known as the Hobbs Act, said Danya Perry, a former prosecutor in the U.S. Attorney's office in New York City. Its definition of "extortion" includes obtaining property using "threatened force, violence, or fear, or under color of official right," meaning using one's official capacity. The crime is punishable by up to 20 years in prison.

---

67. Jeffrey Toobin, "Is His Dealings With Ukraine, Did Donald Trump Commit A Crime?," *New Yorker,* November 1, 2019, https://www.newyorker.com/news/daily-comment/in-his-dealings-with-ukraine-did-donald-trump-commit-a-crime/amp

> The Hobbs Act statute applies to a demand, or a threat, made by a public official in order to obtain something of value in exchange for his or her performance of an official act. This is the very definition of what Trump did.[68]

#5.   Title 18 USC 1503, Obstruction of Justice. Trump ordering Administration employees not to respond to September and October 2019 Congressional subpoenas to testify and produce documents, which was later called illegal by a Federal U.S. District Court Judge on November 26, 2019.[69]

What does obstruction of justice mean?

Obstructing justice, as it sounds, has to do with knowingly interfering in the administration of justice. Known as a "process crime," it's a criminal offense against the judicial process itself, similar to crimes of false and misleading statements, contempt, perjury, and failure to appear.[70]

CBS News pointed out on July 23, 2019, that, according to Special Investigator Robert Mueller, Trump may have obstructed justice ten times.[71]

A District Court ruled on Trump's obstruction of justice. On Nov 25, 2019, **U.S. District Judge** Ketanji Brown Jackson said 'No One Is

---

68. Shirish Date, "Another Term For Trump's Quid Pro Quo? Extortion," *Huff Post*, November 5, 2019, https://m.huffpost.com/us/entry/us_5dc0a6dde4b0bedb2d5149ee/amp?guccounter=1

69. Legal Information Institute, "Influencing or injuring officer or juror generally. 18 U.S.C. § 1503.,"*Cornell Law School*, 20 March 2020, https://www.law.cornell.edu/uscode/text/18/1503

70. Freidman & Nemecek, "18 U.S.C. § 1503: What Exactly is Obstruction of Justice?," *Freidman & Nemecek LLC,* May 17, 2019, https://www.iannfriedman.com/blog/2019/may/18-u-s-c-1503-what-exactly-is-obstruction-of-jus/

71. Will Rahn, "10 Times Trump May Have Obstructed Justice, According To Mueller," *CBS News,* July 23, 2019, https://www.cbsnews.com/news/obstruction-of-justice-10-times-trump-may-have-obstructed-justice-mueller-report/

Above the Law', stating former White House counsel attorney Donald McGahn must comply with U.S. Congressional House subpoena for his testimony. The Judge's ruling is under appeal by Trump and is expected to go to the U.S. Supreme Court.[72]

#6. Title 18 USC 1505 - Obstruction of Congress.[73]

We learn from the Cornell University Law School's Legal Information Institute that **Title 18 USC 1505 states**,

> Whoever corruptly, or by threats or force, or by any threatening letter or communication influences, obstructs, or impedes or endeavors to influence, obstruct, or impede the due and proper administration of the law under which any pending proceeding is being had before any department or agency of the United States, or the due and proper exercise of the power of inquiry under which any inquiry or investigation is being had by either House or any committee of either House or any joint committee of the Congress- Shall be fined under this title, imprisoned not more than 5 years.

Intimidating a witness who may be asked to appear before Congress is obstruction of Congress.

On September 26, 2019, AP News reported, "The chairmen of the foreign affairs, intelligence, and oversight committees say, 'The President's comments today constitute reprehensible witness

---

72. Spencer Hsu & Anne E. Marimow, "Former White House counsel Donald McGahn must comply with House subpoena, judge rules," *Washington Post*, November 26, 2019, https://www.washingtonpost.com/local/legal-issues/former-white-house-counsel-donald-mcgahn-must-comply-with-house-subpoena-judge-rules/2019/11/25/6de26cc8-018d-11ea-8bab-0fc209e065a8_story.html

73. Legal Information Institute, "Obstruction of proceedings before departments, agencies, and committees. 18 U.S.C.§ 1505," *Cornell law school*, 20 March, 2020, https://www.law.cornell.edu/uscode/text/18/1505

intimidation and an attempt to obstruct Congress' impeachment inquiry."[74]

#7. **Title 18 USC 2381 – Treason: Aid /Comfort to an** Enemy.[75]

> Whoever, owing allegiance to the United States …adheres to their enemies, giving them aid and comfort within the United States or elsewhere, is guilty of treason and shall suffer death, or shall be imprisoned not less than five years and fined under this title but not less than $10,000.

Republican Bill Weld says Trump committed treason and mentions the death penalty (USA Today 9/23/2019) Weld says Trump is in violation of Article III, Section 3 of the US Constitution: Treason against the United States. Read the story here:[76]

Trump's Alleged Treasonous Crimes Against America.

THE FACTS:

1. Trump's July 16, 2018, Helsinki press conference lie endorsing Putin's denial of Russian election interference reflects what a Russian agent would do.

2016: The Obama administration informed Trump of Russian interference in the 2016 election.

---

74. Staff, "The Latest: Democrats accuse Trump of witness intimidation," *The Associated Press.* September 26, 2019,
,https://apnews.com/f2f662aa7aa64030bed2dd496dfc3b0b
75. U.S. Code, "Treason. 18 U.S.C.§ 2381," *uscode.house.gov*, March 24, 2020, https://uscode.house.gov/view.xhtml?req=granuleid:USC-prelim-title18-section2381&num=0&edition=prelim
76. Nicholas Wu, "GOP challenger Bill Weld says Trump committed 'treason,' mentions death penalty," *USA Today,* September 23, 2019, https://www.usatoday.com/story/news/politics/elections/2019/09/23/bill-weld-says-donald-trump-committed-treason-amid-ukraine-scandal/2417466001/

Aug. 2016: Washington Post: "Trump first received a classified intelligence briefing as the Republican nominee."[77]

October 2016: The Director of National Intelligence and Department of Homeland Security issued an unusual joint public warning, blaming Russia for election interference.[78]

1/11/2017: According to the NY Times, "President-elect Donald J. Trump on Wednesday conceded for the first time that Russia had carried out cyberattacks against the two major political parties during the presidential election." Trump said, "As far as hacking, I think it was Russia."[79]

100's of publications discussed Russia's 2016 interference in articles that appeared in the year 2017 including:

On 1/11/2017, the NY Times ran this headline, "Donald Trump Concedes Russia's Interference in Election." https://nyti.ms/39whvAI

On 4/26/2017, The Atlantic ran this article, "Russia's Interference in the US Election Was Just the Beginning." https://bit.ly/2PWanFL

On 6/5/2017, The Intercept ran this headline, "Top-Secret NSA Report Details Russian Hacking Effort Days Before 2016 Election." https://bit.ly/38wqWP9

---

77. Philip Bump, "What Obama did, didn't do and couldn't do in response to Russian interference," *The Washington Post,* February 21, 2018, https://www.washingtonpost.com/news/politics/wp/2018/02/21/what-obama-did-didnt-do-and-couldnt-do-in-response-to-russian-interference/
78. Philip Bump, "What Obama did, didn't do and couldn't do in response to Russian interference," *The Washington Post,* February 21, 2018, https://www.washingtonpost.com/news/politics/wp/2018/02/21/what-obama-did-didnt-do-and-couldnt-do-in-response-to-russian-interference/
79. Julie H. Davis & Maggie Haberman, "Donald Trump Concedes Russia's Interference in Election," *New York Times,* January 11, 2017, https://www.nytimes.com/2017/01/11/us/politics/trumps-press-conference-highlights-russia.html

On 10/30/2017, The Guardian ran this headline, "Russia-backed Facebook posts 'reached 126m Americans' during US election." https://bit.ly/2TG6OEI

On 12/20/2017 Politifact ran this story, "2018 Lie of the Year: Russian election interference is a 'made-up story.'" https://bit.ly/336aWCn

Please note all of these headline-generating stories appeared in 2017, the year <u>before</u> Trump met Putin in Helsinki in 2018.

To repeat, all of these articles ran in 2017, long before Trump's July 16, 2018, Helsinki lie.

07/13/18: U.S. Intel gave Trump indisputable facts about Russian interference in the U.S. 2016 Election, including the name and rank of the Russian officer who hacked into U.S. election computers, his office location in Russian government Moscow Towers, his computer IP address, including his actual keystrokes, etc.

07/13/18: Three days before Donald Trump and Vladimir Putin are set to meet in Helsinki, the U.S. Justice Department announced indictments[80] against 12 Russian nationals, accusing them of orchestrating a campaign to "hack" emails and computer networks belonging to the Clinton campaign and Democratic Party in the last U.S. presidential election.[81]

07/16/18: Trump lies at the Helsinki press conference. Trump said, "I have President Putin. He just said it's not Russia. I will say this. I don't see any reason why it would be." This lie by Trump was made three

---

80. US Department of Justice, "Case 1:18-cr-00215-ABJ   Document 1   Filed 07/13/18," *US Department of Justice,* March 24, 2020, https://www.justice.gov/file/1080281/download

81. US Department of Justice, "Three days before Trump sits down with Putin, the U.S. Justice Department indicts 12 Russian military intel officers," *Meduza,* July 13, 2018, https://meduza.io/en/news/2018/07/13/three-days-before-trump-sits-down-with-putin-the-u-s-justice-department-indicts-12-russian-military-intel-officers

days after Trump was given irrefutable facts to the contrary, but also after a two-hour secret meeting with Putin.

05/30/19: 4:57 AM Trump admits Russian interference in a tweet: "…I had nothing to do with Russia helping me to get elected."

2. Trump's White House Press Conference Lie on Russian Venezuela interference reflects what a Russian agent would do. An agent acts on behalf of his controller, and an agent will demonstrate to whom the agent is most loyal.

12/11/18: Russian Tu-160 nuclear bombers land in Venezuela.[82]

03/24/19: Two planeloads of Russian soldiers land in Venezuela.[83]

04/30/19: Sec. Pompeo, on CNN, states Russia is deeply involved in Venezuela. Maduro ready to leave for Cuba on a Cuban plane waiting for him on the tarmac, and Russia convinced Maduro not to leave.

05/3/19: Trump, following a secret phone call with Vladimir Putin, lies at WH press conference saying Russia isn't seeking to "get involved" in Venezuela.

In a separate treasonous act:

Trump, on July 25, 2019, was aiding an enemy, Russia, by ordering the suspension of funds for military defense, that Congress authorized, for Ukraine from being delivered to our ally at war with Russia. The Government Accountability Office called this a clear violation of Federal Law by violating the Federal 1974 Impoundment Control Act.

---

82. Associated Press, "Russia sends two nuclear-capable bombers to Venezuela," *NBC News*, December 11, 2018, https://www.nbcnews.com/news/world/russia-sends-2-nuclear-capable-bombers-venezuela-n946246
83. Staff, "Russian air force planes land in Venezuela carrying troops: report," *UNIAN*, March 24, 2019, https://www.unian.info/world/10490769-russian-air-force-planes-land-in-venezuela-carrying-troops-report.html

Pushing a Russian hoax that can only benefit Russia while providing disinformation to Americans is probably a treasonous act.

Trump sought two investigations by Ukraine President Zelensky in his July 25, 2019 call and with his approaches through intermediaries. Trump sought an announcement of an investigation into the Biden's, and into a non-existent Ukrainian DNC server hypothetically used in the 2016 election, which was a hoax developed by Russia to distract from Russia's own interference in the 2016 US election.

Blocking Ukraine's military aid in 2019 is even more suspicious when you consider the fact that Trump released the aid to Ukraine in 2017 and in 2018 without any strings or discussions about corruption. Yet, "out of the blue" strings got attached as soon as Trump was entering the 2020 election cycle and wanted help in smearing his presumed 2020 opponent, Vice President Joseph Biden.

And, scarily Trump unilaterally, with no support from anyone else in the Administration or State Department, sought to create a false distraction from Russia's interference in the 2016 election by promulgating a hoax invented by Putin.[84]

Trump's most treasonous act occurred on 7/25/2019 and fully admitted to by Donald Trump when he released a transcript of his July 25 phone call with the Ukrainian President. In that phone call, Trump was pushing the Russian CrowdStrike Ukrainian-based DNC server hoax. That hoax has only one beneficiary, Russia. Trump, therefore, is carrying water for Putin. You have to ask yourself, "Why?"[85]

---

84. Annieli, "Guilty Trump: conspiracy to commit Bribery and Extortion because he believes nonsense," *DailyKos.com*, November 09, 2019, https://m.dailykos.com/stories/2019/11/9/1898190/-Guilty-Trump-conspiracy-to-commit-Bribery-and-Extortion-because-he-believes-nonsense

85. Fadel Allassan, "Senators briefed that CrowdStrike theory is Russian-backed disinformation campaign," *Axios*, November 22, 2019, https://www.axios.com/ukraine-election-meddling-briefing-conspiracy-russia-971db9ae-4024-40b9-a04c-aba6029b39ee.html

What's in it for Trump? Clearly, there is something in it for Russia, or they wouldn't be pushing the hoax, and they wouldn't be pushing Trump to push the hoax. But something is motivating Trump because Trump doesn't do anything for anybody for free. It has to be a carrot or a stick. Maybe both. Could the carrot be some promise about building Trump Towers in Russian held territories after Trump is out of the White House? Maybe a Trump Tower in Moscow and in Crimea? Or is there also a stick involved where Putin has something compromising on Trump that would be incredibly embarrassing for Trump to have revealed.

No doubt the Russians have hacked various computers around the world and in the United States and maybe they have a copy of Trump's tax returns. Could that be it?

Or was there some compromising video that exists from when Trump, known as a philanderer, was in Moscow during the Miss Universe pageant. Of course, Russia would never entrap a businessman with a little hot sex video, right? The Russians did not invent kompromat, but they are certainly masters at it. Even the CIA has used sex tapes to blackmail and motivate various people around the world. That's no secret. For more on CIA and Russia using sex for entrapment purposes, you can go to the CIA library at CIA.gov/library and look up the book titled, "The Search For The 'Manchurian Candidate'" by John Marks and Allen Lane. In that book, you will find this report that was acquired from the CIA using the Freedom of Information Act, "In the best tradition of Mata Hari, the CIA did use sex as a clandestine weapon, although apparently not so frequently as the Russians." Or go to https://medium.com/war-is-boring for an article titled, "The CIA and KGB Both Tried to Blackmail This World Leader With Sex Tapes." The world leader in question was Sukarno of Indonesia. The Russians had a small group of professionals pose as flight attendants. The rest of the story is online.

In May 2016, Politico reported, "On June 18, 2013, Donald Trump had some exciting news: He would soon be whisking dozens of the world's most beautiful women to Russia. 'The Miss Universe Pageant will be broadcast live from MOSCOW, RUSSIA on November 9th,' Trump tweeted that day, referring to the beauty pageant he owned at the time. 'A big deal that will bring our countries together! And maybe not just the countries,' Trump also tweeted, 'Do you think Putin will be going to The Miss Universe Pageant? If so, will he become my new best friend?'[86]

So, what are the odds that Trump, who, according to Trump's voice on the Access Hollywood tape, likes to "grab their pussy" may have been seduced by one or more sexy ladies working for Putin and Russia during the Miss Universe Pageant when it was held in Moscow? Obviously, being sexually compromised on tape is not anything new under the sun. But sometimes we need to remind ourselves that in the real world real people get compromised, and they have to do weird things that they wouldn't ordinarily do like lying to the American public and pushing a bazaar hoax that everybody on the planet knows is absolutely false and that it came from Russia. Why would Trump, a very proud man, make himself appear like such a dunce and a puppet of Putin unless he had to for some reason?

Somehow Putin got Trump to promote the Russian-created CrowdStrike Ukraine hoax.[87]

---

86. Michael Crowley, "When Donald Trump brought Miss Universe to Moscow", *Politico*, May 15, 2016, https://www.politico.com/story/2016/05/donald-trump-russia-moscow-miss-universe-223173

87. Fadel Allassan, "Senators briefed that CrowdStrike theory is Russian-backed disinformation campaign," *Axios*, Nov 22, 2019, https://www.axios.com/ukraine-

Somehow Putin got Trump to lie in Helsinki on July 16, 2018 supporting the false story that Russia did not interfere in the 2016 US election.

Somehow Putin got Trump to lie about Russia not being involved in Venezuela after the whole world knew that Russia had sent in troops and two-supersonic TU-160 nuclear-capable bombers into Venezuela.

All of these lies came on the day of, or shortly after, a secret meeting or secret phone call between Trump and Putin with no American translator, or national security personnel, or State Department people present.

On June 28, 2020, we all read this bombshell. Trump was aware that Putin had ordered the murder of American soldiers and was paying a bounty for every American soldier killed in Afghanistan. The Huff Post reported, "'Tre45on' Trends After Report That Trump Knew Putin Put Bounty On U.S. Troops."[88] The byline read, "Joe Biden slammed Trump's record of "deference and debasing himself before Vladimir Putin."
Putin's Puppet finally outed!

Additional reports reveal, despite his denials, President Trump was briefed about the Russian program, yet, in apparent deference to President Putin, took no action, nor has he announced any to date.

Published 31 mins ago on June 29, 2020By David Badash, The New Civil Rights Movement

---

election-meddling-briefing-conspiracy-russia-971db9ae-4024-40b9-a04c-aba6029b39ee.html
88. Mary Papenfuss, "'Tre45on' Trends After Report That Trump Knew Putin Put Bounty On U.S. Troops," Huff Post, June 28, 2020, https://bit.ly/3006xjh

David Badash, "BUSTED: Trump engaged in 3-week 'flurry of communication' with Putin this year – and the White House hid some of the calls," June 29, 2020, https://www.rawstory.com/2020/06/busted-trump-engaged-in-3-week-flurry-of-communication-with-putin-this-year-and-the-white-house-hid-some-of-the-calls/?utm_source=&utm_medium=email&utm_campaign=4883

Another example of collusion with Russia in secrecy: The American people, for example, only learned of Trump's Oval Office meeting with Ambassador Sergey Kislyak and Russian foreign minister Sergey Lavrov, after a Tass photographer who was in the room published the photos.

What is Trump hiding?

'Tre45on' Trends After Report That Trump Knew Putin Put Bounty On U.S. Troops
Joe Biden slammed Trump's record of "deference and debasing himself before Vladimir Putin."

Read in HuffPost: https://apple.news/AwgG2eiW-RxWuSxr3aje_aw

#8. Article I, Section 9, Clause 8 U.S. Constitution: Emoluments Clause; Accepting foreign money placed directly into his company's bank account.

The emoluments law is described here:[89]

---

89. Legal Information Institute, "18 U.S. Code § 1503.Influencing or injuring officer or juror generally," *Cornell law school,* 20 March 2020, https://www.law.cornell.edu/uscode/text/18/1503

Trump's violations discussed:[90]

October 1, 2019 article titled, *Profiting off the Presidency: Trump's Violations of the Emoluments Clauses* by Gabe Lezra, Staff Counsel for Citizens for Responsibility and Ethics in Washington. Lezra calls for impeachment.   Three lawsuits citing Trump's violation of the emoluments clause were filed. The first was filed by a public interest watchdog. The second lawsuit was by the attorney general of Maryland. The third lawsuit was filed by the District of Columbia. Two of the suits were knocked out on technicalities of "standing" of the Plaintiffs without addressing the merits. In the July 25, 2019 phone call between Trump and Ukraine President Volodymyr Zelensky, Zelensky told Trump that the "last time I traveled to the United States I stayed in New York near Central Park and I stayed at the Trump Tower." Clearly, Zelensky was trying to incur favor by saying, in effect, "Hey, I've given money to you and your business." This kind of undue influence, undue leverage, and conflict of interest were precisely the types of compromise and appearance of corruption that the Founders wanted to avoid when creating the emoluments clause.

In another article in the April 2018 New York Magazine titled, "501 Days in Swampland - A constant drip of self-dealing. And this is just what we know so far …"

This article tracks the money from foreign governments pouring into Trump's pockets via his many business interests.

Nowhere has the self-enrichment been more evident than at his Washington hotel, which quickly filled up with the very lobbyists and swamp creatures Trump had railed against during his campaign. Oil

---

90. Gabe Lezra, "Profiting off the Presidency: Trump's Violations of the Emoluments Clauses," *American Constitution Society,* October 1, 2019, https://www.acslaw.org/expertforum/profiting-off-the-presidency-trumps-violations-of-the-emoluments-clauses/

companies, mining interests, insurance executives, foreign diplomats, and defense contractors all rushed to book their annual conferences at Trump's hotels and resorts, where Cabinet members graciously addressed them. After hiking the nightly rate to $653 — 32 percent higher than other local luxury hotels.

"On January 23, 2018, Saudi Arabia holds a bash at the hotel after renting rooms for lobbyists for five months. Trump's haul: $270,000."

And this statistic in the article jumps out, "Trump collected $2 million in profits from the property (his Washington DC hotel) during his first three months in office."[91]

#9. Title 18 U.S. Code § 2101. Incite to violence. Trump allegedly incites one of his devotees to threaten murder.

Trump may have violated the "incite to violence" criminal statute when Trump held up a photo of the Washington Whistleblower's lawyer, Mark Zaid, and read some of Zaid's 2017 anti-Trump tweets at a rally in Louisiana on November 6, 2019. Trump called Zaid a "sleazeball." That act by Trump was followed by a death threat by someone allegedly known as a Trump devotee.

Brittan J. Atkinson is alleged to have sent an email message to attorney Mark Zaid the day after Trump held up a photo of this Washington lawyer and read some of his tweets at a rally in Louisiana in November. This is the news headline that relates to Trump's statements that was reported by NBC News on February 20, 2020, 'Bleed you out' like a pig: Feds accuse man of threatening Trump whistleblower's lawyer." Atkinson's email is reported to state,

> All traitors must die miserable deaths. Those that represent traitors shall meet the same fate[.] We will hunt you down and

91. Joy Crane & Nick Tabor, "501 Days in Swampland," *New York Magazine,* April 2, 2018, http://nymag.com/intelligencer/2018/04/trump-and-co-are-stealing-america-blind-timeline.html

bleed you out like the pigs you are. We have nothing but time, and you are running out of it, Keep looking over your shoulder[.] We know who you are, where you live, and who you associate with[.] We are all strangers in a crowd to you[.][92]

CBS ran this headline 2020, February 20, 2020, "Michigan man charged for allegedly sending death threat to Ukraine whistleblower's attorney."[93]

Newsweek also ran the death-threat story on February 20, 2020, titled, 'You Are Running Out' Of Time: Feds Charge Michigan Man With Threatening Ukraine Whistleblower."[94]

Had it not been for Donald Trump, this alleged incitement and the related death-threat headlines never would have occurred.

Bear this in mind. While in office, Presidents are treated, as a matter of DOJ policy (not Congressionally approved law) as being immune from prosecution for acts performed in the "official" capacity of President. But that does not mean the President is always above the law.

Because this act of incitement to violence was not part of an official Presidential act, Donald Trump, the civilian, may potentially be charged with the crime of incitement to violence.

The Federal Employees Liability Reform and Tort Compensation Act of 1988, commonly known as the Westfall Act, accords federal

---

92. Rich Schapiro, "Bleed you out' like a pig: Feds accuse man of threatening Trump whistleblower's lawyer," *NBC News*, February 20, 2020, ,
https://news.yahoo.com/bleed-pig-feds-bust-man-201100837.html
93. Melissa Quinn, "Michigan man charged for allegedly sending death threat to Ukraine whistleblower's attorney," *CBS News,* February 20, 2020, https://www.cbsnews.com/news/michigan-man-charged-for-allegedly-sending-death-threat-to-ukraine-whistleblowers-attorney/
94. Asher Stockler, "You Are Running Out' Of Time: Feds Charge Michigan Man With Threatening Ukraine Whistleblower Attorney," *Newsweek,* February 20, 2020, https://www.newsweek.com/whistleblower-ukraine-impeachment-threats-1488293

employees absolute immunity from common-law tort claims arising out of acts they undertake in the course of their <u>official</u> duties. See 28 U. S. C. §2679(b)(1)

Next: Four Whistleblower laws were allegedly violated by Trump.

I am grateful for the brilliant and insightful legal resources provided by attorney David K. Colapinto, Co-Founder and General Counsel of the National Whistleblower Center, and Founding Partner of the Washington, DC whistleblower law firm of Kohn, Kohn, and Colapinto located at https://www.kkc.com and https://www.kkc.com/who-we-are/our-attorneys/david-colapinto/. Because of attorney Colapinto, I was able to learn about a number of "whistleblower" related laws. In fact, I had originally included one whistleblower law in the manuscript that attorney Colapinto explained to me was not applicable to members of the intel community. So, thanks to him, I was able to remove it.

Based on the in-depth whistleblower related law resources provided to me by attorney Colapinto including those found at the National Whistleblower Center, NWC, https://www.whistleblowers.org, I was able to add four whistleblower related laws allegedly violated by President Trump.

#10. The Inspector General Act of 1978– Section 7 (c): Violated by revealing confidential Whistleblower information, including the identity of a confidential whistleblower. Trump allegedly violated The Inspector General Act when, on December 26, 2019, Trump tweeted the name of the whistleblower out to his 75 million Twitter followers.[95]

Trump also allegedly violated_The Inspector General Act of 1978– Section 7 (c) when he addressed members of UN staff on September 26, 2019, when on that day AP News reported, that the chairmen of the

---

95. Asawin Suebsaeng, "Trump Pushes Out Tweet Naming Alleged Whistleblower," *The Daily Beast,* December 26, 2019, https://www.thedailybeast.com/trump-pushes-out-tweet-naming-alleged-whistleblower

foreign affairs, intelligence, and oversight committees said, "The President's comments today constitute reprehensible witness intimidation…" This witness intimidation accusation is covered in more detail below at #16. Title 18 U.S. Code § 1512 - Witness Intimidation.[96]

The Inspector General Act – Section 7 requires that confidential Whistleblower information, including the identity of a confidential whistleblower, be kept confidential. Section 7 (c) specifically states,

> Any employee who has authority to take, direct others to take, recommend, or approve any personnel action, shall not, with respect to such authority, take or threaten to take any action against any employee as a reprisal for making a complaint...

The "Inspector General Act of 1978". (Pub. L. 95–452, §1, Oct. 12, 1978, 92 Stat. 1101.)[97] specifically states,

> Section 7: Complaints by employees; disclosure of identity; reprisals.

> (c) Any employee who has authority to take, direct others to take, recommend, or approve any personnel action, shall not, with respect to such authority, take or threaten to take any action against any employee as a reprisal for making a complaint or disclosing information to an Inspector General, unless the complaint was made or the information disclosed with the knowledge that it was false or with willful disregard for its truth or falsity.

#11. Title 5 USC §552a. - The Privacy Act of 1974: Trump allegedly violated The Privacy Act of 1974 by revealing confidential

96. AP Staff, "The Latest: Democrats accuse Trump of witness intimidation," *The Associated Press,* September 26, 2019,
https://apnews.com/f2f662aa7aa64030bed2dd496dfc3b0b
97. Staff, "Inspector General Act of 1978," *Council of the Inspectors General on Integrity and Efficiency*, July 7, 2014,
https://www.ignet.gov/sites/default/files/files/igactasof1010(1).pdf

Whistleblower information, including the identity of a confidential whistleblower. Trump violated The Privacy Act of 1974 when, on December 26, 2019, Trump tweeted the name of the whistleblower out to his 75 million Twitter followers. The Inspector General Act – Section 7 requires that confidential Whistleblower information, including the identity of a confidential whistleblower, be kept confidential.[98]

The Privacy Act of 1974, as amended, 5 U.S.C. § 552a, establishes

> a code of fair information practices that governs the collection, maintenance, use, and dissemination of information about individuals that is maintained in systems of records by federal agencies.[99]

> (b) Conditions of Disclosure. — No agency shall disclose any record which is contained in a system of records by any means of communication to any person, or to another agency, except pursuant to a written request by, or with the prior written consent of, the individual to whom the record pertains

> (i) (1) Criminal Penalties.— Any officer or employee of an agency, who by virtue of his employment or official position, has possession of, or access to, agency records which contain individually identifiable information the disclosure of which is prohibited by this section or by rules or regulations established thereunder, and who knowing that disclosure of the specific material is so prohibited, willfully discloses the material in any

---

98. Asawin Suebsaeng, "Trump Pushes Out Tweet Naming Alleged Whistleblower," *The Daily Beast*, December 26, 2019, https://www.thedailybeast.com/trump-pushes-out-tweet-naming-alleged-whistleblower

99. Legal Information Institute, "Legal Information Institute, Records maintained on individuals. 5 U.S.C. § 552a," *Cornell law school*, March 20, 2020, https://www.law.cornell.edu/uscode/text/5/552a

manner to any person or agency not entitled to receive it, shall be guilty of a misdemeanor and fined not more than $5,000.

#12. Title 50 USC §3234 - Prohibited Personnel Practices In The Intelligence Community. Specifically, when, on December 27, 2019, Trump tweeted the name of the whistleblower out to his 75 million Twitter followers, Trump may have violated Title 50 USC §3234 (d) Enforcement, which states, "The President shall provide for the enforcement of this section." And in related circumstances, Trump may have violated his oath of office and may have violated Title 50 USC §3234 (a) (3) (J), which is designed to protect the whistleblower from experiencing "any other significant change in duties, responsibilities, or working conditions."

Statute information may be read at[100]

#13. Title 18 U.S. Code § 1513. Retaliating Against A Witness, Victim, or An Informant - may have been violated by Trump. Specifically, when, on December 27, 2019, Trump tweeted the name of the whistleblower out to his 68 million Twitter followers Trump may have violated 18 USC §1513(e) which states,

> Whoever knowingly, with the intent to retaliate, takes any action harmful to any person, including interference with the lawful employment or livelihood of any person, for providing to a law enforcement officer any truthful information relating to the commission or possible commission of any Federal offense, shall be fined under this title or imprisoned not more than 10 years, or both.

---

100. Legal Information Institute, "Prohibited personnel practices in the intelligence community. 50 U.S.C. § 3234," *Cornell law school*, March 20, 2020, https://www.law.cornell.edu/uscode/text/50/3234

#14. Vicarious Liability. See respondeat superior[101]. Common law legal doctrine, most commonly used in tort[102] that holds an employer or principal[103] legally responsible[104]for the wrongful acts of an employee or agent,[105] if such acts occur within the scope of the employment or agency. See January 2, 2019, *USA Today* article titled, "Trump Illegally Asked Russia To Help Him Win In 2016. He Shouldn't Get Away With It." Trump's public request for Russian help in finding Hillary Clinton's emails was a violation of US law. There are ways to hold him accountable.[106] [107] [108] [109]

Jul 13, 2018 the New York Times covered the "coincidence" at the heart of the Russia hacking scandal. A new indictment charges that Russians tried to hack Hillary Clinton's emails on July 27, 2016, the same day that Donald Trump publicly asked Russia to do so. Here is part of that news story by the New York times on July 13, 2018,

---

101. Legal Information Institute, "Respondeat Superior," *Cornell Law School*, March 20, 2020, https://www.law.cornell.edu/wex/respondeat_superior

102. Legal Information Institute, "Tort Cornell Law School," *Cornell Law School*, March 20, 2020, https://www.law.cornell.edu/wex/tort

103. Legal Information Institute, "Principal," *Cornell Law School*, March 20, 2020, https://www.law.cornell.edu/wex/principal

104. Legal Information Institute, "Liable," *Cornell Law School,* March 20, 2020, https://www.law.cornell.edu/wex/liable

105. Ibid.

106. Fred Wertheimer & Norman Eisen, "Trump illegally asked Russia to help him win in 2016. He shouldn't get away with it," *USA TODAY*, January 2, 2019, https://www.usatoday.com/story/opinion/2019/01/02/trump-broke-law-russia-clinton-emails-hold-him-accountable-column/2449564002/

107. Legal Information Institute, "Vicarious Liability," *Cornell Law School*, March 20, 2020, https://www.law.cornell.edu/wex/vicarious_liability

108. Legal Information Institute, "Respondeat Superior," *Cornell Law School,* March 20, 2020, https://www.law.cornell.edu/wex/respondeat_superior

109. David Graham, "The Coincidence at the Heart of the Russia Hacking Scandal," *The Atlantic,* July 13, 2018, https://www.theatlantic.com/politics/archive/2018/07/russia-hacking-trump-mueller/565157/

"Russia, if you're listening, I hope you're able to find the 30,000 emails that are missing," Mr. Trump said, referring to emails Mrs. Clinton had deleted from the private account she had used when she was secretary of state. "I think you will probably be rewarded mightily by our press."

As it turns out, that same day, the Russians — whether they had tuned in or not — made their first effort to break into the servers used by Mrs. Clinton's personal office, according to a sweeping 29-page indictment unsealed Friday by the special counsel's office that charged 12 Russians with election hacking." https://nyti.ms/3blRNQn

Michael S. Schmidt, July 13, 2018, New York Times, "Trump Invited the Russians to Hack Clinton. Were They Listening?", https://www.nytimes.com/2018/07/13/us/politics/trump-russia-clinton-emails.html

#15. Title 18 U.S.C. § 1001 (a) (1) (2) (3)– Making False Statements[110]

The law includes the following wording that refers to the "executive" branch.

(a) Except as otherwise provided in this section, whoever, in any matter within the jurisdiction of the executive, legislative, or judicial branch of the Government of the United States, knowingly and willfully--

(1)   falsifies, conceals, or covers up by any trick, scheme, or device a material fact;

(2)   makes any materially false, fictitious, or fraudulent statement or representation; or

---

110. Legal Information Institute, "Statements or entries generally.18 U.S.C. § 1001," *Cornell Law School*, March 20, 2020, 2020, https://www.law.cornell.edu/uscode/text/18/1001

(3)   makes or uses any false writing or document knowing the same to contain any materially false, fictitious, or fraudulent statement or entry;

shall be fined under this title, imprisoned not more than 5 years…"

https://codes.findlaw.com/us/title-18-crimes-and-criminal-procedure/18-usc-sect-1001.html

"In 1,095 days, President Trump has made 16,241 false or misleading claims." That was the Washington Post headline on January 19, 2020. Sometimes these false and misleading statements can dramatically impact the stock market. This article provides an example. In the fall of 2019, Trump was talking about reaching a trade deal with the Chinese that would bring in $50 billion to the farmers in soybean sales. When the deal was finally struck in January 2020, it made a reference to only $32 billion in purchases. Then, the Chinese vice premier said there was no hard number, but that it was all based on the market conditions at the time. This sent soybean stocks tumbling.[111]

On March 17, 2020, we were given another example of a false and misleading statement that could be damaging to many in the American public according to Politifact in an article titled, "Latest False Fact-Checks On Donald Trump." The article reported that Trump said, "insurance companies will waive co-pays for coronavirus treatments." In an environment where many people are worried about how they are going to pay for their insurance, especially when it comes to the new coronavirus, Politifact found out that the statement by Trump was not true.[112]

---

111. Glenn Kessler, Salvador Rizzo and Meg Kelly, "In 1,095 days, President Trump has made 16,241 false or misleading claims," *Washington Post*, Jan. 19, 2020, https://www.washingtonpost.com/politics/2020/01/20/president-trump-made-16241-false-or-misleading-claims-his-first-three-years/
112. Jon Greenberg, "Latest False Fact-checks on Donald Trump," *PolitiFact*, March 17, 2020, https://www.politifact.com/factchecks/list/?speaker=donald-trump&ruling=false

False statements by President Trump can be damaging in many ways, including financially and emotionally.

#16. Title 18 U.S. Code § 1512 - Witness Intimidation, Tampering with a witness, victim, or...[113]

> (b) Whoever knowingly uses intimidation, threatens, or corruptly persuades another person, or attempts to do so, or engages in misleading conduct toward another person, with intent to— (1) influence, delay, or prevent the testimony of any person in an official proceeding;

On September 26, 2019, AP News reported that the chairmen of the foreign affairs, intelligence, and oversight committees said, "The President's comments today constitute reprehensible witness intimidation and an attempt to obstruct Congress' impeachment inquiry." Those Chairmen were referring to President Donald Trump statements earlier on that day to a "crowd of staff from the United States Mission to the United Nations" that he (Trump) wanted to know who the Ukraine whistleblower's source or sources were "because that's close to a spy." Trump then remarked that back in the "old days" spies and traitors were treated "a little differently." In those days, we were "smart," Trump said. The three Congressional Chairmen immediately interpreted Trump's words as witness intimidation and an attempt to obstruct Congress. The intimidation and obstruction were very significant as those White House sources may very well be asked down the line to testify in some form or fashion in front of Congress.[114]

#17. Title 2 U.S. Code § 192, "Refusal To Produce Documents"

---

113. Legal Information Institute, "Tampering with a witness, victim, or an informant.18 U.S.C. § 1512," *Cornell Law School*, March 20, 2020, https://www.law.cornell.edu/uscode/text/18/1512

114. Staff, "The Latest: Democrats accuse Trump of witness intimidation," *The Associated Press,* September 26, 2019, https://apnews.com/f2f662aa7aa64030bed2dd496dfc3b0b

A description of the law can be found here:[115]

The code states,

> Every person who having been summoned as a witness by the authority of either House of Congress to give testimony or to produce papers upon any matter under inquiry before either House, or any joint committee established by a joint or concurrent resolution of the two Houses of Congress, or any committee of either House of Congress, willfully makes default, or who, having appeared, refuses to answer any question pertinent to the question under inquiry, shall be deemed guilty of a misdemeanor, punishable by a fine of not more than $1,000 nor less than $100 and imprisonment in a common jail for not less than one month nor more than twelve months.

Writers for MSN reported, "The White House refused Tuesday (October 8, 2019) to turn over internal documents regarding Ukraine being sought by House Democrats as the Trump administration dug in against their impeachment inquiry."[116]

#18. Title 44 U.S.C. §§ 2201–2207, The Presidential Records Act (PRA) of 1978, is an Act of the United States Congress governing the official records of Presidents and Vice Presidents created or received after January 20, 1981, and mandating the preservation of all presidential records. Federal and constitutional law prohibits the destruction of presidential records. At a minimum, we know Trump has been destroying Presidential tweets.

---

115. Legal Information Institute, "Refusal of witness to testify or produce papers. 2 U.S.C. § 192," *Cornell Law School*, March 20, 2020, 2020, https://www.law.cornell.edu/uscode/text/2/192

116. Shannon Pettypiece and Kristen Welker and Alex Moe and Hallie Jackson, "White House refuses to cooperate with impeachment investigation," *MSN*, October 9, 2019, https://www.msn.com/en-us/news/politics/white-house-refuses-to-turn-over-documents-to-democrats-in-impeachment-inquiry/ar-AAIu1sE

Illegal Misappropriation

On January 16, 2020, the nonpartisan Government Accountability Office stated, in a public announcement, that Pres. Donald Trump had illegally impounded taxpayer dollars in violation of the Impoundment Control Act of 1974.

The facts show that on or before July 3, 2019, and until September 11, 2019, Donald Trump personally and at his direction illegally took control of over three hundred million dollars of American taxpayer dollars for the purpose of pursuing personal gain and benefits that would only accrue to him. A misappropriation is a form of stealing. Because Donald Trump misappropriated American taxpayer dollars, he allegedly violated a number of federal statutes that have to do with illegal misappropriation some of which are now listed below:

These next six criminal codes are derivative charges that might be alleged following Trump's illegally (according to the GAO) taking control of over $300 million US taxpayer dollars. Once you accept the charge made by the GAO that Trump illegally took US Federal funds and applied for his own personal purposes, then the titles of the statutes are self-explanatory as to the alleged crime committed by Trump in relation to that illegal act.

#19. Title 18 U.S. Code Chapter 31 - Embezzlement and Theft.

#20. Title 18 U.S. Code § 641 - Converting Public Money for Personal Gain.

#21. Title 18 U.S. Code § 648 - Custodian Misusing Public Funds.

#22. Title 38 U.S. Code § 6101 - Misappropriation by Fiduciaries.

#23. Title 10 U.S. Code § 921 - Art. 121. Larceny and Wrongful Appropriation.

#24. Title 18 U.S. Code § 666 - Theft or Bribery Concerning Programs.

#25. Title 18 U.S. Code § 912. Impersonating Census Officer.

Whoever falsely assumes or pretends to be an officer or employee acting under the authority of the United States or any department, agency or officer thereof, and acts as such, or in such pretended character demands or obtains any money, paper, document, or thing of value, shall be fined under this title or imprisoned not more than three years, or both.[117]

Trump placed an ad on Facebook that was so egregious that even Facebook took it down because it involved a misleading ad purporting to be part of the US Government 2020 census. The BBC headline said, "Facebook removes 'deceptive' Trump census ads."[118]

The BBC article quotes Vanita Gupta,

> The adverts were 'deceptive' and 'unacceptable,' said Vanita Gupta, president, and CEO of The Leadership Conference on Civil and Human Rights, which helped Facebook craft its policy on census interference. If Trump says a fake census is 'official,' people are going to think its official," she said in a series of tweets. "Trump's deceptive ads will confuse people about how and when to participate in the 2020 Census, threatening their right to get counted and bring resources and political power to their communities.

Follows is an actual screenshot from the Trump tweet where Trump falsely implies he represents the Census Department. There is nothing ambiguous about the official look statement, "Official 2020 Congressional District Census."

---

117. Legal Information Institute, "18 U.S. Code § 912.Officer or employee of the United States," *Cornell Law School*, March 20, 2020, https://www.law.cornell.edu/uscode/text/18/912

118. Tom Gerken, "Facebook removes 'deceptive' Trump census ads," *BBC*, March 5, 2020, https://www.bbc.com/news/world-us-canada-51730185

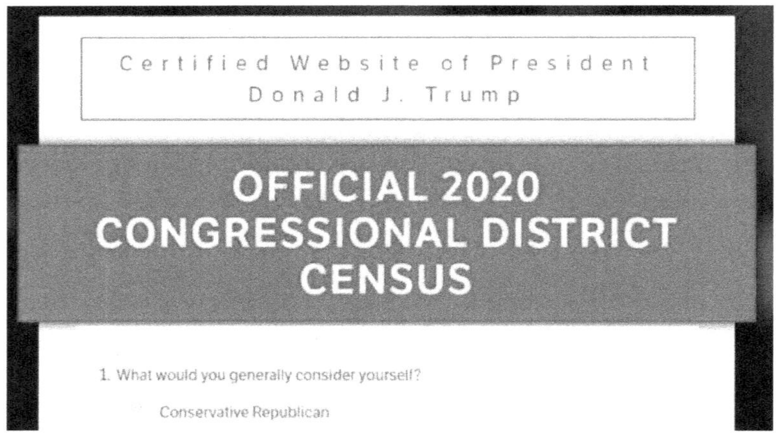

Summary List

All of the following are supported by publicly available evidence.

The 25 Criminal Codes Allegedly Violated by Trump:
1. Title 52 USC § 30121 (a) (2) – Solicitation in violation of FEC.
2. Title X – 1974 Impoundment Control Act - Illegal impoundment.
3. Title 18 USC § 872 – Extortion.
4. Title 18 USC § 201 – Bribery.
5. Title 18 USC §1503 - Obstruction of Justice.
6. Title 18 USC §1505 - Obstruction of Congress.
7. Title 18 USC § 2381 - Treason -Aid /Comfort to an enemy.
8. Article I, Section 9, Clause 8 U.S. Constitution: Emoluments.
9. Title 18 U.S. Code § 2101. Incite to violence
10. The Inspector General Act of 1978– § 7 (a), (b), and (c).
11. Title 5 USC §552a. - The Privacy Act of 1974: Revealed Government confidential secret.
12. Title 50 USC §3234 - Prohibited Personnel Practices In The Intel dept. lists prohibited act allegedly committed by Trump.
13. Title 18 U.S. Code § 1513. Retaliating Against A Witness, Informant.
14. Vicarious Liability under Common Law.

15. Title 18 U.S.C. § 1001 (a) (1) (2) (3) – Making False Statements.
16. 18 U.S. Code § 1512 - Witness Intimidation
17. Title 2 U.S. Code § 192, "Refusal To Produce Documents
18. Title 44 U.S.C. §§ 2201–2207, The Presidential Records Act
19. Title 18 U.S. Code Chapter 31 - Embezzlement and Theft
20. Title 18 U.S. Code § 641 - Converting Public Money for Personal Gain
21. Title 18 U.S. Code § 648 - Custodian Misusing Public Funds
22. Title 38 U.S. Code § 6101 - Misappropriation by Fiduciaries.
23. Title 10 U.S. Code § 921 - Art. 121. Larceny and Wrongful Appropriation
24. Title 18 U.S. Code § 666 - Theft or Bribery Concerning Programs
25. Title 18 U.S. Code § 912. Impersonating Census Office

Before reading this section, many people may have believed that "Yes, it's dirty politics (Trump seeking Ukraine's help in a US election), but no laws were broken." That's not true at all. According to legal analysts, many laws were broken. There is a long list of criminal laws mentioned above that were allegedly broken based on publicly available evidence.

You say, "Yes, but Congress found Trump not guilty. So, Trump was exonerated from any wrongdoing." That's not true at all. Many Senators who voted not to remove Donald Trump from office did not say he was innocent of any wrongdoing.

Upon examination, on February 20, 2020, nearly half of the U.S. Senate jury found Trump guilty of wrongdoing that was so serious he should be removed from office. So, not being removed from office when 48 votes out of 100 said you were guilty and should be instantly removed from office is not an "exoneration." It's a near-death experience.[119]

---

119. Jeremy Herb, "Acquitted: Senate finds Trump not guilty of abuse of power, obstruction of justice," *CNN*, Feb. 5, 2020, https://www.cbs58.com/news/senate-acquits-trump-of-abuse-of-power

With all due respect for the House impeachment prosecutorial team, they lost their case in front of the Senate because they were never able to arouse the public intellectually and emotionally, specifically the preponderance of constituents of the Republican Senators were not swayed. The central theme of the House prosecution team's case had no legal backbone, no criminal law backbone, in the mind of much of the public even though it was sitting there in plain sight. The House impeachment team missed the mark given the available evidence that one could easily allege that at least 10, possibly 25, federal criminal laws were broken by Trump.

The House impeachment prosecutors should have said that they are aware of, and being "informed" by these 24 criminal codes but are not asking the DOJ to file a Federal complaint under them "at this time" because the impeachment clause of the Constitution does not require that a criminal code violation be alleged. In fact, there were no Federal criminal codes at the time the Articles of Impeachment were drafted and approved. It was years later that the first Federal crimes started to be codified. So, although the House prosecution team was technically correct in not having to allege a specific violation of a Federal criminal code, that distinction was way too nuanced for the public, the true jury the House needed to win over, the jury of public opinion. The public wanted to know what laws did Trump break that would justify throwing him out before an election. Well, the evidence is overwhelming that Trump allegedly broke many criminal codes, but the House prosecution team did not effectively highlight any of them in their case presentation. Yes, they highlighted the July 25th call and other actions, but placed all that activity under the umbrella of "attempting to cheat," as opposed to multiple acts of criminal behavior. Big difference there.

Also, all of these alleged Federal "crimes" by Trump formed a solid evidentiary basis for the two articles of impeachment, Abuse of Power, and Obstruction of Congress. The evidence seemed to prove beyond a shadow of a doubt that the identified crime was committed. Read the listed criminal codes. Review the evidence. Many in Congress and numerous legal scholars have indicated that they believe that some, if not all, of those 25 criminal laws had allegedly been violated by Trump. You only needed one solid, un-debatable crime to convince the public. You easily could have *proven* five (illegal impoundment, and violation of four Whistleblower laws, witness intimidation, and Government confidentiality laws.)

Here are just five of the many articles written stating Trump violated the law:

On 10/10/2019: "The Actual Laws Trump Has Broken, Just With the Ukraine and China Affairs, Could Land Him 10 Years in Prison."[120]

On 1/23/20: "What law did Donald Trump break?"[121]

1/16/20: "Trump Broke The Law In Freezing Ukraine Funds, Watchdog Report Concludes."[122]

1/16/20: "G.A.O. Report Says Trump Administration Broke Law in Withholding Ukraine Aid."[123]

---

120. Ryan Grim, "The Actual Laws Trump Has Broken, Just With the Ukraine and China Affairs, Could Land Him 10 Years in Prison," *The Intercept*, October 10, 2019, https://theintercept.com/2019/10/10/trump-crimes-law

121. Allan Lichtman, "What law did Donald Trump break?," *The Hill*, January 23, 2020, https://thehill.com/opinion/white-house/479547-what-law-did-donald-trump-break

122. Ayesha Rascoe, "Trump Broke The Law In Freezing Ukraine Funds, Watchdog Report Concludes," *NPR*, Jan. 16, 2020, https://www.npr.org/2020/01/16/796806517/trump-broke-the-law-in-freezing-ukraine-funds-watchdog-report-concludes

123. Emily Cochrane, Eric Lipton and Chris Cameron, "G.A.O. Report Says Trump Administration Broke Law in Withholding Ukraine Aid," *New York Times*, January 16, 2020, https://www.nytimes.com/2020/01/16/us/politics/gao-trump-ukraine.html

1/2/20: "Unredacted documents show Trump explicitly broke the law."[124]

I invite lawyers, legal scholars, journalists, and law students to send me your own analysis of one or more of the 25 crimes listed (alleged) and others you have identified. DrDavidKingKeller@gmail.com

FYI

Federal Employees and Presidents can be sued.

The Westfall Act, which states that under certain conditions, a Federal employee cannot be sued, does not apply in the above-cited criminal acts in this author's opinion because none of them were as part of an official act in fulfillment of the job's requirements.[125]

Westfall Act is Title 28 U.S. Code § 2679, Exclusiveness of remedy, does not apply because that code states in part the act being cited is excluded from suit if the act is done "while acting within the scope of his office…". So, don't be misled. A Federal employee can be sued for acts committed outside the scope of their office. For example, the Stormy Daniels lawsuit against President Trump was allowed to proceed. It was dismissed because the judge did not accept her evidence, not because she lacked standing.

<u>Twenty-Five Laws Broken (Allegedly)</u>

The number of laws allegedly broken by Trump actually exceeds 25. If you add in "conspired to violate" as an added allegation in front of the title of the criminal statute, because conspiring to break the law is also

---

124. Quinn Hillyer, "Unredacted documents show Trump explicitly broke the law," *Washington Examiner,* January 2, 2020, https://www.washingtonexaminer.com/opinion/unredacted-documents-show-trump-explicitly-broke-the-law

125. US Department of Justice, "Federal Tort Claims Act, Personal Liability Tort Litigation Against Federal Employees," *US Department of Justice*, November 2010, https://www.justice.gov/sites/default/files/usao/legacy/2010/12/06/usab5806.pdf

illegal, then you have another whole list of alleged crimes. The "conspiracy to commit" 'X' covers the "tried to" break the law but got caught in the process is still an illegal act if proven. So, Trump trying to cheat in a US election by allegedly committing or conspiring to commit an illegal act is also a federal crime. Yet, as Trump's attorney said, no crimes were alleged.

And yet, the easily reported and blatantly obvious federal crime committed by Trump according to the non-partisan GAO has gone largely unreported since the GAO's original January 16, 2020 statement on the matter because the Dems lack a proper messaging apparatus that incorporates all media. For this reason, most Americans and most radio talk shows still talk about Trump as not having broken any laws.

But it gets worse. Where was the legal team of white-collar criminal lawyers and former Federal prosecutors assembled by the Democratic leadership that could have been featured in the media and on a website titled www.TrumpsAllegedCrimes.com? (This domain has been reserved by this author and is available for use.)

This website, www.TrumpsAllegedCrimes.com, should have been created and populated well BEFORE the impeachment hearings. This would have given journalists, TV news anchors, Congresswomen/men, Senators, attorneys, legal scholars, and average citizens a place to go for background information on all of Trump's alleged crimes and Trump's alleged un-American activities. This should have been a central part of all the tactics and strategies incorporated to lay the groundwork for the gravest act a Country can contemplate, the removal of an elected President.

That TrumpsAllegedCrimes.com website would read like a formal court-filed complaint by a Federal prosecutor on each of the federal criminal statutes. Anyone preparing their case for Trump's alleged criminal code violation could learn from the well-crafted legal discussion prepared by Law Professor and Co-Director of the Institute of Judicial Administration at NYU School of Law Samuel Estreicher and his associate Christopher Owen, in their highly detailed and well documented presentation on the charge of bribery against Trump printed up on the website verdict.justia.com at this URL:[126]

There are over 25 federal crimes that could have been alleged as crimes committed by Donald Trump, which are supported by substantial public evidence.

Despite this large body of criminal evidence, because of the Democrats' incredibly poor communication apparatus, the average American believes Trump committed no crime and broke no laws. The majority may not like him, but they haven't been educated on any crimes committed by Trump that they could cite over coffee with a friend. Had Obama allegedly committed those 25 crimes, you can bet the Republican-echo chamber would have the average American capable of citing at least 6 of them within three weeks.

The Dems need their own version of Kellyanne Conway, along with a team of communication specialists who feed the voracious appetite of the 24/7 news world, including social media with this list of all the possible crimes committed by Trump. The majority of sound bites should not have been left just to Representative Nancy Pelosi and Senator Chuck Schumer, as talented as they are, the media needs a variety of faces and voices to keep their audiences engaged. Yes, I know many Representatives and Senators gave interviews, but
the Democratic leadership should have found a leading expert in each of the above criminal areas and had them on a well-publicized media stand-by list. For example, in discussing the four Whistleblower laws allegedly broken by Donald Trump, you could have had the brilliant whistleblower attorney David Colapinto on call for media comments

---

126. Samuel Estreicher & Christopher Owens, "Did President Trump Commit the Federal Crime of Bribery?," *Verdict Justia*, December 3, 2019, https://verdict.justia.com/amp/2019/12/03/did-president-trump-commit-the-federal-crime-of-bribery

and interviews, as well as directors from the National Whistleblower Center.

It would have been very easy to secure testimonials from retired Federal prosecutors willing to describe the 25 alleged crimes of Donald Trump. There's already a list of 1,000 former prosecutors that say, but for being President, Trump would have been indicted.[127]

These Federal prosecutor testimonials could have appeared on the DNC website, and each one could have been an individual YouTube release circulating the Internet. The prosecutors, themselves, could be making the rounds of all of the cable news channels and the various talk shows. Had all of this exposure of Trump's alleged crimes taken place before the impeachment hearing, would a different person be sitting in the White House? Had all of these alleged crimes been properly publicized, would twenty-five percent of America believe that Trump did nothing wrong?

One reason the Democrats may lose the 2020 election was their failure to publicize Trump's 25 alleged federal crimes.

---

127. Alexandra Hutzler, "Former Federal Prosecutors Renew Statement That Trump Would Have Been Indicted If he Weren't President," *Newsweek*, May 30, 2019, https://www.newsweek.com/former-federal-prosecutors-trump-indicted-wasnt-president-1439716

CHAPTER 4

12 STEPS TO A DEMOCRATIC VICTORY

The Democrats may lose the 2020 election if they fail to include the following twelve elements in pursuit of a 2020 victory.

The Victory Plan.

Brief Summary of the 12 Steps

1. Re-Brand Trump

2. Re-Brand Republican Party

3. Turn Base into Raving, Super-Committed Voters

4. Vote Acquisition Strategy of Moderate Republicans

5. Winning Available Independent Votes

6. Nine State Strategy

7. Issues: Something for Every Demographic (almost):

8. Celebrities Galore

9. Entertainment, Games, Prizes, and Rewards

10. Biden: Increase Favorable Rating; Reduce Unfavorable Rating; Increase Enthusiasm Level

11. Media Blitzed 24/7 by Dems Large National Media Team

12. Money. Lots of it. $10 Billion.

Expanded Summary of the 12 Steps

1. Re-Brand Trump:

Point out the undesirable side of Trump using short memes.

Don-the-Con, Traitor-Trump, Tax Dodger Trump, and Dark-Secrets Trump. Short word memes downgrading Trump are discussed below and elsewhere within this book. See Table of Contents and Index.

Two-Faced Liar Trump said, "Border wall money will come from Mexico," then demands billions in the US budget for the wall. See "Chapter 3" regarding the alleged crime of providing false and misleading information. Two-Faced Liar Trump tweeted, "President Obama wasting time golfing," then spends more money and more time golfing than Obama ever did. See the Trump golf cartoon with a reference source.)

Don-first-America-second Trump diverts military aircraft through Scotland for refueling, so, they stay at his resort).[128] See also "Chapter 3" on alleged Emoluments crime.

Heartless Don. He caged babies and separated children from parents then lost the location of the babies' parents. Trump wants to reduce social security to pay for tax benefits to rich.[129]

We need to create even greater nagging doubt about Trump, the person, his actions, and his policies.

---

128. Kenneth Garger, "Trump had a deal with Scottish airport that sent Air Force crew to his resort: report" *New York Post*, (2019, Sept. 9). ,https://nypost.com/2019/09/09/trump-had-deal-with-scottish-airport-that-sent-air-force-crew-to-his-resort-report/

129. Ryan Devereaux, "The U.S. Has Taken More Than 3,700 Children From Their Parents — and Has No Plan for Returning Them," *The Intercept*, June 19, 2018, https://theintercept.com/2018/06/19/children-separated-from-parents-family-separation-immigration/

Trump turned blue-collar workers into economic slaves for the rich. See *Appendix 4, 5, and 12* for an explanation and data sources.

Metric to determine success: increase Trump's unfavorable rating in polls by 10 points.

Trump's unfavorable rating in Gallup poll on 2/27/20 = 50% unfavorable; Quinnipiac University Poll on March 9, 2020= 58% unfavorable.[130] [131]

Target: by October 30, 2020, you want Trump unfavorable rating in Gallup poll =70%.

Be aware of this important background data:

Trump's unfavorable rating on October 30, 2016, was 61%, and he still won.[132]

If Trump's unfavorables were so high, at 61% in 2016 compared to Clinton's 52%, why did Trump still win? The answer is Electoral math.

Although Clinton did win the popular vote by almost 3 million (thanks to big voter margins in California, New York, Illinois, and Massachusetts), she lost the Electoral College vote by 304 (Trump) to 227 (Clinton). You need 270 Electoral College votes to win.

Trump won the majority of Electoral College votes with strategic messaging into the swing states of Wisconsin, Michigan, and

---

130. Victor Hanson, "Trump's Chances for Re-Election Are Looking Better and Better," *RealClear Politics,* Feb. 27, 2020, https://www.realclearpolitics.com/articles/2020/02/27/trumps_chances_for_re-election_are_looking_better_and_better_142494.html

131. Quinnipiac University Poll, "Biden Crushes Sanders In Democratic Race, Quinnipiac University National Poll Finds; More Disapprove of Trump's Response To Coronavirus," *poll.qu.edu,* March 9, 2020, https://poll.qu.edu/national/release-detail?ReleaseID=3657

132. Lydia Saad, "Trump and Clinton Finish With Historically Poor Images," *Gallup,* November 8, 2016, https://news.gallup.com/poll/197231/trump-clinton-finish-historically-poor-images.aspx

Pennsylvania, capturing their combined 46 Electoral College votes. Trump, by leveraging Russian-hacked DNC emails that formed the basis of a false but effective negative ad campaign in the last three weeks saying Hillary was anti-Catholic. Although false, the message may have resonated with those three heavily Catholic states. Analysts will remind you that Clinton never visited Wisconsin during the entire campaign. Clinton never visited Wisconsin during the general election campaign, while Trump visited six times. Oops.

You will recall Clinton lost those three states of WI, PA, and MI by a combined total of only 78,000 votes out of a total of nearly 14 million votes cast in those three states. So, it was close, but Trump won them and, as a result, won the election. Did Trump's false "Hillary is anti-Catholic" attacks swing the one-half of one percent of total voters that decided those three states to give him the White House? It's possible, right?

The anti-Catholic email is discussed in the first four minutes of "The Asset" podcast, Episode 9, titled "Winning." It will blow your mind. It is produced by the Center for American Progress Action Fund's Moscow Project.[133]

Also, note, and this is critical, there were two other polls that came out a week before that "unfavorable" poll of 18+ adults (with no reference as to whether or not they were voters.). The "likely voter" preference poll and the "strong enthusiasm" poll.

The "likely voter" preference level for Clinton dropped below Trump's in the last week of the campaign. In fact, according to the ABC News/Washington Post poll support for Clinton was 12 points above Trump on October 23, 2016, 50% to 38%; but by October 30, 2016, Clinton went down 5 points, and Trump went up 8 points in just one week to 46% in favor of Trump to Clinton's 45%. That same poll also

---

133. The Asset Podcast, "Center for American Progress Action Fund's The Moscow Project," *The Asset Podcast*, April 13, 2020, https://theassetpodcast.org/

measured "strong enthusiasm." In that enthusiasm poll, Clinton was significantly behind Trump on October 30th (8 days before the election), Trump was 53% to Clinton's 45%, for a strong enthusiasm gap of 8%. That is a huge gap. People will look for reasons not to vote, and in a close race, the enthusiasm gap can predict a winner.[134]

The take away from the above information is this: one, Electoral College math decides everything. So, do what Trump did, let go of the states you have no chance to win, and focus on your battleground / "swing" states, those that can go either way. Two, enthusiasm level is next in importance if voter preference of "likely voters" is close. Three, unfavorables will predict a winner in a close race if the voter preference and enthusiasm levels are about the same (within the statistical margin of error), and must be looked at within a given precinct, state, and nation with particular focus on where these three indicators (likely voter preference, strong enthusiasm, and unfavorable gap) line-up in the swing states.

To conclude, you need to eat away at Trump's enthusiasm level by increasing his unfavorables in the nine battleground states I identified: PA, WI, MI, FL, AZ, NC, NM, MN, and GA.

Highlight Trump's "let'em eat cake" moment:

When Governors around the Country were asking Trump to use his federal powers to help get more supplies out to their citizens to address the coronavirus crisis, Politico reported that Trump said, "'We're not a shipping clerk': Trump tells governors to step up efforts to get medical

---

134. ABC News/Washington Post poll, "Strong Enthusiasm Ebbs for Clinton; Trump is +1 in Vote," *Langerresearch.com*, November 1, 2016, https://www.langerresearch.com/wp-content/uploads/1184a102016ElectionTrackingNo10.pdf

supplies. The president's remarks amounted to a rebuke of governors' recent pleas for greater federal intervention."[135]

There were over 100 ways to re-brand Trump. I've listed just a few.

In a tight race, it's the "unfavorables" that determine the winner. See "Reason #21" in the companion book, *Why Trump Won The 2020 Election 21 Reasons The Democrats Lost*, and Chapter 4's "Polls That Count" in this book to learn how to predict an election.

How do you raise Trump's unfavorables 10 points?

You have iconic celebrity images making simple, yet powerful remarks.

30-second TV spot:

Clint Eastwood or someone with that level of gritty true American reputation while stepping into a used pick-up truck with an American flag painted on the door turns to the camera saying:

"Lately, I have been asking myself, "Is Donald Trump a traitor to our Country?"

In Helsinki Trump lied to us denying Russia interfered in our 2016 election, Trump lied to us, denying Russia had sent troops into Venezuela. Now, Trump is promoting a blatant Russian lie that it was Ukraine, not Russia, that interfered in our 2016 US election.

So, I'm asking myself, "Is Trump a traitor to our Country?" Paid for by "Is Trump a Traitor?" political action committee.

---

135. Quint Forgey, "'We're not a shipping clerk': Trump tells governors to step up efforts to get medical supplies," *Politico*, March 19, 2020, https://www.politico.com/news/2020/03/19/trump-governors-coronavirus-medical-supplies-137658

Bloomberg's Trump Parody 48-second YouTube video:

Twenty-five celebrities participated in this Dump Trump video.[136]

---

136. Mike Bloomberg, "We're not done with you yet, Donald," *Twitter*, March 5, 2020,
https://twitter.com/MikeBloomberg/status/1235638018641465347?utm_source=She
ekey%2BDaily%2BRead&utm_campaign=ae2c2995ec-
EMAIL_CAMPAIGN_2020_03_04_06_34&utm_medium=email&utm_term=0_731
9d2fc05-ae2c2995ec-185866581

This 48-second #DumpTrump YouTube video sponsored by Michael Bloomberg featured 25 celebrities including Tom Hanks, Robert DeNiro and 23 others.

Here's the original YouTube link to that celebrity video: https://www.youtube.com/watch?v=p9KQGQe6vVk

15-second TV spot:

Judge Judy, a friend of Mike Bloomberg, says:

"Why isn't Trump is pushing the Senate to pass legislation passed by the House to protect our 2020 election from Russia. No true American patriot would act like that. Is Trump a Russian Traitor?

Paid for by, "Is Trump a Russian Traitor?" political action committee.

30-Second TV spot:

Governor Arnold Schwarzenegger sitting on his motorcycle wearing a leather coat with an American flag patch on it:

"When it comes to Trump not showing his tax returns, is he a girly man? A chicken? A tax dodger? An honest American would show his tax returns to someone like the non-partisan Congressional Joint Committee on Taxation to verify Trump has paid his fair share and isn't doing business with some country like Russia or China that might be creating a serious conflict-of-interest."

Paid for by the, "What is Trump Hiding?" political action committee.

Bloomberg, Steyer, Soros, Sussman, Schultz. Can any of you contribute to messages like this?

If re-branding is done properly, it's done at a core belief level and at a core values level. If you can cause Trump supporters to start to question Trump at a core belief level, then you can begin to dampen their enthusiasm. That would be a big win for the Democrats.

The kind of advertising described above gives impetus and rationale to fence-sitting moderate Republicans and Independents to come down on the side of a patriotic American, all-American Joe Biden.

Messages that highlight "Trump-First-America Second" help to re-brand Trump, like burning up U.S. taxpayer dollars by diverting military aircraft to refuel at Prestwick Airport near his failing Scottish golf in order to get flight crews to spend their overnight at his Trump Turnberry resort increasing his business income by over $200,000.

Background on that statement:

On September 18, 2019, Business Insider reported that,

259 military crews have refueled at Scotland's Prestwick Airport just this year, according to a report from The New York Times.

Over the past two years, US military refueling at Prestwick has earned the airport $17.3 million. And since Trump has been in office, overnight stays by military crews have earned his resort nearly $200,000.

Politico reported on September 12, 2019, that forty Air Force crews have stayed at Trump Turnberry on overnight refueling trips. Trump's golf resort is 54 miles away from the airport, a long drive for a tired aircrew. There are accommodations right at the airport.[137]

According to another Business Insider report, President Trump's organization entered into a quid pro quo business partnership in 2014 with a Scottish airport [Prestwick Airport]. Trump directs military craft to refuel there and, in exchange, the airport promotes Trump's Turnberry property.

The business arrangement was that Trump would promote refueling at the Prestwick airport in exchange for the airport promoting Trump's

---

137. Ellen Ioanes, "Trump's Turnberry resort has made nearly $200,000 from US military visits since he took office," *Business Insider*, September 18, 2019, https://www.businessinsider.com/259-air-force-crews-refueled-at-the-airport-trump-turnberry-2019-9

Turnberry resort as a place to stay for flight crews, even though there are plenty of other places to stay that are closer and cheaper.[138]

Those ideas above were just a few of the ways The Democrats could re-brand Trump.

Failed to Protect Americans When He Was Told of Virus.

Trump Endangered Americans by Firing WH Pandemic Officials.

Trump's closing down the White House pandemic office and his slow response to coronavirus warnings may have killed many Americans, and possibly caused many more to become seriously ill. That's not leadership. Citizens were ignorant of a danger about which, Trump was fully informed. Yet, initially, Trump did nothing.

As of April 2, 2020, Trump had not yet recommended a national shelter-in-place like California, New York, Nevada, and Illinois. Even while the front page of the New York Times showed a graph of how many more Americans would die by failing to take this action. (March 31, 2020 NYTimes front page graphs and text.)

This CNN headline speaks volumes, "Washington Post: US intelligence warned Trump in January and February [2020] as he dismissed coronavirus threat."[139]

Trump's refusal to heed these warnings about the virus may have severely endangered American lives. The article goes on to state:

---

138. Kenneth Garger, "Trump had a deal with Scottish airport that sent Air Force crew to his resort: report," *New York Post*, September 9, 2019, https://nypost.com/2019/09/09/trump-had-deal-with-scottish-airport-that-sent-air-force-crew-to-his-resort-report/

139. Caroline Kelly, "Washington Post: US intelligence warned Trump in January and February as he dismissed coronavirus threat," *CNN,* March 20, 2020, https://www.cnn.com/2020/03/20/politics/us-intelligence-reports-trump-coronavirus/index.html

President Donald Trump ignored reports from US intelligence agencies starting in January that warned of the scale and intensity of the coronavirus outbreak in China, The Washington Post reported Friday. Citing US officials familiar with the agencies' reports and warnings, the Post reported that intelligence agencies depicted the nature and global spread of the virus and China's apparent downplaying of its severity, as well as the potential need for government measures to contain it — while Trump opted to dismiss or simply not address their seriousness. 'Donald Trump may not have been expecting this, but a lot of other people in the government were — they just couldn't get him to do anything about it,' the official noted to the Post. 'The system was blinking red.'[140]

Politics USA reported,

On February 28, 2020, at a rally, Trump claimed that he had no idea that the coronavirus was coming even though the CDC had been warning about it for months before that Trump statement.

Trump shut down the White House pandemic office in 2018. On May 10, 2018, Rear Adm. Timothy Ziemer, the senior White House official responsible for leading the U.S. response in the event of a deadly pandemic, had his office closed down by Trump's NSC Director John Bolton. In a prophetic article on that same day in May 2018, Bipartisan Report stated that shutting down the White House pandemic office "comes at a time when many experts say the country is already unprepared for the increasing risks of a pandemic or bioterrorism attack.

---

140. Caroline Kelly, "Washington Post: US intelligence warned Trump in January and February as he dismissed coronavirus threat," *CNN*, March 20, 2020, https://www.cnn.com/2020/03/20/politics/us-intelligence-reports-trump-coronavirus/index.html

When Trump fired the White House pandemic officials, observers warned that the administration was weakening global health security. In a Politics USA article titled, "Top White House official in charge of pandemic response exits abruptly. His exit comes against the backdrop of other administration actions critics say have weakened health security preparedness, including dwindling financing for early preventive action against infectious disease threats abroad. Ironically, on that same day, May 10, 2018, an Ebola crisis broke out in the Congo."[141]

According to Front Page Live,

> In 2018, the government's entire pandemic response chain of command was let go. Trump shut down the global health security unit within the NSC, and the DHS epidemic team was also pushed out. No one was ever replaced. Trump's budget request for 2021 cuts the budget for the Centers for Disease Control and Prevention (CDC) by nearly 16%. The CDC is responsible for disease prevention and control in the United States. But Trump isn't worried about cutting funds to the entity that stops disease prevention because he says, "it will all work out well." Trump keeps repeating a false claim that Americans don't have to worry because the Coronavirus will be defeated by warm weather.
>
> On February 10, 2020, the President tweeted, "The heat generally speaking kills this kind of virus," Ron Klain, for one, has been telling the Trump administration for two years that the United States was not capable of handling a pandemic. Klain

---

141. Jason Easley, "Trump Lies About Coronavirus Warning After Removing Pandemic Officials," *Politics USA,* February 29, 2020, https://www.politicususa.com/2020/02/29/trump-lies-about-coronavirus-warning-after-removing-pandemic-officials.html

served as Chief of Staff for two U.S. Vice Presidents and was also the Ebola response coordinator in 2014.

Even Bill Gates, the philanthropic billionaire, repeatedly met with John Bolton (Trump's former Chief of Staff) about the issue. Bill Gates warned that ongoing cuts to the global health disease infrastructure would make the United States vulnerable to the "significant probability of a large and lethal modern-day pandemic occurring in our lifetimes. The CDC's global health section had been cut back so drastically that staff members had to be laid off in droves. The section used to work in 49 different countries, but now they have a presence in just 10.

When the Country was blind to the deadly viral danger that lurked around the corner, only one man stood in the way of warning Americans of what was coming, Donald Trump.

The typical Trump supporter I interviewed said the virus was not Trump's fault, and he was doing a good job responding.

Cracking the "Trump Trance" and securing some of the Trump base in a very targeted campaign has to be a clearly defined goal. One way is to re-brand the Republican party.

The Socialist Republican Party Dedicated to the Rich must become the Socialist Party Dedicated to the Rich (SPDR) tactic: Every reference to that Party must be "the SPDR." This forces the media to accept and explain SPDR. That's the trick, don't explain SPDR. Just say it, like it's an everyday phrase. Trump is the leader of the SPDR, SPIDER for short, the Socialist Party Dedicated to the Rich. Trump runs the SPIDER Party. SPDR, "spider" for short.

Never say "Republican," and never say "GOP." You have to be very disciplined about this. It's the "SPIDER Party."

This strategy reframes that party in the minds of Americans. It also very effectively turns the word "socialist" back on the Spider Party. So, it diminishes the value of labeling Democrats "socialist" when "socialist" is now part of the name for Trump's party. You can never say the word "Republican" or "GOP," again. Not as long as Trump is in office. Why? Because it falsely connects Lincoln to Trump.

You can no longer use the elephant image anymore to represent the Trump Spider Party. You have to use the Spider. Don't fight this messaging tactic if you truly want to beat Trump. It's an essential part of re-branding.

Another benefit is that it will help embarrass the few remaining "decent" members of the Spider Party to want to disassociate from that characterization. When their constituents start referring to them as members of the Spider Party, you're halfway to victory.

The SPDR puts Corporate profits before the welfare of average American Citizens. The SPDR takes money from the poor and gives it to the rich. *Appendices 3,4,5 and 12* elaborate on this fact.

The Spider animation.

Follows is a description of a 30-second TV spot, complete with production notes on what the announcer says in the voiceover and what the animators need to draw to put on the screen when creating the supporting animation.

This **Spider** animation and narration, described below, will go viral and help to win not only Florida's 29 electoral votes, but all states with a large older population..

There is a 30-second version, a 60-second version, and a 90-second version.

This one 30-second TV spot can Win 2020 for Democrats

The SPIDER Trump Animation

VO: Voiceover narration script for the narrator:

"Donald Trump turned the Republican Party into the **Socialist Party Dedicated to the Rich** which gives government welfare to the richest corporations at the expense of the poor and the middle class.

Trump's Socialist Party Dedicated to the Rich, **S-P-D-R** are the letters, or **SPIDER** for short. Trump's **SPIDER** party gave $4.3 Billion of our taxpayer dollars as a CASH refund to 60 Corporations that made $79 Billion in profit and paid zero taxes. Paid for by Stop the Spider PAC."

Visual: Animation to accompany the above voiceover.

Trump's full body with coat and tie and legs sitting in the middle of a spider's web.

On one side of the spider's web it says, "Socialist **P**arty **D**edicated to the **R**ich."

Under those words are the words Republican Party scratched out. ~~Republican Party~~.

Under those words it says, **SPIDER Party**

Trump spider: on his back it says "**SPDR.**"

Trump turns into (morphs into) a creepy black widow spider but keeps his head with orange hair and red tie.

Spider walks over to 3 people: all blue-collar workers, 1 man, 1 woman and 1 older man that says "Retiree." [Eddie suggests we not put him in a wheelchair.]

The Trump spider takes money out of their pockets and puts it in a bag labeled $4.3B.

The Trump spider then crawls over to a shiny Rolls Royce.

Under the distinctive RR [similar] logo and or on the side of the vehicle are 3 lines of text:

$79 Billion Profit.
$0 Taxes.
$4.3B Refund.

and the Trump-spider hands the money in a bag labeled "$4.3B" to the smiling pig-faced, pink-faced driver behind the wheel of the Rolls.

The Trump-spider crawls back to the web and re-emerges as Trump and the words on the web say Socialist Party Dedicated to the Rich = SPDR = SPIDER.

[End of 30-second SPIDER Trump animation]

That animation could go viral and could turn the Country against Spider Trump. Particularly the people in Florida who are hard-working and retirees on a fixed income. These senior citizens are still paying Federal taxes and would be repulsed to learn that their precious dollars are being given by Trump to the elite rich under Trump's new tax laws.

In response to the question, "Why do you keep calling them the **SPIDER** party and the Socialist Party Dedicated To The Rich and not the Republican Party?"

Answer: There are no more Republicans. Republicans used to respect our Country and our Constitution, and in treating everyone fairly. They used to be hard-working people that believed in paying their fair share of taxes. They used to believe in a balanced budget. They used to believe in protecting us from our enemies like Russia. But now the new Socialist Party Dedicated to the Rich founded by Trump has forced all Republicans to join the Socialist Party Dedicated to the Rich. This new SPIDER party believes in giving away taxpayer dollars to the wealthiest in the Country. The elite rich corporations and the elite wealthy people were the beneficiaries of the 2017 tax overhaul that put the country into $1 trillion in debt in 2018 and 2019 and headed for the same in 2020. No real Republican would do that. These SPIDER folks are RINOs. Republicans-In-Name-Only. Moreover, they don't even deserve to be called RINOs because they don't deserve to be associated with the word Republican. "Republican" used to be an honorable word associated with people who wanted to preserve and to protect the environment, True Republicans were conservatives and conservationists. The old school Republicans used to protect America from its enemies like Russia. Russia invaded our 2016 election, and with Moscow Mitch and Trump's help, the Russians are invading the 2020 election. And Republicans used to be the ones that wanted to protect the budget from debt; now, they're the ones that put us in the greatest debt in the history of the United States. Just when we needed that trillion dollars taken from the Treasury by Trump 2017 tax heist to fight the coronavirus pandemic, that money was gone because the SPIDER party took it and gave it to all the rich people. 55 corporations under Trump's **SPIDER** party, the **S**ocialist **P**arty **D**edicated to the **R**ich, made $79 billion in net profit and paid no taxes. These are the same corporations that have 18 wheelers running up and down our highways and tearing up our infrastructure and paying zero taxes. Now, we're the ones paying for the roads that their trucks beat up, creating potholes. We are the ones providing them with lighting on the highways, traffic lights, police protection, and military protection, and free airports built and maintained with our Federal tax dollars, Federal Aviation Controllers for their corporate planes. We, the average taxpayer, are the ones paying for all that infrastructure. They made $79 billion in profit and paid zero taxes, but Trump's welfare-for-the-rich gets worse for the average American.

The Trump **SPIDER** party has reached into our pockets and taken our taxpayer dollars that we worked by the sweat of our brow to earn and then pay on time to the Feds under threat of imprisonment and fines. The Trump **SPIDER** party then took that money from our wallets and gave $4.3 billion of it to the same corporations that paid no taxes. WTF, right?! That is government welfare for the rich in its most grotesque form. This is an example of that black widow **SPIDER** coming into our homes taking money out of our wallets, walking out, and giving it to the richest corporations and the richest people in the Country. That's the **SPIDER** party, the **Socialist Party Dedicated to the Rich**. That's the Trump party.

Well, many of us believe in exterminating dangerous venomous spiders. The **SPIDER**, in this case, is dangerous and harmful and venomous. Venomous to our society. They raised our debt by over a trillion dollars, especially at a time when we needed the trillion to fight off the coronavirus pandemic, and people are being laid off left and right. This is when we needed that treasury money. But in 2017 when the formerly known as Republicans, now known as the **SPIDER** party, had majority control over the House of Representatives and over the Senate and controlled the Executive Branch, they passed this bogus tax reform law where they gave over a trillion dollars to the richest corporations and the richest elite in America at the expense of the poor and the middle class That's what the Trump **SPIDER** party did.

The Socialist Party Dedicated to the Rich, the Spider party, took trillions from the poor and middle class who pay taxes, and they gave it to the rich while running up the national debt by trillions. This new un-American party is a venomous spider, and it needs to be exterminated.

My old high school classmate asked this question when he heard about this SPIDER Trump animation.

"Who is the audience for the Spider Trump animation?"

Answer:

Audience: Independents: People on the fence about Trump who can be moved to Biden and Dem down ticket.

Audience: Trump supporters who can be turned to Biden by understanding what Trump is doing to average American - them.

Audience: Trump supporters who can have their enthusiasm turned down, and won't vote if it's a hassle. Trump has a 29% edge over Biden on enthusiasm poll.

Audience: Fire up Dems to increase their enthusiasm to go through the maze of voter suppression that the Trump machine will throw at them.

Audience: Fire up Dems to reduce doubts about Biden when compared to Trump.

Audience: Republicans who can be shamed into understanding what their Party has become and leave it or try to change it from within.

Primary AUDIENCE: To educate the DNC leadership: to give them a basis to start describing the Republican Party as the SPIDER Party, which forces the conversation in the media and in TV interviews as to the origin of the "SPIDER" description. When that happens on a large scale, the Dems WIN. That SPIDER messaging will begin to build a more solid momentum with a large segment of the American voting population. Many people dislike the "give-away Democrats". They see the Dems as taking their hard-earned tax dollars and giving it to illegal immigrants and welfare cheats.

The Republicans have a 3-pronged attack on Dems: they are socialists, supporting open borders and large tax hikes. Multiple messaging from different Republican sources show this.

AUDIENCE: All of the American voters are being told that "Socialists are bad and Democrats are Socialists." By branding Republicans as SOCIALIST, you kick out one leg of the anti-Dem campaign.

Trump's first TV ad branded Dems as "socialists." You can view images from that TV commercial in this book's companion book, *Why Trump Won The 2020 Election, 21 Reasons The Democrats Lost*. It's a central theme drumbeat that MUST be diluted and watered down by obfuscating the issue by calling Republicans the true SOCIALISTs. If the message is loud enough, it will blunt and neutralize that foundational Republican attack on Dems. The Socialist description of Dems underpins all the other attacks as the "radical left give-everything-away-to-everybody-for-free Party." (That's a quote from a college PoliSci major!) The truth is the Republicans give far more Government welfare away, but they give it to the rich. That has to come across, and there is little time left to do it. So, we NEED a quick short phrase and visual that conveys the message. The phrase is "SPIDER Party." The visual is Spider Trump taking money from hard-working blue-collar Americans and giving it to rich fat cats.

The average American associates the word "socialism" with communism. So, Trump and reactionary talk show hosts have conflated those two terms and stuck them on the back of every Democrat. The only effective way to combat that atomic bomb attack is to turn it back on them with equal force. It will take a big commitment on DNC / Biden leadership to do this effectively, but for now, it's a battle the Dems have lost and will cost them millions of votes unless they can blunt that "socialist" attack. The only way to do that is to place that "socialist" label so big and so loud on Republicans that the average voter goes neutral on that term as to Dems and hopefully does a 180 and holds it against the Republicans.

A second question asked by old high school classmate of author:

"How do you intend to deliver the Spider Trump animation?"

Answer:

Delivery: Place on YouTube and then send the link to all Dem leadership. So, they can start drum beating about the "SPIDER Party".

Delivery: Hopefully a PAC chair will pick up and fund TV placement; and/or fund a higher budget version and place that one on TV.

Delivery: Send to PRESS as a TV spot created by **"Artists Against Trump"** and co-sponsored by the Keller Research Institute (KRI), that will hopefully generate interviews with the available artists and co-sponsor Dr. David King Keller, founder of KRI and best-selling legal author with 3 books on the 2020 election

Delivery: Encourage other artists via social media to produce their own SPIDER Trump spots and images.

Delivery: Create a Facebook page or web site where artists can place their visual versions of the SPIDER Party.

Delivery: Place SPIDER Trump-30 links on Twitter, Instagram, other.

The SPIDER Trump spot has the potential to re-brand Trump and the Republican Party. It's a big task. It's also an essential task to assure victory in 2020.

More Issues And Soundbites To Promote

Moscow Mitch won't protect our election from Russia.

Why? Is it because Senator Mitch McConnell's State of Kentucky is getting a $200 million investment from a rich Russian Oligarch, who was somehow exempted from the 2016 election interference sanctions by Trump?

#MassacreMitch and SPDR put Corporate gun profits before American family's lives by refusing to take up the bipartisan House-approved background check bill.

By constantly referring to *Socialist* Republican Party for the Rich, you water down and blunt Trump's biggest weapon against Dems, "they're socialist;" "they're radical left-wing socialists." Trump's party is the extreme radical right-wing Socialist Republican Party for the Rich. That has to be the Democratic mantra.

Re-branding Trump can take place by raising a number of fact-based issues. Trump's un-American. Trump's a Russian Asset. Trump admitted that Russia helped get him elected in a Tweet, and therefore was indebted to Putin. What is Putin demanding from Trump in return? Why are there all of these secret meetings and phone calls between Putin and Trump with no other American present?

Consider this visual to present to America that captures part of what is taking place before our very eyes. A Trump-look-a-like wraps his arms around the American flag but reveals a Russian flag under his coat, so, actually, Trump is wrapping a Russian flag around the US flag.

News journalist Dan Rather had a stark reaction to the news that Trump has known for months that Russia had put a bounty on US soldiers in Afghanistan, and Trump had done nothing about it. Rather said in a June 27, 2020 Tweet, " Reporters are trained to look for patterns that are suspicious. And time and again one stands out with Donald Trump. Why is he so slavishly devoted to Putin? There is a spectrum of possible answers, ranging from craven to treasonous. One day I hope and suspect we will find out."[142]

---

142. Mary Paperfuss, "'Tre45on' Trends After Report That Trump Knew Putin Put Bounty On U.S. Troops," Huff Post, June 28, 2020, https://www.huffpost.com/entry/trump-russia-putin-bounty-us-soldiers_n_5ef8C417c5b612083c4e9106

Trump exhibits evidence that he is Putin's Puppet. Trump publicly lies for Putin. Why? What is Putin's carrot? What is Putin's incentive for Trump? What is Putin's stick? What threat does Putin hold over Trump's head?

Why is Trump and Mitch McConnell allowing Russia to have fairly unfettered access to our election process? Why is Trump and Moscow Mitch blocking legislation passed in a non-partisan way in the House from coming before the Senate for a vote? Why is Trump refusing to protect our election and our form of government?

Here is a short TV spot (convertible to radio):

Harley Davidson rider says, "Why is Trump letting Russia run roughshod over America's election? That ain't right."

Why is Trump blocking Congress from passing laws to keep Russia out of our American election process? That ain't right. And it's Un-American."

Allowing Russia to destroy our Democracy set up by our Founding Fathers is Un-Patriotic, and it puts Russia ahead of America. You have to ask yourself what kind of "leader" do we have who bold-faced lies to Americans after a secret meeting with Putin? After a secret meeting with Putin in Helsinki, Trump said Russia "did not interfere" in our 2016 US election. Lie! Later, after a secret phone call with Putin Trump said Russia was not involved in Venezuela. Lie! What's worse was that everyone listening knew those were lies. What does that say about America? What does that say about Trump? What does say about the people around Trump who are supposed to be his advisers while also acting as America's second line of defense when a President veers off course?

Trump is a Coward. He is afraid to show his tax returns like other patriotic Presidential candidates. What is Trump hiding?

Trump is a Two-Faced Liar. *Candidate* Trump said, "Mexico will pay for the Wall," a solid border wall along the shared border between Mexico and the United States. *President* Trump shut down the U.S. Government over his demand that US tax dollars be used to pay for the Wall.

Have you forgotten the December 2018 headlines? Like this headline in Fortune magazine, "Federal Government Shuts Down, as Trump, Senate Clash on Border Wall Funding."[143]

Trump joined #Massacre Mitch and put Corporate gun profits before American family lives by supporting the Senate in blocking firearm safety legislation passed in a bipartisan fashion in the House.

Consider this visual: #MassacreMitch with a 100 round mag AK-47 standing next to a schoolyard sign. Massacre Mitch says, "We have to protect the Second Amendment right of bat-shit crazy people with 100-round magazines attached to an AK-47 to walk along the sidewalk next to our schools because in Trump's America gun sale profits come before children's lives. "

A strategy that attacks Trump at such a core belief and core value level that it shakes the faith of those in the Trump trance to the point where they actually start to open their mind to the point where they start to consider that maybe they might need to consider another option other than Donald Trump and his pal, Massacre-Moscow-Mitch.

If you're going to shake someone out of their Trump Trance, the only way to do that is to shake them up at their core belief and core value

---

143. Glenn Fleishman, "Federal Government Shuts Down, as Trump, Senate Clash on Border Wall Funding," *Fortune*, December 22, 2018, https://fortune.com/2018/12/22/wall-funding-partial-government-shutdown-midnight/

level. It is the only thing that will get a Trump "Trancer" to consider an alternative choice, and it won't be easy, and it won't be fast, but it can be done.

By addressing the Trump Trancer with ads that demonstrate that Trump's loyalties are certainly not to America first, you are also addressing two other groups at the same time: Republicans and Independents who are on the fence about Trump.

What is that core belief in core value that must be appealed to in a deep emotional level in order to shake someone in a Trump trance out of their trance and open their mind up just enough so you can get other messages into their brain that will cause them to not only think twice about voting for Trump but actually turn their back on him? This is a very challenging but doable strategy.

Here is a description of that strategy.

What is the core belief and the core value that must be appealed to and must be leveraged in order to pull a voter away that is Velcro-ed to Trump? It is the belief by that voter that she or he is a true patriot and a true American, and so is Trump. The other candidates are not true Americans and true patriots and therefore do not deserve their vote and will not get their vote. In fact, a candidate that is not a true American and a true patriot is to be vilified. And that has been the successful tactic used by Donald Trump.

If your core belief is that you are a true American, a true-blue American through and through and that you are a true patriot and you love your country, and you love your flag above all else. And that you believe, "it's love it or leave it." And you firmly believe your man Trump is a true patriot and a true American. Isn't Trump the one that keeps saying, "America First"? In contrast, the Republican echo chamber mantra machine has painted the Democrats as un-American, unpatriotic, putting illegals ahead of Americans, and, therefore, should be vilified and run out of the country, if at all possible. That is a very intense statement.

This is the level of emotion that we're dealing with when we are dealing with someone's core beliefs and core values. There is only one way to break into an emotion that is that intense. You must attack it head-on, full force, and in such a manner that there is no escaping the "new truth" about Donald Trump.

Here's the strategy:

You have to convince the Trump Trancers that Trump is not a true American, is not a true patriot, and does not put America first. If you can do that, then you can get their attention. Then, you can start to create a hairline crack in the solid concrete wall that surrounds this core belief that is tied to their core support of Donald Trump. In the beginning, it's an almost invisible hairline crack. You need a clear and consistent message that is delivered over and over and over again. You must use multiple channels of communication and multiple sources of communication. Those sources must have complete credibility with your audience. You must provide various forms of evidence supporting your claim. Then, and only then, can you start to crack that impenetrable granite wall that has been set up to shield a Trump Trancer's emotional attachment to, emotional support for, and undying belief in their one true hero, their candidate, Donald J. Trump.

Donald Trump is going to have to become almost equivalent to "the enemy" for a true Trump Trancer to come out of that trance and open their mind long enough to receive an alternative message about their "America first hero."

Follows is a description of different approaches in the communication process with a Trump Trancer. These would be considered as a form of "message testing" with actual members of the target audience in preparing a TV spot, or a flyer, or a social media campaign.

Message #1: "Trump is a Russian asset."

Trump Trancer Response #1: "Bullshit!" will be the immediate and instant response of those in a Trump Trance.

Message #2: If a tough-looking guy on a Harley-Davidson wearing a black leather jacket with an American flag on it says, "Trump is a Russian asset."

Trump Trancer Response #2: "Oh, why would he say that?"

See the difference in the two responses? Can you hear the difference in tone of this second response compared to the first?

Message #3: A man and a woman wearing a MAGA hat looks directly into the camera, and they both say, "We're very sorry to report that upon reviewing the evidence, Trump is a Russian asset."

Trump Trancer Response #3: Now your voter who is in a Trump Trance says, "Oh come on, this is some kind of a Democratic trick, that can't be true."

Do you hear in the background of that Trump Trancer response is an inquiry that says, "No way that can be true, *right*?"

Big difference from the first response, right?

As you shake up a Trump Trancer at their core belief level, at their core value level, you are also solidifying your base, and you're also pulling those away that were leaning toward Trump or going to vote for Trump while holding their nose. You are starting to give all of these groups second thoughts. Those "second thoughts" are a direct result of and a measure of your messaging success. Polls can track this attitudinal shift.

So, I will give you more details on how to turn a Trump Trancer into a reluctant yet committed Democratic voter. I just wanted to give you a sense of how this can be done and why it must be done and why there is no other way.

I can give you lots of scientific research and a number of psychological studies to support what I am saying. You can simply do the research yourself and use a keyword phrase like, "how do you get a true believer to change their mind?"

If you go to Google and put in the key phrase "how do you appeal to someone's core values," you will come across a 2014 article in Forbes magazine titled, "To Change Minds Appeal To Values, Not Attitudes" by Sebastian Bailey. You may also come across 2012 research titled, "Circumventing Resistance: Using Values To Indirectly Change Attitudes." The research states that <u>directly attacking people's attitudes rarely works and that it's far more effective to target the values which relate to that attitude.</u>

If you ask anyone who has studied the neuroscience of communication, or Neuro-Linguistic Programming (NLP), or Neuro-Associative Conditioning (NAC) or any of the belief and attitude change modalities, they will all tell you that the best and most effective way to change an attitude is to address it at the level of the person's core values.

My background includes three international Master's level certifications in the neuroscience of communication. Because of that research and training, I can usually support a person in getting rid of a deep-seated phobia in less than an hour over the phone. Why? Because deep-seated beliefs can be changed. And a deep-seated belief in Trump can be changed. But it will take a laser focus on the core values of those that are currently in a deep Trump Trance.

Psychologists, hypnotists, and human behaviorists who study the art and science of trance induction also learned that in order to snap somebody out of their trance, especially if it's a deep trance, you need a strategy that "breaks" that trance.

"Trump is a Russian asset" presented by a credible source, over and over and over again, can, if done properly, can serve to break that Trump trance.

Ask any Trump supporter, whose core value is American patriotism, and they will tell you that anyone who wants to be President of the United States must first be a true patriot and a true American.

That's why Trump started running a very effective TV ad on July 31, 2019, that depicts the Democratic candidates as putting illegal foreigners, illegal immigrants ahead of Americans, and ahead of the needs and concerns of American citizens. This is an extremely persuasive ad for those that hold the core value that anyone who wants to lead this country must be a true American and a true patriot and put America and Americans first and foremost, basically, every Trump Trance voter.

Tactics:

When someone is in a deep trance, like your basic Trump supporter, you need to approach them from every possible angle of stimulus and communication in order to secure their attention long enough and over a long enough period of time to break their trance and deliver a different message.

[PS: When a Trumpista says, "You have TDS, Trump Dysfunction Syndrome," (a meme they use to blow you off), you respond, "No, *you* have TDS, Trump Devotee Syndrome, you're like a member of the Manson cult, you're in a hypnotic trance and have lost control of the ability to think for yourself.]

Specifically:

All media and all mediums must be used: TV, radio, print, US mail, social media, Facebook page, Facebook ads, Instagram, Twitter, emails, and texts, etc.

TV and Radio:

Here's a sample of a 10-second TV and radio ad that must be presented by a recognizable and respected person, like a Meryl Streep, and for radio, the person must have a recognizable voice that is so distinct it does not require an image, for example, Arnold Schwarzenegger.

Follows is the narrative script for the 10-second TV and/or radio commercial message.

Speaker says

"Trump is a Russian asset. For the facts on U.S. Traitor Trump, go to Trump is a Russian asset (dot) com."

Frequency:

Weekly: for 52 weeks starting November 2019. The Dems are getting off to a slow national campaign. Ads began in earnest in June and July in a few battleground states. Nationally? No.

Spokespersons: Celebrities.

The ads would feature a different celebrity every week. There are more than 52 Hollywood celebrities (see the list) and other instantly recognizable celebrities who, I believe, would gladly offer 10 seconds of their time for this effort, given the public comments they have made in the past about Donald Trump.

Running the ad weekly is not very often. Running the ad more frequently more would be better. But after every new celebrity makes her or his 10-second statement then that 10-second spot can go viral on YouTube and be sent out via Twitter and via Instagram and via Facebook and so there will be multiples upon multiples of their 10 seconds that will be transmitted throughout the United States and the world. Also, with each new celebrity spokesperson, you can issue a press release announcing that so and so of such and such fame just released a campaign ad against Donald Trump that says, "Trump is a Russian asset. For the facts on U.S. Traitor Trump, go to Trump is a Russian asset (dot) com."

Follows is a partial list of celebrities who have spoken out against Trump, according to Harper's Bazaar:

Meryl Streep, Robert DeNiro, Miley Cyrus, Rob Reiner, Cher, Jon Stewart, Madonna, Arnold Schwarzenegger, Tom Steyer, George Soros, Mark Ruffalo, George Clooney, J.K. Rowling, Cher, Sarah Silverman, Alex Baldwin, Stephen Colbert, Jimmy Kimmel, Chrissy Teigen, Chelsea handler, John legend, Lady Gaga, Aziz Ansari, Olivia Wilde, John Oliver, Lena Dunham, Seth Meyers, Kim Kardashian, Shonda Rimes, Debra Messing, America Ferrara, Stephen King, Gabrielle Union, Lebron James, Ben Stiller, Laverne Cox, Samuel L Jackson, Arianna Huffington, Bette Midler, Shakira, Jennifer Lawrence, Kerry Washington, Richard Gere, Lauren Jauregui, Ava DuVernay, Jessica Chastain, Zoe Kazan, Don Cheadle, Camilla Cabello, Demi Lovato, Kumail Nanjiani, Mandy Moore, Chris Evans, Lin-Manuel Miranda, Samantha Bee, Alyssa Milano, Amy Schumer, Matt Damon, Margaret Cho, Amber Rose, Ashley Judd, Shonda Rimes, George Takei, Kate Walsh, Jennifer Lawrence, Eva Longoria, Lena Dunham, Andy Cohen, Ariel Winter, Johnny Depp, Jaime King, Mac Miller, Rashida Jones, Seth McFarlane, Jessica Chastain, Amanda Seyfried, Will Smith, Barbra Streisand, Gabrielle Union, Kerry Washington, Louis C.K., Elizabeth Banks, Susan Sarandon, George R. R. Martin and you., From *Harper's Bazaar*, 10/2/2017, "50 Celebrities Who Spoke Out Against President Trump." You can click through a photo gallery and read details about each.[144]

Apparently, you can add Tom Hanks to the above list as he allowed his image to be in the #DumpTrump Bloomberg sponsored YouTube video referenced above. Mia Farrow sent a Tweet calling Trump to task for

---

144. Harper's Bazaar Staff, "50 Celebrities Who Spoke Out Against President Trump," *Harper's Bazaar*, October 2, 2017, https://www.harpersbazaar.com/culture/politics/g12502906/donald-trump-celebrity-statements/

touting the re-opening of his golf course rather than attending to the thousands of Americans dying of COVID-19.

If you know you belong on this list. Please contact the author, and I will add your name to the list in V2.0 of this book, or simply put you on a private list of people to contact for very targeted and specific participation. Thank you.

DrDavidKingKeller@gmail.com.

Best use of celebrity talent as of this writing is on this YouTube video sponsored by Michael Bloomberg: link in the footnote:[145]

Message to Michael Bloomberg: We need you. America and the world need you, Mike, and we need more of your creative messaging. You are a brilliant man and a humanitarian. We need you.

Now, under cover of the coronavirus crisis, the Spider party is running through a $2 Trillion package that will, once again, make sure the rich don't suffer while only providing a meager hand out to the poor and middle class.

Look at the coronavirus crisis airline bailout, for example. According to *Live and Let's Fly*, American and Delta CEOS make approximately $12 million and $15 million a year, respectively.[146]Pay attention and notice if these CEOs receive hard-earned taxpayer dollars from people who are not sure how they are going to pay the rent, or buy food, and these two CEOs are getting their companies bailed out, which is "good" for the

---

145. Mike Bloomberg, "We're not done with you yet, Donald," *Twitter*, March 5, 2020, https://twitter.com/MikeBloomberg/status/1235638018641465347?utm_source=She ekey%2BDaily%2BRead&utm_campaign=ae2c2995ec-EMAIL_CAMPAIGN_2020_03_04_06_34&utm_medium=email&utm_term=0_731 9d2fc05-ae2c2995ec-185866581

146. Mathew Klint, "How Much Did U.S. Airline CEOs Make In 2018?," *Live and Let's Fly,* May 30, 2019, https://liveandletsfly.com/2019/05/30/airline-ceo-pay-2018/

Country, but will they be asked to take any pay cut as part of receiving American taxpayer largesse, and commit that not one dime of those precious tax dollars goes to them personally?

Trump has made it easy to re-brand him. All you have to do is examine the facts.

See "Reason # 15- Trump, The "Generous" Rebel Hero" and "Reason #19 – Putin & Trump Partnership" in the companion book, *Why Trump Won The 2020 Election, 21 Reasons The Democrats Lost*, to see what the Dem campaign is up against.

2.   Re-Brand Republican Party:

The Socialist Republican Party Dedicated to the Rich, SRPDR. Delete "Republican" because the current party has no resemblance to Lincoln's Republican Party. So, it's actually the Socialist Party Dedicated to the Rich, which has been riding the coattails of the once honorable Republican name.

Socialist **P**arty **D**edicated to the **R**ich, SPDR, pronounced "SPIDER" for short. And switch out the popular elephant for the black widow SPIDER image.

Demonize. Cause doubt.

There are no longer any RINOs, Republicans-In-Name-Only, but SPIDERS. SPIDERS are radical rip-off artists stealing American tax dollars from hard-working Americans. The SPIDER party has now turned blue-collar workers into economic slaves for the rich. See *Appendices 5a, 5b, 5c, 6, 7, and 10* for examples, details, and reference sources.

Americans need to hear "The Socialist Republican Party For the Rich" so often that they actually believe the Republicans have changed their name. By doing this, you water down the impact of the constant barrage of the reference to Democrats as socialists by the Republican echo-chamber. You'll know you've successfully conflated the word socialist with the Republican Party when those socialist Democrat messages stop.

The words "socialist," "radical," "extreme" need to be repeatedly used as descriptors of the SPIDER Party. Why? Because those are the adjectives being used to attack the Dems. The descriptors lose their power when they are applied to both sides equally. Currently, under the RINO Party and the Democrats, as well, we have a Plutocracy run by the rich just pretending it's a democracy. It's just done in a more flagrant manner under the RINOs

Part of the RINO group are rich firearm safety legislation killers

Both weapons used in Dayton and El Paso were illegal from 1994 to 2004 under the *Public Safety and Recreational Firearms Use Protection Act*. The killers would never have been able to purchase their weapons when that Act was in effect. But the Socialist Republican Party of the Rich put corporate gun profits ahead of family lives and re-legalized those weapons and put them back on the street for sale. Since then, FBI records show mass shootings increased 500%. Politifact reports, "The death toll from mass shootings went from 4.8 per year during the ban years to 23.8 per year afterwards."[147]

RINO, Republican In Name Only, Republicans used to be fiscally responsible and conservative with taxpayers money - not today's Socialist Republikans who are running up the highest deficits in American history. The Socialist Republikans are dedicated to the rich at any cost to the U.S. Treasury, not the party of fiscally conservative true Republicans of years past.

---

147. Jon Greenberg, "Bill Clinton: After (the assault weapon ban) passed in 1994, there was a big drop in mass shooting deaths. When the ban expired, they rose again," *Politifact,* August 7, 2019, https://www.politifact.com/factchecks/2019/aug/07/bill-clinton/did-mass-shooting-deaths-fall-under-1994-assault-w/

There are no more "Republicans." The members of today's Socialist Republican Party Dedicated to the Rich have abandoned the principles once held by real Republicans in years past.

Previous Republicans watched every penny of the hard-earned American taxpayers' dollars, not today's Socialist Republikans.

Previous Republicans thought saving innocent American lives from slaughter by weapons of war was a fundamental obligation of a Party dedicated to its citizens. Not today's Socialist Republikans led by "Massacre Mitch." Today's Republicans, as represented by their elected leaders, are blocking HR-8 bi-partisan firearm safety legislation on background checks. Republicans act as if protecting assault weapon manufacturers' profits is a higher priority than protecting mothers and their children from having their skulls splattered across an entire room by a bullet.

For a brief period when real Republicans passed an assault weapon and high capacity magazine ban, from 1994 to 2004, mass murders dropped dramatically, but the RepubliKKKan controlled congress of 2004 lifted the ban, and mass murders increased by 500%.[148] Following killings using the mass-murder weapons they legalized, real Republicans would be on their knees begging forgiveness from those families who lost their parents and children, and brothers and sisters. Oh no, today's Republikans, denying the black and white statistics, say it has nothing to do with the easy and free access to these assault weapons of mass destruction and magazines that hold 100 bullets. The August 2019 Dayton, Ohio killer used an assault weapon with 100 magazine capacity and killed and injured 37 people in 30 seconds. When the 2nd Amendment was passed, the maximum number of people you could kill

---

148. Jon Greenberg, "Bill Clinton: After (the assault weapon ban) passed in 1994, there was a big drop in mass shooting deaths. When the ban expired, they rose again," *Politifact,* August 7, 2019, https://www.politifact.com/factchecks/2019/aug/07/bill-clinton/did-mass-shooting-deaths-fall-under-1994-assault-w/

in that same time frame with a musket was just one. The Republican Party that used to represent everyday Americans has vanished.

Previous Republicans were nature-loving fishermen who knew the impact of drought and fire and would take measures to reduce those occurrences by working with Earth's natural resources, not against them. But today's Socialist Republikans dedicated to the rich believe protecting the profits of fossil fuel corporations is more important than developing job-creating alternatives to protect farmers from drought, California from fires, Kansas from tornadoes, and Florida from hurricanes. Rich first, everybody else second.

Previous Republicans believed in minimizing the government's role. But today's Socialist Republikan Party For The Rich believes it's OK for a President to have unlimited and dictatorial control over trade and tariffs and war. The name "Executive Branch" comes from the word "execute," which originally meant the Executive Branch executes the will of the people as expressed by Congress. Now, today's Socialist Republikan Party For The Rich believes Trump should have dictatorial powers; and Trump only has to inform Congress what he's doing, if he feels like it.

Previous Republicans believed in "all people are created equal" and should be treated with respect. Today's Socialist Republi**KKK**an Party For The Rich believes it's OK for the leader, the LEADER of the United States of America, to make blatantly racist remarks against members of Congress. The former head of the KKK applauds Trump and today's Republi**KKK**an Party while Lincoln spins in his grave.[149]

---

149. Staff, "Ex-KKK Leader Praises Trump's Speech," *The Daily Beast*, July 22, 2016, https://www.thedailybeast.com/cheats/2016/07/22/white-supremacist-praises-trump-s-rnc-speech

There are no more "Republicans." The members of today's Socialist Republican Party Dedicated to the Rich have abandoned the principles once held by real Republicans in years past.

It's no wonder a founder of the conservative Republican Congressional Freedom Caucus, Congressman Justin Amash, not only quit the "conservative" caucus group but quit the Republican party and called for Donald Trump's impeachment. Real Republicans won't be identified with today's Socialist Party Dedicated to the Rich, the Socialist Party Dedicated to the Rich, SPR, the **SPIDER** party.

3.　　　**Turn Democratic Base into Raving Voters**

The Democratic leadership must turn the Democratic base into Super-Committed, evangelistic voters.

Using Pain/ Pleasure motivators. Carrot and Stick. Fear and Joy.

Skin in the game tactics: include getting a contribution no matter how small give the voter a sense of greater identity. Elicit a $1 contribution and a one-minute survey. Once "engaged" gradually up engagement level until you have achieved a level of support that is equivalent to the targeted voter making a simple one-minute auto-dial call to Moscow-Mitch's Senate Office demanding passage of election protection legislation.

Simple, easy, volunteer activities like that make people feel like they are part of the Team, and that "they matter," because they do. Tom Steyer's Need To Impeach group has this software and used it very effectively.

The goal would be to get 70 million voters to contribute "just $1." Use various messages, including Trump text tactics such as "Become a Trump Gold Card Member." Review all of the Trump engagement texts and emails for a template on engagement. Change the previous text to "Become a #DumpTrump Gold Card Member!" Better yet get various celebrities to sponsor various cards, such as "Get an Official 'Barbra

Streisand #DumpTrump Gold Card.'" Contributor provides their email or text number, and they are sent a classy looking gold card to print. Ask 100 celebrities to make up a card. Maybe with a photo and signed "Thank you" autograph. Donor provides their first name, and the card is now personalized to them. "Thank you, David, for your contribution to help our Country – Cher." Team up with a pro bono design agency and watch the donations pour in.

Also, ask for a response to a one-word survey. Forward to 3 friends. Again, just get the voter involved, engaged. Use Trump techniques, citing their importance and the need to defend our Country. "Trump wants to take away your social security and Medicare. Is that OK with you?" Yes / No [button]. Simple acts of engagement like that make people feel like their voice counts because it does.

Now they are an active member of the Team. Big Welcome and acknowledgment. Reward with acknowledging "We cannot save our Country, Climate and Retirement and Healthcare without YOU, ________" (Capture their first name and use it.) Personalize all emails and texts. If you study the text and email streams from Trump since July of 2019, you would have a very robust sampling of how to accomplish the above two tactics of motivating using the avoidance of pain and acquisition of pleasure techniques. I have all of the Trump texts and emails as part of my research.

Once you have the smallest level of engagement, then you build on that. Learning from Trump, you are constantly texting and emailing your base with things that list the pain that could be caused by the Republicans that must be avoided at all cost, and while celebrating the pleasure of current and future successes of our Team. Many of the texts say we "need" you. Many texts say your donation will be matched 1:1. 2:1, 3:1 and for just the next "x" hours "4:1". We are excited to announce a special match, so, that your $10 contribution will instantly grow to $40, if you donate in the next "x" hours. You're never told who is doing the "matching." But no doubt, this strategy is effective on many levels.

Using Pain/ Pleasure motivators; Carrot and Stick; Fear and Joy. Skin-in-the-game tactics:;$1 contribution; 1-minute surveys; Simple 1-minute auto-dial calls, etc. Simple, easy, volunteer activities like that make people feel like they are part of the Team, and that "they matter."

There were dozens of ways to turn a registered /leaning Dem into a "raving fan" where nothing will stop them from voting.

When both parties have close to the same percentage of declared or leaning voters, and if the Independents split 50/50, then it is the party who gets the largest number of their base out to vote that wins. In some cases, you can overcome a deficit on the Independent voter side if you overachieve in getting your base out to vote.

Gallup in a February 2020 poll put Dems and Republicans both close to each having 46% of the adult population. The numbers are higher than in some "party affiliation" stats because Gallup is including not just those "registered" with a given party but also those Independents that have, after testing, expressed specific party leanings.

Here is a link to a poll on Independents describing the percent who "lean" Democrat or Republican.[150]

All things being equal on party base participation, then it's the Independents who can swing the victory margin. See "Reason #21" in the companion book, *Why Trump Won The 2020 Election, 21 Reasons The Democrats* Lost, which describes the power of the Independent voter. If you cannot win over the "swing" Independent voters, then there's only one way to neutralize their power, and that is by creating a surge in the turnout of your base that is so large it nullifies the impact of the "swing" Independent voter.

There are many ways to galvanize your base. Trump has demonstrated the emotional techniques of fear and pleasure to galvanize his base. And

---

150. Staff, "Party Affiliation," *Gallup*, 27 March 2020,
https://news.gallup.com/poll/15370/party-affiliation.aspx

anger. When Trumped talked about a "caravan" headed to the southern border that included criminals, that is a perfect example of motivating your base out of fear and anger.

Who is more motivated, a calm, happy-go-lucky person or an angry person? Notice how much anger plays a role in motivating the Trump base.

Trump Tweeted on November 21, 2018, "There are a lot of CRIMINALS in the Caravan. We will stop them. Catch and Detain! Judicial Activism by people who know nothing about security and the safety of our citizens, is putting our Country in great danger. Not good!"

Democrats need to find the "fear" motivators for their base. For many, it will simply be to remind them of all the ways Trump first prevented, then slowed the US response to the looming coronavirus pandemic that has killed so many Americans.

There are a number of ways to use the carrot and the stick to motivate one's base. I will list a few more as we proceed.

Exciting the Democratic base, which includes non-socialist moderates, and Bernie-AOC socialists must be done with a variety of appeals.

 You had to bring the Democratic base to a boiling point of emotion equivalent to the emotional commitment of a Trump Trancer, so, that nothing would stop them from casting their vote.

How?

Targeted messaging to specific constituencies.

Men: real men, off the battlefield and in the general population, don't use assault weapons and high capacity magazines. Only cowards and murderers, who are emboldened by #MassacreMitch and his bought-and-paid-for-gun-cartel-campaign-money-recipients in the Socialist Republican Party, feel the necessity to carry a 100 round capacity AK-47.

Women: pro-choice. Gun violence. Retirement protection by protecting Medicare and Social Security from Socialist Republicans who want to defund Medicare and Social Security in order to pay for more welfare-for-the-rich and bloated defense spending on private contract killers and secret spending programs (see Commonsense Tax Policies at taxpayer.org.)

In order to beat Donald Trump you have to, of course, solidify your base to the point where they are not just willing to vote for the Democrat but they need to be so enthusiastic that they get up and out to vote no matter what the weather, coronavirus-related voting changes, or what impediments that the Republicans will put up.

To defeat the potential voter participation drop caused by fears around the coronavirus of 2020, you need to make mail-in balloting available and easy. So, is it any wonder that our "America First" (LOL) President opposed making voting easier. Trump doesn't care if waiting in line for hours puts you at risk of dying from COVID-19. Trump doesn't care if parents can't spend hours in a voting line because they have children that need their care. Trump doesn't care if people can't wait in long lines because they are working two and three jobs to make ends meet following the largest level of unemployment since the great depression. On April 3, 2020, The Hill ran this headline, "Trump says he opposes mail-in voting for November."[151]

Vote by mail works. Oregon, Washington, and Colorado) conduct their elections completely by mail. Over 20 other states permit voting by mail as an option. Of course, the military and other out-of-state citizens have always been allowed to vote by mail. According to the US Election Assistance Commission, six states reported over 50 percent of their

---

151. Brett Samuels, "Trump says he opposes mail-in voting for November," *The Hill*, March 4, 2020, https://thehill.com/homenews/administration/491126-trump-says-he-opposes-mail-in-voting-for-november

votes as absentee ballots: Arizona, California, Florida, Hawaii, Montana, and Utah.[152]

If national vote-by-mail is implemented, how is Russia going to hack into the precinct-level voting booth computers?

It's no wonder Trump indicated he was opposed to an all-mail vote option. The Guardian carried this headline on March 30, 2020, "Trump says Republicans would 'never' be elected again if it was easier to vote."[153]

This comment by Trump brings me back to my New Mexico Russian-hacking prediction in *Appendix 4 – Predictions*. You need electronic voting booths hooked to computers to make hacking easier. A 100% vote by mail, similar to what Oregon has had for twenty years, eliminates the hackable voting booth. In twenty years, Oregon has had virtually ZERO fraud.

There is absolutely no incentive for an individual to commit voting fraud because it's a criminal violation of federal law, 52 U.S. Code § 2051, with up to a 5-year prison sentence and a $10,000 fine.

Although, there is plenty of incentive for GRU officers in their Moscow military headquarters to hack into the voting systems because there is no extradition clause between Russia and the US. But they need an electronic computer system to hack. They can't hack a paper ballot.

So, yes, Trump wants to prevent easy paper ballot mail-in voting. Trump wants to stifle the Democratic base from voting because Trump knows his base will cross over alligator pits to make sure their man is

---

152. Staff, "EAVS Deep Dive: Early, Absentee and Mail Voting," *US Election Assistance Commission*, October 17 , 2017, https://www.eac.gov/documents/2017/10/17/eavs-deep-dive-early-absentee-and-mail-voting-data-statutory-overview
153. Sam Levine, "Trump says Republicans would 'never' be elected again if it was easier to vote," *The Guardian,* March 30, 2020, https://www.theguardian.com/us-news/2020/mar/30/trump-republican-party-voting-reform-coronavirus

re-elected, but Democrats are not registering the same level of enthusiasm, which I point out a little later under Biden.

My point is that you need to have a strategy that not only solidifies your base but excites your base to the point where they will overcome any challenge to make sure their vote for you gets in, and they will enthusiastically enroll others to do the same.

The other strategy you need in order to win is to have a strategy that can peel off millions of the Trump Trancers, the people that are in a Trump Trance, and believe that Trump is near god-like in their eyes. One lady I met as we both waited at a Jacksonville, Florida car wash told me, "Trump brings light into darkness." Do you think she is going to let a little thing like a Florida hurricane stop her from voting for Trump?

And there are millions that don't worship Trump. In fact, there are millions that don't even like him but will vote for him because he offers them policies that they prefer over those being offered by the Democrats.

Of course, the ultimate strategy will achieve both: solidifies and excites your base and pulls voters from the other side.

4. **Strategy to Acquire Moderate Republican Votes** Make America Proud Again, MAPA Hats. Blue hat. Gold Letters. Same letter design. Confuse the MAGA hat and slogan issue by conflating similarities. It puts a little damper on MAGA hats and twists the phrase into something better. It fits with Biden's battle for the soul of America campaign theme. Not "proud" of racist past, but proud of great leadership moments in the past. Leadership in world peace, NATO, environment, people, jobs, infrastructure, WHO and more.

Yes, moderate Republicans who are not happy with Trump can be swayed over to the blue column if the Dem platform is reasonable and not riddled with anything "socialist." Plus, a strong National- Debt-Be-Gone plan message to appeal to the fiscal conservatives long abandoned by the SPIDER party (Socialist Party Dedicated to the Rich, SPR, SPIDER).

Republicans no longer have exclusive use of the word "socialist" to attack Dems. This is critical and essential re-branding. Now when Republicans say "socialist": many will think, well, Republicans are "socialist" as well, as they give free welfare tax handouts to the rich at the expense of all of us who have to bear the cost of welfare

 Make America Proud Again- Same hat design, same letter design, different third letter, MAPA. Confuse the issue a little and take the unique specialness off the MAGA hats. You can really capture the genre with a red, white, and blue designed hat. Red bill. White hat. Blue letters. Or, if you insist, make the hats blue with gold MAPA letters. The parody factor is priceless.

5.   Win over Available Independents.

The primary way to do this is based on the research discussed in the companion book, *Why Trump Won The 2020 Election, 21 Reasons Democrats Lost*. Specifically, in "Reason #21 – Failure to Win A Majority of Independent Voters," we discuss the most effective strategy to win over "swing" Independents. This is done by creating more negatives about your opponent in the mind of the Independent voter than they have created about your candidate. With Independents, to a large degree, it's all about the "unfavorables."

The Dems needed to have pursued a Mega-Neg Don assault, meaning a mega, massive, unrelenting negative campaign against Don-the-Con, Traitor Trump, Trea45son Trump, and Social Security Killer Trump.

Winning over Independents of various stripes. How to do this is clearly delineated in *Why Trump Won The 2020 Election, 21 Reasons Democrats*

Lost, "Reason #21 – Failure to Win A Majority of Independent Voters." Various strategies to win over Independents is explained along with the actual sub-set of Independents that will decide the election.

6.   Nine State Strategy – WI, PA, MI, FL, NC, AZ, NM, GA, and MN. These are "swing" battleground states.

Bloomberg's Team, Kevin Sheekey, et al., believe the focus needed to be on six states: WI, PA, MI, FL, NC, and AZ. They were 67% correct. There are good reasons to include NM, GA, and MN.

New Mexico: In Electoral College math, it's chess, not checkers, and in *Appendix 4 – Predictions*, I expose what I call the Republican-Russia "New Mexico" gambit. In that scenario, Trump can lose both Pennsylvania and Michigan and still win, if he wins New Mexico. Remember, in 2016, Trump won with 304 Electoral College (EC) votes. 34 more than the minimum EC needed of 270. All things being roughly equal in 2020, except Trump lost Pennsylvania (20 EC votes) and Michigan's (16 EC votes), which brought Trump down 36 EC votes, or 304 minus 36 = 268. That was 2 EC votes shy of the 270 minimum EC votes needed to win, except "miraculously" Trump won the "blue state" New Mexico with its 5 EC votes. Now Trump wins with 268 + 5 = 273 Electoral College votes. New Mexico can give Trump a 2nd term in the White House.

The Dems needed to win New Mexico in 2020, and didn't. But, according to this theory, the Dems were never going to win NM because the "fix" was in. Moscow-Mitch blocked legislation to protect voting machines and computers from being hacked by Russia, and it is theorized that it was Russia not the voters who delivered New Mexico to Trump. See *Appendix 2– Predictions* where I predicted this loss.

Georgia: The Dems lost the Governorship by only 55,000 votes when African-American Stacey Abrams ran for that seat. Extensive voter suppression has been alleged that denied Abrams a possible victory. The point is the Dems need to convert GA to the Blue column with its 16

EC votes, thus blunting any Republican win of Wisconsin (10EC) and New Mexico (5EC).

The new EC math: Trump loses PA +MI = 36 + GA (10) = 46. Trump 2016 with 304 less PA+MI+GA = 46; puts TRUMP at 304 − 46 = 258, and even with NM (5EC), Trump only hits 258+ 5 = 263 because Trump lost GA's 10 and did not win even with 273 using the New Mexico gambit, but lost GA (10EC) and therefore lost with only 263 total Electoral College votes.

MI- Union AFL-CIO CHAIR 24/7- message "Biden Admin saved MI

FL: Republicans want to take away Social Security and Medicare – 24/7

PA: Biden is Blue-collar / Catholic / Hometown Boy – Messenger: Bruce Springsteen.

NM: Hispanic Latino Leaders and Celebrities praise Biden, point out Trump's racism.

GA- trying to take your vote away. Putting GA in play would force Republicans to spend resources there that they had wanted to place elsewhere.

WI- issues to highlight: health care, environment, trade policy, roads, and gun violence prevention.

AZ – In 2018, Democrats won by focusing on Trump's broken promises, according to DNC Chair Tom Perez.

NC - In 2018, a federal court ruled that all 13 of North Carolina's congressional districts were unconstitutionally gerrymandered in favor of the GOP. The redistricting will help Dems, but may not be enough to turn state blue.

The MN-NM gambit.

Minnesota (MN) is in play. Trump only lost MN by 45,000 votes, 3.4% of the total vote, in 2016, and Trump is being hailed in parts of MN as bringing back manufacturing and mining jobs to that State, and why is MN so important? MN has 10 Electoral College votes, and Trump only lost MN by 45k votes out of nearly 2.9m cast. In a Politico article on March 22, 2020, titled, "Minnesota on the edge: 'I've voted Democrat my whole life. It's getting tougher'" writer Adam Behsudi states, "In a mining town in the heart of Humphrey, Mondale and Wellstone territory, Trump stakes his claim."

With MN's 10 Electoral College votes, and NM's 5 EC votes, Trump, following the 2016 EC results can afford to lose, PA, MI, and Wisconsin, states he won in 2016, and still win the election with 273 Electoral College votes. So, MN is definitely a "swing" state.

7. Issues: Something for Every Demographic (almost): These are serious policy proposals that will win over large segments of Republican constituency.

The author has 14 policies which are available in a secret "eyes only" memo for Vice President Biden, as well as, Michael Bloomberg, Tom Steyer, George Soros and a small group of major financial players who want to bet on the Democratic nominee.

The author was not going to let Republicans dilute impact of these far-reaching and across-the-ideological-aisle-appealing policy proposals. One is a headline grabber with endless news-cycle appeal. A different one will galvanize the BLM movement and virtually assure that every minority in America will come out to vote along with every LGBTQ supporter.

All of these are designed to kick-up the enthusiasm factor, which is sorely needed.

One of these secret campaign statements will suck the air out of one of Trump's strongest demographics. Many who would NEVER have voted Democrat will switch to Biden with this announcement. That same policy proposal would eliminate one of the biggest and most successful attack messages always launched against a Democrat.

One of the 14 policies will lock in millennials.

Many conservatives unenthused about Trump will be motivated by a few of these policies to enthusiastically vote Democrat.

People with war fatigue will be given a policy solution that will prevent an "endless war" from ever occurring again.

Veterans, current military, and those with ties to the military will rave and loudly cheer one of the policies in particular.

One policy will gut and replace one of Trump's signature policies.

In political campaigns, we know that even one really great, news grabbing policy statement can move an election toward that candidate.

Do I really have more than a dozen useful policies that can generate millions of enthusiastic voters for the Democratic nominee? There's a simple way to find out.

Some of these policies are lifted from my next book, *20 Ways To Improve America*, which I have been working on for more than 15 years.

If you think this book has any gravitas, then you know there probably is a there, there with these policy proposals.

Back to messaging. To quote Howard LaGardé, one of my coaches, "Listen to learn." That's easier said than done. Don't listen while at the same time creating your witty retort or your insightful add-on. "Listening to learn" is a form of meditation, the type that involves focused attention. You must direct your mind and truly listen to what the other is saying. Your only intention must be to learn from what is being said. You can only create effective messaging to your audience from a reservoir of deep listening to what your audience is saying. Clearly, Trump has "listened" to his base. The Democrats needed to listen to Trump's base and to everyone else in order to develop a proper national message. What is the Country saying? Are there some common themes that emerge?

By listening, the Democrats hit on a messaging strategy that resonated. "Save our Jobs. Save our Money. Save our Social Security. Save our Healthcare. Save our Medicare. Save our Medicaid. Save our Students. Save our Country. Save our Species."

Save our Jobs. The Democrats rocked America with a promise, "Anyone who lost a job will get a job*" Anyone who lost a job due to the pandemic is guaranteed a job or 6 months of prior income per W-2 or 2019 tax return. Federal infrastructure programs in co-operation with States will seek to fill the gap on prior jobs that don't come back at the end of the pandemic with Federally-funded Federal-State infrastructure job programs that will last 12- 36 months or longer with full benefits.

Save our Money from continuing to be stolen by the Socialist Republican Party for the Rich, the SPR, SPIDER party, in order to fatten the pockets of their elite rich friends. We will replenish the cost of the pandemic by "patching holes in the TCJA that are leaking government revenue."

Save our Healthcare, Medicare. Medicaid, Social Security, and our retirement infrastructure that the Socialist Republican Party for the Rich want to defund in order to give more money to their elite rich friends.

Third Rail Social Security Threatened by Trump

Save Social Security:

On February 4, 2020, President Trump said, "We will always protect your Medicare and we will always protect your Social Security. Always."

Six days later, on February 10, 2020, Trump released a budget that has cuts to Social Security.

Are you scared about the future of Social Security? With this administration in power, you should be.

Treasury Secretary Steve Mnuchin said on Capitol Hill,

"It's not a cut, it's a reduction in the rate of increase." Who do they think they're fooling?[154]

Biden will guarantee America's seniors don't have their retirement security taken away by Trump and the SPIDER party.

Republicans were proposing to cut back on Medicare, Social Security, and other essential programs in order to recover funds being given to the wealthy.)[155]

Nathaniel Weixel, "Ryan eyes push for 'entitlement reform' in 2018," *The Hill.* December 6, 2017, available at https://thehill.com/homenews/house/363642-ryan-pledges-entitlement-reform-in-2018[156]; Steven T. Dennis, "McConnell Blames Entitlements, Not GOP, for Rising Deficits," *Bloomberg*, October 16, 2018, available at https://www.bloomberg.com/news/articles/2018-10-16/mcconnell-blames-entitlements-not-gop-for-rising-deficits.[157]

---

154. Jake Johnson, "Steve Mnuchin admits Trump's budget cuts Social Security even as president claims he is 'not touching' the program," *Raw Story*, February 13, 2020, https://www.rawstory.com/2020/02/steve-mnuchin-admits-trumps-budget-cuts-social-security-even-as-president-claims-he-is-not-touching-the-program/

155. Andrew Schwartz & Galen Hendricks, "One Year Later, the TCJA Fails to Live Up to Its Proponents' Promises - Center for American Progress," *Center for American Progress*, December 20, 2018, https://www.americanprogress.org/issues/economy/reports/2018/12/20/464534/one-year-later-tcja-fails-live-proponents-promises/

156. Nathaniel Weixel, "Ryan eyes push for 'entitlement reform' in 2018," *The Hill,* December 6, 2017, https://thehill.com/homenews/house/363642-ryan-pledges-entitlement-reform-in-2018

157. Steven T. Dennis, "McConnell Blames Entitlements, Not GOP, for Rising Deficits," *Bloomberg,* October 16, 2018, https://www.bloomberg.com/news/articles/2018-10-16/mcconnell-blames-entitlements-not-gop-for-rising-deficits

Save our Country from the Russian invasion supported by Moscow Mitch, Putin-Puppet-Trump, and the anti-American pro-communist dictator Republicans.

Save our species by saving our farms from drought, our coastal cities from floods, and our forests from fire by creating 100's of thousands of climate-improving jobs of all types.

Save our student generation from crippling debt by creating free college classes in new-century job-creating courses. Student debt elimination programs and student loan programs that allow loans to be paid off at an affordable pace are essential. For example, no more than 3% of net income after rent, food, and transportation deduction can be allocated toward student debt reduction. This program would be underwritten by the same group that underwrites the GI-Loan program, which will allow complete loan forgiveness for those who join an approved service in the interest of US Health, Security, and Welfare.

Stop the economic enslavement where the poor and middle class are forced to give their tax money, under threat of imprisonment and fines, to subsidize the rich corporations and the wealthy. This is economic slavery by the Republican-supported rich over the democratic poor and middle class.

<u>When addressing issues with Independents:</u>

Remember, in a close race, Independent voters decide elections. See "Reason #21" on the Independent voter in the companion book, *Why Trump Won The 2020 Election, 21 Reasons Democrats Lost* for a deep appreciation of this fact.

Here's advice from a PAC chair who has studied independent voting behavior for a long time: if you want to describe a policy without alienating an Independent you need to say "earth," not climate; "background checks," not guns; "healthcare," not Obamacare; and talk about providing coverage for pre-existing conditions, not a government takeover of health care.

Keller Research Institute (KRI) shows that Trump supporters have trouble defending or responding to certain issues and topics. There are a number of issues to feature in any debate and in any media strategy based on KRI research. Here are the nine issues summarized with a more detailed description to follow:

1. Trump de-funding Social Security.

2. Helsinki Lie saying Russia did not interfere in the 2016 election.
3. Trump's 2017 tax restructure primarily benefited the rich and ran up the national debt.
4. Trump broke the law according to the GAO. See Chapter 3.

5. Trump says he can murder you and not be liable. See note below.

6. Trump fired the entire White House Pandemic Office in 2018, which severely hampered the Country's ability to quickly and effectively respond to the coronavirus pandemic. As result the US has over 30% of global COVID-19 deaths but only 4.2% of global population. See the April 16, 2020 Newsweek article by Neil Baron titled, "Could Trump Be Criminally Liable for His Deadly Mishandling of Coronavirus?"[158]

7. Promoting Putin-sponsored hoax that the 2016 DNC server was hacked from Ukraine. In fact, it was Russian GRU military intelligence officers in Moscow Towers, and the Mueller report reveals the IP address of the computers used and the names of the Russian officers who did the 2016 hacking of the DNC computer.

---

158. Neil Baron, "Could Trump Be Criminally Liable for His Deadly Mishandling of Coronavirus?," *Newsweek*, 4/16/20, https://www.newsweek.com/could-trump-criminally-liable-his-deadly-mishandling-coronavirus-opinion-1498146

8. Lying about Russia not "getting involved" in Venezuela on May 3, 2019, with detailed press announcements by Secretary of State Mike Pompeo and national security adviser, John R. Bolton, to the contrary just two days earlier.[159]

9. Trump lied about eliminating the national debt. Quote his 2016 pledge. Under Trump's money giveaway to the rich, we have experienced the largest increase in our national debt in US history. $1 Trillion. This was BEFORE the cost of the coronavirus. The January 2, 2020, Politifact headline reads, "Federal debt is up, not down, under Trump's watch,"[160]

10. Trump's delayed and inept response to the Covid-19 pandemic. US military warned Trump about virus dangers back in November 2019.

11. Trump's life-threatening suggestion on April 23, 2020, that Americans consider injecting disinfectant to kill Covid-19 virus. This was followed by a number of calls into poison control centers around the Country. The Forbes headline read, "Calls To Poison Centers Spike After The President's Comments About Using Disinfectants To Treat Coronavirus." Robert Glatter, MD reported on April 25, 2020, "One call involved someone using a sinus rinse consisting of a detergent-based solution, and another

---

159. Mark Landler, "Trump Says He Discussed the 'Russian Hoax' in a Phone Call With Putin," *New York Times*, May 3, 2019, https://www.nytimes.com/2019/05/03/us/politics/trump-putin-phone-call.html?login=email&auth=login-email&login=email&auth=login-email

160. Louis Jacobson, "Federal debt is up, not down, under Trump's watch," *Politifact*, January 2, 2020, https://www.politifact.com/truth-o-meter/promises/trumpometer/promise/1418/eliminate-federal-debt-8-years/#:~:text=In%20a%20March%2031%2C%202016%2C%20interview%20with%20the,how%20much%2C%20Trump%20failed%20to%20provide%20a%20figure.

individual who gargled with a mixture of mouthwash and bleach intended to kill the coronavirus."[161]

Katie Rogers in the New York Times informed us in an article discussing the outcry following Trump's disinfectant remarks, "Injecting bleach or highly concentrated rubbing alcohol 'causes massive organ damage and the blood cells in the body to basically burst,' Dr. Diane P. Calello, the medical director of the New Jersey Poison Information and Education System, said in an interview. 'It can definitely be a fatal event.'"[162]

12. #TREA45SON. Trump praising Russia and inviting Russia back into G7 even after knowing Russia was paying bounties to kill American soldiers. Biden hammered Trump on this egregious dereliction of duty and cruel insult all soldiers and veterans in his June 30, 2020 press conference. This makes Trump an accomplice and accessory to murder of American soldiers. As of this writing there are three soldiers whose murder in Afghanistan seemed to be linked to payments from Russia's GRU.[163] [164]

---

161. Robert Glatter, MD, "Calls To Poison Centers Spike After The President's Comments About Using Disinfectants To Treat Coronavirus," *Forbes*, April 25, 2020, https://www.forbes.com/sites/robertglatter/2020/04/25/calls-to-poison-centers-spike-
-after-the-presidents-comments-about-using-disinfectants-to-treat-
coronavirus/#dfd787b11574
162. Katie Rogers, Christine Hauser, Alan Yuhas and Maggie Haberman, "Trump's Suggestion That Disinfectants Could Be Used to Treat Coronavirus Prompts Aggressive Pushback," *New York Times*, April 24, 2020, https://www.nytimes.com/2020/04/24/us/politics/trump-inject-disinfectant-bleach-
coronavirus.htm
163. Charlie Savage, Eric Schmitt and Michael Schwirtz, "Russia Secretly Offered Afghan Militants Bounties to Kill U.S. Troops, Intelligence Says," *New York Times*, June 26, 2020, https://www.nytimes.com/2020/06/26/us/politics/russia-afghanistan-
bounties.html
164. Charlie Savage, Mujib Mashal, Rukmini Callimachi, Eric Schmitt and Adam Goldman, "Money Transfers Bolstered Belief In Russian Scheme, Intercepted Data

Attorney Neil Baron wrote an op-ed for Newsweek titled, "Could Trump Be Criminally Liable for His Deadly Mishandling of Coronavirus?" He points out, "The definition of involuntary or negligent manslaughter encompasses unintended killing through negligence. Attorney Baron stated that "Dr. Anthony Fauci has said, it didn't have to be this bad in the U.S.," and "The U.S. accounts for just 4.2 percent of the world's population but 30 percent of COVID-19 cases…"[165]

Trump Defunding Social Security: Trump lied about protecting Social Security. On February 4, 2020, in the State of the Union address, President Trump said, "We will always protect your Medicare and we will always protect your Social Security. Always." On February 10, 2020, Trump releases a budget that has cuts to Social Security.

"Trump budget cuts trillions from Social Security, Medicare, and Medicaid" was the February 11, 2020, headline in People's World in an article by Mark Gruenberg.[166]

Business Insider reported, "Trump's latest budget proposal called for $130 billion less to be spent on prescription drugs under Medicare and a $70 billion cut resulting from constricted eligibility rules for Social Security disability benefits."[167]

Links Intelligence Unit to Afghans Who Killed U.S. Troops," *New York Times*, July 1, 2020, https://static01.nyt.com/images/2020/07/01/nytfrontpage/scan.pdf

165. Neil Baron, "Could Trump Be Criminally Liable for His Deadly Mishandling of Coronavirus?," *Newsweek*, 4/16/20, https://www.newsweek.com/could-trump-criminally-liable-his-deadly-mishandling-coronavirus-opinion-1498146

166. Mark Gruenberg, "Trump budget cuts trillions from Social Security, Medicare, and Medicaid," *People's World*, February 11, 2020, https://www.peoplesworld.org/article/trump-budget-cuts-trillions-from-social-security-medicare-and-medicaid/

167. Joseph Zeballos-Roig, "Trump says he's willing to cut entitlements to shrink the $23 trillion national debt," *Business Insider,* March 6, 2020, https://markets.businessinsider.com/news/stocks/trump-cut-funding-entitlements-social-security-medicare-national-debt-reelection-2020-3-1028972301

A former Health and Human Services employee with whom I spoke thought implementing "constricted eligibility rules for Social Security disability benefits" might harm a lot of already marginalized citizens.

On February 9, 2020, The Washington Times reported, "The plan would reduce spending by $4.4 trillion equally from discretionary and mandatory programs such as Medicare over the next decade."[168]

These cuts will help offset the debt creating tax give-a-ways to the rich in the 2017 TCJA tax restructure where the rich corporations and richest Americans received trillions in tax deductions.[169]

The Helsinki Lie: on July 16, 2018, after a secret meeting with Vladimir Putin, Trump went in front of the world press and promoted Russia's lie that Russia did not interfere in America's 2016 election. That lie by Trump severely damaged the reputation of the American intelligence community around the world. What made it worse was that the whole world knew it was a lie. In the previous year, there been numerous public articles, hearings, statements on TV, and criminal indictments against Russians by the federal government for their Putin-directed interference in the 2016 election.[170]

---

168. Dave Boyer, "'Shrink' government: Trump's budget reduces spending by $4.4 trillion, makes 2017 tax cuts permanent," *Washington Times,* February 9, 2020, https://www.washingtontimes.com/news/2020/feb/9/trump-budget-cuts-44-trillion-medicare-discretiona/

169. Ron Bieber, "Opinion: Trump's tax cuts benefit top 1%, hurt working class," *Detroit News,* December 10, 2019, https://www.detroitnews.com/story/opinion/columnists/labor-voices/2019/12/11/opinion-trump-tax-cuts-benefit-one-percent-hurt-working-class/2631031001/

170. Jon Swaine, & Marc Bennetts, "Mueller charges 13 Russians with interfering in US election to help Trump," *The Guardian,* February 17, 2018, https://www.theguardian.com/us-news/2018/feb/16/robert-mueller-russians-charged-election

Trump's 2017 Tax Restructure Benefited The Rich and Ran Up National Debt by Trillions. The middle class was hurt in the long run, with corporations making billions in profits and paying no taxes. The Detroit News ran this headline in December 2019, "Opinion: Trump's tax cuts benefit top 1%, hurt working class."[171] *See Appendix 4, 5, and 12.*

Trump Broke the Law According to the GAO. The United States Government Accountability Office (GAO) declared that Trump had broken the law by violating the Impoundment Act, the illegal impoundment of US appropriated funds by a President. Go to:[172]

Trump Says He Can Murder You And Not Be Liable. Donald J. Trump told a US Federal Judge in the Second Circuit Court of Appeals on October 23, 2019, through his attorney, that he had the legal right to murder anyone of us. That would include murdering our families and pets. Trump said he could murder us and could not be held accountable as long as he was President. Listen to the audio by finding the white audio arrow in the article:[173] That link is also here: https://bit.ly/3ijNo4k.

Trump Fired White House Pandemic Office in 2018.

Trump shut down the White House pandemic office in 2018. On May 10, 2018, Rear Adm. Timothy Ziemer, the senior White House official

---

171. Ron Bieber, "Opinion: Trump's tax cuts benefit top 1%, hurt working class," *Detroit News*, December 10, 2019, https://www.detroitnews.com/story/opinion/columnists/labor-voices/2019/12/11/opinion-trump-tax-cuts-benefit-one-percent-hurt-working-class/2631031001/
172. Emily Cochrane, Eric Lipton and Chris Cameron, "G.A.O. Report Says Trump Administration Broke Law in Withholding Ukraine Aid," *New York Times*, January 16, 2020, https://www.nytimes.com/2020/01/16/us/politics/gao-trump-ukraine.html
173. Ian Millhiser, "Trump's lawyer: If Trump shoots someone on 5th Avenue, nothing could be done," *Vox*, October 23, 2019, https://www.vox.com/2019/10/23/20928680/nothing-could-be-done-trump-fifth-avenue-immunity-mazars-vance

responsible for leading the US response in the event of a deadly pandemic, had his office closed down by Trump's NSC Director John Bolton. In a prophetic article on that same day in May 2018, the Bipartisan Report stated that shutting down the White House pandemic office, "Comes at a time when many experts say the Country is already <u>unprepared for the increasing risks of a pandemic</u> or bioterrorism attack."[174]

Trumped lied about Russia not interfering in Venezuela in a White House press briefing. This lie occurred right after a secret phone call with Vladimir Putin on May 3, 2019. The lie was made all the worse because of detailed press announcements by Secretary of State Mike Pompeo and national security adviser, John R. Bolton, to the contrary just two days earlier.[175]

On May 3, 2019, Trump, following a secret phone call with Vladimir Putin, lies at a WH press conference saying Russia isn't seeking to "get involved" in Venezuela.

On that same day, May 3, 2019, the New York Times reported,

> On Wednesday, [May 1, 2019], Secretary of State Mike Pompeo called the Russian foreign minister, Sergey Lavrov, to warn him that his country's *intervention* in Venezuela was "destabilizing" for that Country and for the United States-Russia relationship.

---

174. Jon Easley, "Trump Lies About Coronavirus Warning After Removing Pandemic Officials," *Politics USA,* February 29, 2020, https://www.politicususa.com/2020/02/29/trump-lies-about-coronavirus-warning-after-removing-pandemic-officials.html
175. Mark Landler, "Trump Says He Discussed the 'Russian Hoax' in a Phone Call With Putin," *New York Times*, May 3, 2019, https://www.nytimes.com/2019/05/03/us/politics/trump-putin-phone-call.html?login=email&auth=login-email&login=email&auth=login-email

Other officials portray Venezuela as a Cold War-like proxy battle between Washington and Moscow.[176]

Trump lied about eliminating the national debt.

Candidate Donald Trump promised to eliminate the US national debt. The October 2019 Newsweek headline under President Trump was this, "Donald Trump Promised to Eliminate the Deficit in 8 Years. So Far, He Has Increased it by 68%."[177]

The headline from NPR on February 19. 2019 was, "US National Debt Hits Record $22 Trillion."[178]

Another headline proving Trump's lie to control debt was this one, "At the end of FY 2019, the federal deficit was **$984** billion, or **4.6%** GDP." Nearly $1 Trillion in debt in just one year.[179]

6. Celebrities Galore

Blanket campaign with famous faces.
Local and nationally admired Celebs must be a centerpiece along with big-name endorsements within each State. Work with a list of top 100 State Influencers.
    a.   Virtual Parties with Celebrities.
    b.   Win Photos w their favorite celebs through online technology.

---

176. Mark Landler, "Trump Says He Discussed the 'Russian Hoax' in a Phone Call With Putin," *New York Times*, May 3, 2019, https://www.nytimes.com/2019/05/03/us/politics/trump-putin-phone-call.html?login=email&auth=login-email&login=email&auth=login-email

177. Shane Croucher, "Donald Trump Promised to Eliminate the Deficit in 8 Years. So Far, He Has Increased it by 68%," *Newsweek*, August 10, 2019, https://www.newsweek.com/trump-deficit-debt-cbo-data-obama-1463802

178. Bill Chappell, "US National Debt Hits Record $22 Trillion," *NPR*, February 13, 2019, https://www.npr.org/2019/02/13/694199256/u-s-national-debt-hits-22-trillion-a-new-record-thats-predicted-to-fall

179. Staff, "At the end of FY 2019 the federal deficit was **$984** billion, or **4.6%** GDP," *US Government Spending,* April 19, 2020, https://www.usgovernmentspending.com/debt_deficit_history

   c. Win memorabilia from celebrities' movies and songs, etc.

   d. A plethora of 15-second celebrity TV-spots must be released.

   e. Precincts with the highest percentage of registered base participation win a live Zoom party with a famous celebrity and can select from a list of celebrities.

   f. Counties with the highest percentage of registered base participation win a live virtual party with a famous celebrity and can select from a list of celebrities.

   g. States with the highest percentage of registered base participation win a live virtual party with a famous celebrity and can select from a list of celebrities.

   h. Remember we have a list of over 50 celebrities listed above in the re-branding Trump with TV spots section including Meryl Streep, Robert DeNiro, Miley Cyrus, Rob Reiner, Cher, Jon Stewart, Madonna, Arnold Schwarzenegger, Tom Steyer, George Soros, Mark Ruffalo, George Clooney, J.K. Rowling, Cher, Sarah Silverman, Alex Baldwin, Stephen Colbert,

7. Entertainment is a Focus

Make Politics fun and cool.

   a. For all, but primarily the millennials.

      i. Adopt a millennial in another town.

         1. 75% saturation metric. Meaning we need 75% of eligible millennial voters participating.

         2. Set up social media sites, hubs, virtual meet-ups, etc. Run by full time paid social media millennial experts in every county in every state. Minimum 2 per county. According to usgs.gov, there are 3,141 counties in the 50 States. That

means 6,282 students with a Summer-Fall job. Excellent!

3. These 6,200 will be in charge of games, virtual parties, press conferences, and two dozen award categories in every state plus national award contests with real prizes picked out by a vote of the 6,200. Pop quizzes on election facts. Each county gets to pick their favorite "celebrity sponsor" from any medium. Each county competes for the best summary of the issues. Participants vote on the top 10 national legislative proposals. Each county votes on a spokesperson. Then each state. Then nationally, they vote on four national spokespersons. At least one woman, one man, one minority, and one LGBTQ. They can overlap.

4. Awards for the best 2020 election game.

5. Awards for highest level of registered voter participation 18- 29 year olds.

6. These 6,200 receives texts or recoded calls every day from a different celebrity from all walks of life. From Meryl Streep to Robert DeNiro.

ii. Adopt-a-voter

This is an unprecedented effort. But the life of our planet is at stake, so it calls for an unprecedented effort.

1. 70 million as a metric. Contact author for details. In general, you need 7 million voters to reach out to 10 others. People sign up via email or text. They are given a link. These programs already exist. (I used one in the 2018 Democratic

candidate for Florida Governor campaign.) On that link is one name with a phone number. If a person answers they say," Hi my name is ___ and I am a 2020 election volunteer, may I have 1 minute of your time?" After calling that person they click on one of the multiple results: OAS: out of service number; BS: busy signal; NA: No answer, NVM: no voice mail; LVM: left voicemail; VB: spoke w_voting B; VT: spk w voting T; V3G: spk w voting3rd prty-Green; V3L: spk w voting3rd prty-Libertarian; V3O: spk w voting 3rd prty-other; VU: spk w voting but undec; NV: spk w not voting; R: spk w refuse to discuss 2020; 10: will be one of my 10- 2020 buddies (exchange name, ph #'s and best time to speak and prefer Ph, email, or text; J10: will; join program to find 10 election buddies: send info and call app; considers self D, R, I, 3: 3rd prty, NP: non-partic; HIT SUBMIT. A thank you message and sound occurs. Then another name with phone number appears.

b.   VR (Virtual Reality) visits with your fav star; photos with your fav star.

c.   Use the Celebrity-Dem Connect App. Celebrities give OK to limited access, and fans select times to connect for live chats, webinars, VR photos, etc.

a.   Entertainment, Games, Prizes, and Rewards is a Focus to Keep Younger Voters and many others Interested. Especially for the "Quarantined" election.

b.   Treasure hunts (vote hunts: where are the votes… can you find them?) Issue hunts: find the key issues in your community.

   d. Creative programs are specifically designed for the "Quarantined" election.

   e. I voted proof = enters voter into big sweepstakes. Of course, no proof of who you voted for is required. Entries can include texting or emailing a photo of you mailing absentee ballot or in front of the precinct.

   f. "I voted" Instagram posting and texting that photo enters that person in a very cool drawing.

Virtual Parties with Celebs

Win Photos with their fav celebs through online technology: using "e-z match-up" app on Dem website.

Win memorabilia of famous stars who donate them to Dem to be placed on Dem website. Including the "Big Prize" – lunch with your favorite star sweepstakes. (Trump has been doing this by offering dinner with him and a separate sweepstakes that offered dinner with Melania. Using all caps, the text from Melania read, "I would LOVE to have dinner with you in Beverly Hills."

Imagine a sweepstakes that offer lunch (when it can be done safely post-pandemic) with Star Wars characters and four dozen other famous celebrities from TV, theatre, cinema, and music with all travel expenses paid. Awesome publicity. Also offer lunch with famous GEEKS and Silicon Valley superstars, as well as other famous business people.

Lunch with Oprah !!! Lunch with Michelle Obama! Lunch with famous NBA and NFL superstars. In fact, have one sweepstake where you Name Your Fantasy Lunch Partner, and DNC pledges to try and secure that lunch if you make a donation of at least $x. The Dem website posts photos of the lucky winners with their celebrity. Those photos are sent to their hometown paper and their local TV station to maximize the PR boost. You can create a donor gift page. People agree to donate "X" if the donor contributes "Y." ACT BLUE verifies donation but does not process the donation until UPS/FedEx verifies the delivery of the gift package.

The idea, people, is engagement!!! Engaged people will absolutely 100% vote and tell their friends to vote now that they have skin-in-the-game.

8. Biden

Reduce Biden's Unfavorable Rating by 5 points minimum. Go for a 34% Unfavorable rating (a 10% drop). It was at 44.8% in March 2020 according to Real Clear Politics average of six polls.[180] In June 2020, according to the New York Times, "polls aggregated by RealClearPolitics found that 45% of those surveyed had a favorable view of Biden, and 46% had an unfavorable view." Biden's "<u>very unfavorable</u> rating" in June 2020 was 25%.[181]

> a. How do you reduce Biden's unfavorable rating? For Biden: pursue the "six headlines strategy" of favorables. The six headlines strategy used effectively by Trump and his Team is simply overwhelming the media with multiple headlines, three minimum, and ideally, with six in your pocket when you need to take over the news cycle to squash a negative event.
>
> A perfect example of the "six headlines" strategy was when the Trump Access Hollywood "grab-their-pussy"

---

180. Staff, "Joe Biden: Favorable/Unfavorable," *Real Clear Politics*, March 27, 2020, https://www.realclearpolitics.com/epolls/other/joe_biden_favorableunfavorable-6677.html#!

181. Amy Walter, "Trump Is in a Deep Hole. Can He Dig Himself Out Before November?" *The Cook P{olitical Report*, June 26, 2020, https://cookpolitical.com/analysis/national/national-politics/trump-deep-hole-can-he-dig-himself-out-november

and "I-tried-to-f-her" tape came out, just 29 minutes later Wikileaks released a trove of hacked DNC emails. 29 minutes! That, by any definition, is the epitome of people working together in coordination, collaboration, and collusion.

The Center For American Progress' initiative titled The Moscow Project released this statement, "The 'Access Hollywood' tape of Trump boasting about sexually harassing women is released at 4:03 pm. At 4:32 pm, WikiLeaks begins posting Clinton campaign chairman John Podesta's stolen emails."[182]

Most people remember "grab their pussy," but forget Trump also said on the Access Hollywood tape, "I did try and fuck her. She was married. And I moved on her very heavily." He was referring to TV hostess Nancy O'Dell.

That was a very lucky circumstance for Donald Trump, or was it coordination, or another c-word, collaboration, or another c-word, collusion? Nobody in the communication world would think that it was a lucky circumstance. That leaves you to pick one of the other c-words.

In any case, it was a perfect example of the six-headline strategy of overwhelming a negative media event with a tsunami of other headlines that tends to push your undesirable headline into the background, and that quiets the potential noise around your negative news.

---

182. Staff, "WikiLeaks Releases Podesta Emails Shortly After "Access Hollywood" Tape Released," *The Moscow Project*, October 7, 2016, https://themoscowproject.org/collusion/wikileaks-releases-podesta-emails-shortly-access-hollywood-tapes-released/

How efficient is your media messaging machine when you can hit a crushing negative headline with a tidal wave of opposing news within just 29 minutes?

It makes you wonder who was pulling the levers behind the curtains on that one, doesn't it?

b. Fight off Trump's negative ads and comments as more lies from Don-The-Con because Trump knows he killed Americans with his slow response to coronavirus. Just ask the Director of Global Health at Harvard.

Ashish Jha is the director of the Harvard Global Health Institute. In an April 2020 article in Vox writer, German Lopez states,

"Jha described the Trump administration's messaging on coronavirus so far as "deeply disturbing," adding that it's "left the country far less prepared than it needs to be for what is a very substantial challenge ahead."

The Lopez article goes on:

The Trump administration, with John Bolton newly at the helm of the White House National Security Council, began dismantling the Team in charge of a pandemic response, firing its leadership and disbanding the Team in spring 2018.

The cuts, coupled with the administration's repeated calls to cut the budget for the Centers for Disease Control and Prevention (CDC) and other public health agencies, made it clear that the Trump administration wasn't prioritizing the federal government's ability to respond to disease outbreaks.

That lack of attention to preparedness, experts say, helps explain why the Trump administration has consistently botched its response to the coronavirus pandemic.[183] Improve Biden's "enthusiasm" rating. This is critical.

March 29, 2020, The ABC/ Washington Post enthusiasm poll had Biden trailing Trump by 29 percentage points in the high-level enthusiasm segment.[184]

That is a bone-crushing difference and bodes ill for Biden.

There are people who can turn this around — one in particular. Contact me, and I'll give you his name.

c. Flag. Country. Family. Seniors. Children. Pets. Charity. Salary to revolving charities: list a few, cancer research, (Beloved Top 5 neutral). Gladiator fighting for you. (Offset Trump's "Rocky" body.) Harley w/ flag-waving off back of cycle. Video demonstrating firearm safety to girl scouts/boy scouts. Iconic images. Biden walking senior lady across the road, or off curb. Making Joe more loveable / likeable.

    i. Best-Bet Biden
    ii. Sunny Bright Joe
    iii. Joe Knows Mo'
    iv. Siden' w Biden
    v. Mojo Joe
    vi. Joe with the mojo
    vii. Bright Biden
    viii. Country Joe

---

183. German Lopez, "The Trump administration's botched coronavirus response, explained," *Vox*, April 2, 2020, https://www.vox.com/policy-and-politics/2020/3/14/21177509/coronavirus-trump-covid-19-pandemic-response

184. Sofi Sinozich, "Biden consolidates support, but trails badly in enthusiasm: Poll," *ABC News,* March 29, 2020, https://abcnews.go.com/Politics/biden-consolidates-support-trails-badly-enthusiasm-poll/story?id=69812092

There are many qualified women for Biden's VP position.

Biden was smart to consider Val Demings as his VP running mate.

> d. She's a gun-totin', badge wearin', motorcycle ridin' woman, and she's an African American who reduced crime by 40% when she was Police Chief of Orlando, Florida. She is now a Congresswoman who won in a key battleground District in the key swing state of Florida. Her husband is a Sherriff. The photos and news clips go on forever.
> See her Gov. Bio:[185]
> US Congresswoman (FL-10)
> Former Chief of Police in Orlando, Florida.
> Husband is a Sherriff
> Val was born into a 2-room wooden home. Her mom was a maid. Her Dad was a janitor.
> Val was one of the House Managers for the Impeachment prosecution team handling the national spotlight well.
> Rep. Demings enjoys spending her very limited free time riding her Harley-Davidson Road King Classic motorcycle.
> Great imagery!
> A great role model.
> Val is An African-American woman who has broken many glass ceilings.
> Val brings a strong Florida presence.
>
> If some #BlackLivesMatter and some progressives have concerns about Demings as a VP due to her "police" background, then Biden should consider Val Demings in another national role. For example, Demings could be the National Law Enforcement Relations Director, a new

---

185. Staff, "About: US Representative Val Demings," *United States House of Representatives,* March 19, 2020, https://demings.house.gov/about

Cabinet-level position, in charge of rooting out systemic-racism in all areas of American life with an emphasis on law enforcement.

TV spot: A strong black woman pulling up on her Harley Davidson motorcycle and endorsing Biden is a powerful image.

9. Media Blitzed 24/7: using a Massive National Media Team

a. Massive national media team supported by a very large team in each State.

b. Large Media team with experts in every area guided by PR, Advertising, and Marketing pros; Heavy twitter FB Instagram and social media presence— 75% young folks run this.

c. Must match Russian trolling 2:1 [not easy]

    i. Huge Team required:
        1. State Dir/ 4 state-co-Dir.
        2. Dir. per County / 4 reg co-dir.
        3. Every major media outlet, print, TV, radio, has a coordinator

d. Non-stop letters to editors.

e. Non-stop calls to talk shows.

f. Continuous Celeb appearances in every State, and
    i. especially in every down-ticket district in play.

g. See "Reason #13 – Outmedia-ed" in the companion book, *Why Trump Won The 2020 Election, 21 Reasons Democrats Lost*, to see what campaign is up against.

h. Biden's digital divide between himself and Trump is massive.

i. Trump has a huge social media advantage that Dems must find a way to overcome. Trump has 75 million Twitter followers and 28 million Facebook followers.

Biden, for example, has 4.6 million Twitter followers and 1.7 million Facebook followers.[186] That is a huge deficit. So, Biden needs to team up with a number of media and business celebrities to increase his Twitter following so that, with re-Tweets it will add up to 300 million (with many overlaps, of course). Same strategy with FB. Committed stars like Oprah and Michelle and 100 other celebrities guarantee to re-post any FB posting taking Biden up to 300 million impressions with every post.

j. At least four studies, detailed in *Why Trump Won The 2020 Election*, and in *Racism and Racial Resentment, Their Role In Trump's Election*, that demonstrate that nearly half of Trump's voters have some degree of motivation around racial resentment. Given that, we should do something to address this before the November 3, 2020 election. It can be estimated that as many as 40 million people who voted for Trump are experiencing racial resentment.

Dear Mike Bloomberg, given the dramatic impact that racial resentment had in 2016 and will have on the 2020 election, what series of 30-second TV spots can we create to tamp down racial resentment in key swing states? I have some ideas. One series would be "African-American Heroes Who Made America Great!" Specifically, African-American heroes who made huge contributions within the various swing states. Of course,

---

186. Jim Rutenberg & Matthew Rosenberg, "Trump Won the Internet. Democrats Are Scrambling to Take It Back," *New York Times,* March 30, 2020, https://www.nytimes.com/2020/03/30/us/politics/democrats-digital-strategy.html

you can lead with all that Obama did for various swing states. I know the linkage between "Who Made America great," and "Make America Great" and Afro-Americans is not lost on you. That linkage will have a conscious and below conscious impact on the MAGA crowd in a way that heals while at the same time greatly reducing a Trump-motivator for many. Also include living Blacks who "Make America Great."

10. Money: $10 Billion

    a. $10 Billion is required to match the $10 Billion the Trump-PAC-Russia partnership will muster.

    b. The Democrats desperately need the resources that only a Michael Bloomberg can bring to the table. Bloomberg was worth $61 billion, according to Forbes magazine. Yes, Tom Steyer, Soros, and others are absolutely essential, as well.

    c. See "Reason #11 – Outspent" in the companion book, *Why Trump Won The 2020 Election, 21 Reasons Democrats Lost*, must be reviewed to see what the campaign was up against financially. Just $2.99 on Kindle. A small price to pay for my 3,000 hours of research and writing, wouldn't you say?

    d. When Bloomberg dropped out of the campaign for the Democratic Presidential nomination in March of 2020, he gave an $18 million donation to the DNC. All hoped that was not his last financial contribution.

The Democrats may lose the 2020 election because they failed to start an aggressive <u>national</u> anti-Trump campaign by November 2019. They let the Democratic primary candidates attack themselves instead of Trump. This self-inflicted wounding party went on until April 2020 when Biden became the "presumptive" nominee. Biden secured enough primary delegates to become the official Party nominee on June 2, 2020.

Due to the shelter-in-place COVID-19 pandemic, Biden started his national campaign by broadcasting from his basement. It would seem that both parties are operating with their hands tied behind their backs. This is actually a big advantage for Biden as Trump is seemingly restricted from having big rallies. Trump's first attempt on June 20, 2020, at an intra-pandemic rally at Tulsa's Bank Of Kentucky Center, fizzled. And recent reports suggest many attendees acquired the COVID-19 virus.[187] But the Democrats need to seize the national moment, and the above *12 Steps To Victory* are essential components of that strategy.

Polls That Count

Four in 10 voters said that the most important quality in a candidate was one that "can bring change." Among that group, Trump beat Clinton 82% to 14%." [188]

The four polls that count in this order:

1. The enthusiasm poll: T beating B by 28 pts
2. The "double hater" poll 2016 trump beats Clinton ….
3. The "Change wanted" poll
4. The unfavorable poll

---

187. Will Steakin and Olivia Rubin, "Trump rally likely contributed to surge in COVID-19 cases, Tulsa health official says," *ABC News*, July 9, 2020, https://abcnews.go.com/Politics/trump-rally-contributed-surge-covd-19-cases-tulsa/story?id=71680180

188. Chris Cillizza, "How Donald Trump wins again, in 3 sentences," *CNN*, May 18, 2020, https://www.cnn.com/2020/05/18/politics/donald-trump-james-woods-2020-reelection/index.html

Republicans Testing Their Primary Messaging

The overall preference poll: B beats T 6% means nothing compared to the other four polls.

The Early summer messaging by Republicans is along the lines this author has predicted.

Email from New Gingrich on May 29, 2020:

---------- Forwarded message ---------
From: **Newt Gingrich** <contact@victory.donaldtrump.com>
Date: Fri, May 29, 2020 at 3:47 PM
Subject: The Big Government Socialist Party
To: <DavidKeller>

David,
The Democratic Party doesn't exist anymore.

They're now the Big Government Socialist Party. <u>They've moved so far left that they make Cheatin' Obama look like a moderate.</u> The Party that wants open borders, gun confiscation, and skyrocketing tax rates for the middle class will **NEVER** control the White House.

Right now, it is too important for Patriotic Americans, like YOU, to sit on the sidelines while Joe Biden and his Fake

News friends are threatening everything we've worked so hard for.

That Gingrich email is your entire SPIDER campaign in one sound bite.

This above email from Republican Newt Gingrich contains the 3 BIG SPIDER PARTY LIES about open borders, gun confiscation, and skyrocketing taxes.

No one in Democratic leadership wants "Open Borders."
No one in Democratic leadership wants "Gun Confiscation."
No one in Democratic leadership wants "skyrocketing tax rates for the middle class."

"Open borders" attack is designed to attract the 73 million Americans who don't like illegal immigrants.

"Gun confiscation" attack is designed to attract the owners of 393 million guns in America.[189]

"Skyrocketing tax rates for the middle class" is designed to attract the 173 million shareholders in America, and all Americans who fear for their dwindling disposable income and the millions who are barely getting by from month-to-month. And it's a dog whistle to the rich corporations and rich elite who receive the majority of benefits under Trump's new 2017 "Tax Heist" TCJA law.

As to the open border and illegal immigration issue, the Democrats should listen to the American fears and concerns about illegal

---

189. Wikipedia, "Gun ownership," *Wikipedia,* last edited on June 29, 2020, https://en.wikipedia.org/wiki/Gun_ownership#:~:text=The%20Small%20Arms%20S urvey%20stated,firearms%20for%20every%20100%20residents.%22

immigration and open borders. One solution: set up immigration recruiting and interview offices in Mexico paid for by those benefiting from new immigrant labor.

Trump Travesty: Pandemic: Less Testing = More Deaths

On June 20, 2020, in a half-filled BOK Center stadium rally in Tulsa, Oklahoma Trump said,

"When you do testing to that extent, you're going to find people, you're going to find more cases. So, I said to my people, 'slow the testing down.'"

Many were aghast at this admission of leadership malfeasance, which, in effect, puts American lives at risk. People who have COVID-19, but don't know it because they were not tested, and therefore don't receive proper medical care, could die from that failure to test and properly diagnose.

@BrooklynDad_Defiant! Tweeted, "I'm not a doctor or lawyer, but it sure seems like a "president" admitting he intentionally slowed down testing of the most deadly disease we've seen is a pretty big fucking crime."

Trump Travesty: Killing ACA = millions uninsured.

Last month, Donald Trump reaffirmed his commitment to ripping healthcare coverage away from millions of Americans with no replacement, saying, "we want to terminate healthcare under Obamacare."[190] Now, the Trump administration and 18 Republican

---

190. Andrea Haverdink, "Trump Vows Complete End of Obamacare Law Despite Pandemic," *Washington Post*, May 6, 2020, https://www.washingtonpost.com/

state attorneys general have filed briefs with the U.S. Supreme Court to repeal the ACA.

In the midst of a pandemic, we cannot allow critical ACA provisions—including protections for people with pre-existing conditions, the expansion of Medicaid for low-income people, and tax credits to help millions better afford healthcare coverage—be struck down by a heartless administration intent on undoing every single aspect of the Obama administration.

The Supreme Court has upheld the ACA before. We're going to have to fight like hell to defend it once again.

Andrea Haverdink
Digital Director
Americans for Tax Fairness Action Fund

Point To Major Republican Groups Against Trump

Republicans for the Rule of Law

https://www.ruleoflawrepublicans.com

The Lincoln Project. Involves veteran Republican strategists like Stu Stevens, a top adviser for now-Utah senator Mitt Romney's 2012 presidential campaign, and George Conway, the husband of Trump adviser Kellyanne Conway, is also a co-founder of the group. Sarah Lenti, the Lincoln Project's executive director and a self-described former Republican who worked for George W. Bush and Condoleezza Rice.

https://lincolnproject.us/

Republican Voters Against Trump is a group led by Bill Kristol, a well-known neoconservative and former chief of staff to then vice-president Dan Quayle, and Republican consultants Sarah Longwell and Tim Miller. Per Wikipedia: **Republican Voters Against Trump** is a political initiative launched in May 2020 by Defending Democracy Together for the 2020 US presidential election cycle.[1][2] The project was formed to produce a US$10 million advertising campaign focused on 100 testimonials by Republicans, conservatives, moderates, right-leaning independents, and former Trump voters explaining why they would not vote for Donald Trump in 2020. The advertising campaign targets white college-educated suburban voters in Pennsylvania, Wisconsin, Michigan, Florida, North Carolina, and Arizona.

https://en.wikipedia.org/wiki/Republican_Voters_Against_Trump

Republican National Security Officials Against Trump. A set of Republican national security officials has also emerged in opposition to Trump. That group hasn't given itself a name yet, and includes the former Bush homeland security adviser Ken Wainstein, and John Bellinger III, who served in the state department. The group is looking to rally national security officials away from Trump – either by supporting Biden or writing in someone else.

Veterans Against Trump. https://www.votevets.org/

43 Alumni for Biden. A Super Pac called "43 Alumni for Biden" aims to rally alumni of George W Bush's administration to support the Democrat. John Farner is an organizing committee member with a new group called 43 Alumni for Biden that launched earlier this month and has brought in hundreds of former Bush staffers. (Bush was the country's 43rd different person to hold the office of president.)

https://43alumniforjoebiden.com/

Wisconsin decides the winner.

90% of the whole election boils down to Wisconsin.

In 2016 Trump won with 304 to Clinton's 227 Electoral College votes.

If we assume everything is the same as 2016 except:

Michigan (16 EC) and Pennsylvania (20 EC) go to Biden, and the two faithless 2016 electors in Texas go back to Trump and the five 2016 Clinton faithless electors go back to Biden you have:

Biden: 227 + 5 + 36 = 268.

Trump: 304 + 2 - 36 = 270.

Trump wins.

But if Wisconsin (10 EC) leaves Trump and goes Biden:

Trump: 270 − 10 = 260

Biden: 268 +10 = 278

Biden wins.

Wisconsin is the ultimate 2020 battleground state.

Most important States: WI, PA, MI, FL, AZ, and NC.

What if there is no Electoral College winner?

No winner in the Electoral College puts the election in the hands of the House of Representatives per the 12th Amendment.

Hypothetically, if the vote went to the House in 2020, Trump would win, but a 12th Amendment vote to determine our next President will not take place in 2020. I will explain. There is a scenario where Biden wins the popular vote, and Bidens wins more Electoral College votes than Trump, but still shy of the 270 Electoral College votes needed to win, and still Biden could lose the presidency.

Here's how.

See the next chapter, "Chapter 5 - Trump's 'Nuclear Option' to Win 2020."

CHAPTER 5

TRUMP'S "NUCLEAR OPTION" TO WIN 2020

Trump's "Nuclear Option" to steal the 2020 election is a strategy that neutralizes the Electoral College and forces the election into the House of Representatives. Let's examine how that could happen.

The 12th Amendment to the Constitution states that if no candidate receives at least 270 Electoral College votes, then the election leaves the realm of the general public and is decided by a vote in the House of Representatives.[191] There is precedent for this. In 1800 and in 1824, the presidential winner was decided by a vote in the House.[192]

Before we delve into the nuances of Trump's 12th Amendment "Nuclear Option" gambit, we need to do a deeper dive into understanding the Electoral College. This is because the Electoral College lays the groundwork for Trump's "Nuclear Option."

As long as the Electoral College exists as currently structured, Electoral College math normally determines who wins and who loses the presidential race. This is true regardless of who the majority of voters wanted for president. Five times in our history a presidential candidate has won the popular vote and lost the election in the Electoral College: Andrew Jackson in 1824 (to John Quincy Adams); Samuel Tilden in 1876 (to Rutherford B. Hayes); Grover Cleveland in 1888 (to Benjamin

---

[191] https://constitution.congress.gov/constitution/amendment-12/

[192] https://history.house.gov/Institution/Electoral-College/Electoral-College/ Go to "Contingent Elections."

Harrison); Al Gore in 2000 (to George W); and Hillary Clinton in 2016 (to Donald J. Trump).[193]

In order to understand Trump's "Nuclear Option," we must start thinking like a national campaign strategist and examine various Electoral College math scenarios.

The Electoral College has a combined total of 538 votes. This number comes from adding 100 (total number of US Senators) plus 435 (total number of representatives in the House) plus 3 (from the District of Columbia). To win the election, a candidate needs a simple majority. In this case 269 +1, or 270 Electoral College votes.

Let's explore a couple of possible 2020 scenarios.

Foundationally, if the states cast their combined 538 Electoral College (EC) votes as they did in 2016, then Trump wins with 304 to Clinton's 227 EC votes. There were 7 "faithless" electors in 2016. Five who did not vote for Clinton and 2 (in Texas) who did not vote for Trump. 304 + 227 + 7= 538.

In 2020 we will not have any faithless electors. On July 6, 2020, the US Supreme Court made their ruling, and the New York Times headline read, "Supreme Court says a state may require presidential electors to support its popular-vote winner."[194] Therefore, there will not be any "faithless electors" when the Electoral College votes in 2020.

---

193. United States House of Representatives History, Art and Archives, "Electoral College Fast Facts," *United States House of Representatives,* Retrieved on June 24, 2020, https://history.house.gov/Institution/Electoral-College/Electoral-College/
194. Robert Barnes, "Supreme Court says a state may require presidential electors to support its popular-vote winner," *Washington Post*, July 6, 2020, https://www.washingtonpost.com/politics/courts_law/supreme-court-electoral-college-faithless-electors/2020/07/06/cf88f706-bf8f-11ea-b178-bb7b05b94af1_story.html

Had there been no faithless electors in 2016, the results would have been Trump's 306 to Clinton's 232. 306 + 232 = 538 total Electoral College votes. We will use those results as our "adjusted 2016 results."

The 2020 presidential voting results are, of course, expected to be different from 2016. In 2020 we don't have Hillary Clinton as the Democratic candidate. We have former Vice President Joseph Biden. He is Catholic. He is from Pennsylvania, which has a large Catholic population. The Obama - Biden administration bailed out the auto industry in Michigan. Michigan also has a large Catholic population. In 2016 Hillary Clinton lost Pennsylvania, Michigan, and Wisconsin.

In our 2020 election Scenario "A," Pennsylvania (20 EC votes) and Michigan (16 EC votes) go to Biden. Using the adjusted 2016 EC scenario as our base, that adds 36 EC votes to Biden. 232 + 36 = 268 total EC votes. In that circumstance, we take away 36 EC votes from Trump. 306 - 36 = 270 EC votes. In Scenario "A" Trump wins.

In 2016 Trump won Wisconsin by a mere 22,748 votes or 1.6% of the total votes cast.

What happens, in the above scenario, if Trump were to lose Wisconsin's 10 EC votes to Biden? Trump drops another 10 EC votes from Scenario "A" or 270 -10 = 260. And Biden adds 10, or 268 +10 = 278. Biden wins.

Assuming for a moment that Pennsylvania and Michigan will go Biden, that makes Wisconsin the single most important battleground state in the 2020 election.

Trump knows he could lose Michigan, Pennsylvania, and Wisconsin and therefore the 2020 race. To prevent a 2020 loss, Trump has a "Nuclear Option" plan.

If the Trump camp sees that WI, PA and MI will probably go Biden, and Biden is the presumed 2020 winner, then Trump does what a football quarterback does when he sees the need to quickly change the game plan at the line of scrimmage, he calls an "audible." If a loss looks imminent, Trump calls an audible. Trump calls for the "Nuclear Option," where his enablers scuttle the Electoral College vote forcing the election to go to the House of Representatives under the 12th Amendment.

The less informed Democrats in the audience will say, "Yippee! Democrats control the House, so, Biden will win the House vote and become president." Sorry, wrong logic. In fact, the opposite would be true if that House vote were held in 2020. Those same loyal Democrats say, "What? How can that be?" We'll review the answer to that question in just a moment.

First, let's examine how we get to where the House votes on who becomes President. How could Trump "scuttle" the Electoral College vote when a Biden victory seemed to be at hand? There are a number of ways.

In the "Nuclear Option," Team Trump has two or more Republican-controlled states declare an election snafu so extreme as to prevent the state from submitting a pledged group of electors to the Electoral College vote. How can that happen? Simple. The Upper and Lower chambers of a state-controlled by Republicans point to "a series of irregularities and machine malfunctions so great it makes it impossible to render an accurate vote count." So, the Republican-controlled chambers pass legislation stating that no accurate vote tally could be reached. Therefore, no slate of electors pledged to Trump or Biden could be appointed. So, the Republican-controlled legislative body appoints a new slate of electors and instruct them to vote, "no one."

Why vote "no one?" Why vote at all? The attorney that oversees the Electoral College records and filings for the National Archives Records Administration (NARA) provided the following bit of critical information. The Constitution says that the candidate who wins the majority of Electoral College votes that are actually <u>cast</u> becomes president. So, part of this "Nuclear Option" strategy is to vote in order to preserve the 538 total number of votes "cast." If those states just didn't show up, then it would be possible that Biden could win a majority of the Electoral College votes that were actually cast. Preserving the number 538 as total Electoral College votes cast is an important fact when considering Trump's "Nuclear Option" gambit.

Here's a Trump "Nuclear Option" example. Trump gives an "audible" to two of the 29 states where Republicans control the upper and lower chambers, and therefore control any legislation that needs to be quickly passed.

For example, both Wisconsin and Michigan have state legislatures controlled by the Republicans. That would mean that Wisconsin, with its 10 EC votes, and Michigan, with its 16 EC votes, could both withhold any pledged electors from being certified to vote for Biden. In the only scenario above where Biden wins, if Biden loses WI and MI's combined 26 Electoral College votes, then Biden now drops down to 278 - 26 = 252 Electoral College votes. In that same scenario, Trump is also below the 270 Electoral College vote minimum threshold with only 260 EC votes. This forces the election to go to the House of Representatives under the 12th Amendment.

In Trump's "Nuclear Option," even though Biden wins the popular vote and exit polling showed that Biden "would have won" both WI and MI, the vote goes to the House of Representatives, where Trump plans to win. We examine how that could happen in a moment.

Russian hackers also play a role in Trump's "Nuclear Option." A headline in the July 25, 2019 New York Times read, "Russia Targeted Election Systems in All 50 States, Report Finds."[195] Combine that fact

---

[195] David E. Sanger and Catie Edmondson, "Russia Targeted Election Systems in All 50 States, Report Finds," *New York Times*, July 25, 2019,

with this one. In 2018, at a hacker conference, an 11-year old child hacked into a replica of the Florida Secretary of State's election website and altered the results in just 10 minutes.[196] Other children at this conference, which was overseen by a University of Pennsylvania professor, had similar results when hacking into other State's election websites. Can you imagine what the Russian cyber geniuses could do?

Trump's "Nuclear Option" disrupts the Electoral College process and forces the election into the House, where Trump plans on winning. There are 29 Republican-controlled state legislatures. A quick analysis of exit-polls election day November 3, 2020, will inform the Republicans how many and which Republican-controlled states need to declare election counting "malfunctions" beyond any ability to reach a clear legal consensus. We can easily imagine a scenario where a coded signal to the Russians can have any number of election systems "fail" to the point of making a legally defensible result impossible, preventing Biden from hitting the minimum required number of 270 Electoral College votes.

Russia has come to Trump's aid in the past after receiving a "signal" that their man needed help.

Do you remember when Trump said on July 27, 2016, "Russia, if you're listening...?" Trump asked Russia to locate Clinton's emails. <u>Within hours</u> of that request, Russia "made their first effort to break into the servers used by Mrs. Clinton's personal office," according to a New

---

https://www.nytimes.com/2019/07/25/us/politics/russian-hacking-elections.html)

196. Michael D. Regan, "An 11-year-old changed election results on a replica Florida state website in under 10 minutes," *PBS*, August 12, 2018, https://www.pbs.org/newshour/nation/an-11-year-old-changed-election-results-on-a-replica-florida-state-website-in-under-10-minutes

York Times article on July 13, 2018, referencing the Mueller investigation.[197]

On October 7, 2016, another Trump "signal" went out, and the Russians immediately responded. On that day, just 30 days before the 2016 election, a big red "Trump needs help" flare went up when the *Washington Post* released the Access Hollywood "pussy tape." On that tape, Trump is heard saying women would let him "grab-their-pussy" and "I-tried-to-fuck-her," referring to a married TV hostess. That tape came out at 4:03 pm. Just twenty-nine minutes later, at 4:32 pm, the first of 20,000 Russian-hacked Clinton emails are released.[198]

Comrade Trump received a lot of help during the 2016 election from Putin's Russia. Facebook informed Congress that 126 million Americans were exposed to content generated on its platform by the Russian government-linked troll farm known as the Internet Research Agency between June 2015 and August 2017. Twitter reported that during the same period, 36,746 accounts associated with Russia generated election-related content of approximately 1.4 million tweets, which together received 288 million impressions.[199]

It would be naïve to think that Putin will not put even more effort into re-electing his White House pal.

---

197. Michael S. Schmidt, "Trump Invited the Russians to Hack Clinton. Were They Listening?" *New York Times*, July 13, 2018,
https://www.nytimes.com/2018/07/13/us/politics/trump-russia-clinton-emails.html
198. Staff, "WikiLeaks Releases Podesta Emails Shortly After "Access Hollywood" Tape Released," *The Moscow Project*, October 7, 2016,
https://themoscowproject.org/collusion/wikileaks-releases-podesta-emails-shortly-access-hollywood-tapes-released/
199. Dylan Byers, "Facebook estimates 126 million people were served content from Russia-linked pages," *CNN Money*, October 31, 2017,
https://money.cnn.com/2017/10/30/media/russia-facebook-126-million-users/index.htm

So, fabricating a "national election emergency" caused by failed election systems would be a simple task for the Trump-Putin partnership.

Attorney Jerry Goldfeder is an elections expert. In a recent July 1, 2020, **New York Law Journal** article Goldfeder said, "Considering Trump's recent fabricated national emergency to get money for his Mexican border wall, it is not far-fetched to think that he will continue the drumbeat about supposed election fraud and declare another emergency to hold onto power."[200]

Trump's "Nuclear Option" forces the election into the House under the 12th Amendment, where Trump has a second chance to win 2020 and doesn't plan to lose.

Since the Democrats have a majority of seats in the House, why doesn't Biden surely win in a 12th Amendment House vote scenario? Because it's not a majority of total House seats that decides who wins. And a 12th Amendment House vote would not occur in 2020.

When a Presidential election goes to the House, the 12th Amendment allocates one vote for each state. This means that Wyoming and South Dakota have as much voting power as New York and California. Each

---

[200] Jerry H. Goldfeder, Attorney, 180 Maiden Lane, New York, NY 10038, D: 212.806.5857, M: 917.680.3132, https://www.law.com/newyorklawjournal/2020/07/01/still-no-plan-for-a-smooth-election/; https://www.usatoday.com/story/opinion/2019/03/14/donald-trump-peaceful-transition-or-coup-if-he-loses-2020-column/3141268002/; https://www.stroock.com/news-and-insights/a-donald-trump-coup-if-he-loses-in-2020-with-all-the-norms-hes-busted-dont-rule-it-out

state gets one vote. The candidate who achieves a simple majority, i.e., 26 votes out of 50 cast, becomes president.

Most states have a mix of Republican and Democratic representatives. The House representatives for a given state will typically cast their vote along party lines. Here's a fact most people don't know. In today's 116th Congress, the Republicans have a majority of House representatives in 26 states.[201] If a 12th Amendment vote for President were held in today's 116th Congress, Trump would be expected to receive 26 state votes out of 50, a majority, and, therefore, win. But the 116th Congress will not be involved in any vote for President.

If the 2020 election triggers the 12th Amendment and the vote for President goes to the House, it will be the 117th Congress elected on November 3, 2020, that will decide who wins the 2020 election. Let's review the chronological steps.

In this election cycle, the Electoral College meets at noon on December 14, 2020, to cast their ballots.

In Trump's "Nuclear Option" scenario, the Country will know on or before December 14, 2020, that no candidate will receive the mandatory minimum of 270 Electoral College votes, thereby sending the vote for President to the House.

The results of those Electoral College votes are placed in a sealed envelope. Then they are sent to the President of the Senate. Those

---

[201] Ballotpedia, "United States Congressional Delegations by State," *Ballotpedia*, Retrieved June 24, 2020, https://ballotpedia.org/United_States_congressional_delegations_from_Alabama Go to the web page indicated by this URL. Find the section in a column on the right side of opening page titled, "United States Congressional Delegations by State," and then click on the state desired to learn House seats by party for that state. Dr. Keller has an EXCEL spreadsheet of all 50 states.

Electoral College votes are not officially counted until January 6, 2021, at 1 pm by the President of the Senate in a joint session of Congress meeting in the House chambers.

So, immediately following that January 6, 2021, Electoral College vote count, if no candidate receives at least 270 EC votes, then the House stays in session per the 12th Amendment. Winners of the November 3, 2020, Congressional district elections, who officially started their term on January 3, 2021, are now responsible for deciding who becomes President. So, it will be the newly elected House representatives, the 117th Congress, that will vote on January 6, 2021, if the vote for President comes to them under the 12th Amendment.

So, who wins in that case? Trump or Biden?

The winner of a 12th Amendment House vote for President will depend upon how many States are controlled by which Party after the November 3, 2020 election. So, we have to wait until the results are known for all 435 Congressional districts.

If the 117th Congress has the same make-up as the 116th, then Trump will win by a vote of 26 to 24. 26 being the minimum threshold required to win.

Nobody expects the 117th Congress to look exactly like the 116th Congress because too many Congressional Districts are vulnerable to being flipped on November 3, 2020. Can we make an educated guess as to which Party will control a majority of States in the House after the November elections?

After careful analysis, this writer-researcher has determined that the majority control of the states in the House will be decided by 38 Congressional District elections.

How did we go from 435 Congressional District races down to just 38 that will decide who becomes President?

First, we identify those states where a Party in majority control is vulnerable to losing that control if just one seat within that state flips to the opposing Party. This process reduces 50 states down to 24. Twenty-four states "are in play," when it comes to winning the Presidency in a 12th Amendment vote in the House. In essence, this author using publically available data on Ballotpedia.com identified 24 states where one Party controls the majority of House seats within that given state, but that majority can be neutralized into a tie, or the majority control flips to the opposing Party if just 1 House seat within that state changes to the opposing Party.

Within those 24 states, there are 127 congressional districts.

Now, of course, certain states have only one representative in the House, like Wyoming or North Dakota. But there is zero likelihood that those heavily Republican congressional districts can be flipped on November 3, 2020. So, how do we narrow down those 127 congressional districts to those which are most vulnerable to being flipped to the opposing party? If only there was a rating system out there somewhere that could tell us which congressional seats are more vulnerable to be flipped than another. There is. This takes us to a second step.

Second, we use the Cook Partisan Voting Index to determine which Congressional Districts are most vulnerable to being flipped.[202] The Cook Political Report is an independent, non-partisan newsletter that analyzes elections. The Partisan Voting Index (PVI) rates all Congressional districts as to their vulnerability to being flipped. How do they do that? This is done by analyzing recent voting trends during recent presidential and congressional elections by the voting population within that specific district. PVI then assigns a rating. A rating of "even" means that there is a 50/50 chance the seat will remain with the

---

202. The Cook Political Report, "PVI Map and District List," *The Cook Political Report*, Retrieved July 10, 2020, https://cookpolitical.com/pvi-map-and-district-list

incumbent. From there the rating goes toward the "R" Republican side of average percentages, or over to the "D" Democratic side of average percentages. So, a district with R +13 is statistically more likely to vote R than a district with a D+5 rating. As Charles Cook, the founder of the Cook partisan voting Index, says, "these are only guidelines." There are a number of variables that can impact those guidelines, but PVI provides a reasonable guideline that will help us pinpoint those districts that are most vulnerable to flipping within those 24 states that we have identified.

By factoring in the PVI guideline, we are able to reduce those 127 congressional districts that could potentially flip down to 38.

By integrating the data from both searches, there are only 38 Congressional seats that fit our two criteria. Criteria one, they are in a state whose House majority can be flipped to a tie or to control by the opposing Party by the loss of one House seat. And two, that particular seat shows that it is vulnerable to being flipped given an examination of voting results in that district since 2012.

Those 38 Congressional seats reside within 13 states.

So, after careful analysis, there are 38 Congressional Districts within 13 states that, if flipped, can change the outcome of a 12th Amendment vote to the opposing Party.

How are those 38 congressional districts broken up by party and state?

There are 7 Republican House seats within five states that are most vulnerable to being flipped and causing a 12th Amendment vote to create a Democratic winner. Those five states are FL, MI, MN, PA, and WI.

And there are 31 Democratic House seats within 13 states that are most vulnerable to being flipped and causing a 12th Amendment vote to create a Republican winner. Those 13 states are AZ, CO, FL, IA, KS, ME, MI, MN, NH, NV, PA, UT, and WI.

The seven most vulnerable Republican Congressional District seats are FL-18-Brian Mast (R), FL-25-Mario Diaz-Balart (R), MI-06-Fred Upton (R), MN-01-Jim Hagedorn (R), MN-08-Pete Stauber (R), PA-01- Brian Fitzpatrick (R), and WI-01-Bryan Steil (R).

The thirty-one most vulnerable Democratic Congressional District seats (in alpha order by state) are AZ-01-Tom O'Halleran (D), AZ-02-Ann Kirkpatrick (D), AZ-09-Greg Stanton (D), CO-06-Jason Crow (D), FL-07-Stephanie Murphy (D), FL-09-Darren Soto (D), FL-13-Charlie Crist (D), FL-27-Donna Shalala (D), IA-01-Abby Finkenauer (D), IA-02-Dave Loebsack (D), IA-03-Cindy Axne (D), KS-03-Sharice Davids (D), ME-02-Jared Golden (D), ME-02-Jared Golden (D), MI-05-Daniel Kildee (D), MI-08-Elissa Slotkin (D), MI-09-Andy Levin (D), MI-11-Haley Stevens (D), MN-02-Angie Craig (D), MN-03-Dean Phillips (D), MN-07-Collin Peterson (D), NH-01-Chris Pappas (D), NH-02-Annie Kuster (D), NV-03-Susie Lee (D), NV-04-Steven Horsford (D), PA-06-Chrissy Houlahan (D), PA-07-Susan Wild (D), PA-08-Matt Cartwright (D), PA-17-Conor Lamb (D), UT-04-Ben McAdams (D), and WI-03-Ron Kind (D).

Of the Republicans PA-01- Brian Fitzpatrick (R) is the most vulnerable, followed by MI-06-Fred Upton (R), and MN-08-Pete Stauber (R).

Of the Democrats, MN-07-Collin Peterson (D) and UT-04-Ben McAdams (D) are by far the most vulnerable as the voters in their districts have a strong history of supporting Republicans.

The 2020 campaign goal for the Democrats is to retain all of their existing Democratic seats and win over at least two seats in 2 different states out of the seven defined Republican-held seats within those five identified states.

The campaign goal for the Republicans is to retain all of their existing Republican seats, which would give them a 26 majority control over who becomes president in a 12th Amendment vote on January 6, 2021. But for good measure, Republicans will seek to flip as many of those vulnerable 31 Democratically held congressional seats within 13 identified states.

If Trump is going to go so far as to scuttle the Electoral College vote and force the vote for president into the House of Representatives, then you can bet the Trump-Putin partnership will leave nothing to chance as to what the outcome will be in that House vote. The stakes are too high in the minds of Putin and Trump to "cross their fingers" and just hope for the best. That's not how that posse rides.

Based on 3,000 hours of writing and research, this author believes that Vladimir Putin will put his GRU finger on the election scales in favor of Trump. Remember, if an 11-year-old can hack the election systems, there is little doubt Russia can make enough changes in a Congressional seat's vote tally to help Putin's "comrade" in the White House.

The Republican-controlled Senate Intelligence Committee said that Russia invested $1.25 million a month to influence the 2016 election in Trump's favor.[203] That kind of money buys a lot of hacking. If you were Putin, would you not increase the 2016 budget by at least 10 times? So, at a minimum, you can estimate that Russia will invest $12.5 million a month, and probably a lot more, to swing the 2020 election over to Donald Trump.

Bills passed in the House in a non-partisan fashion to protect the 2020 election machinery from being hacked by Russia have been blocked

---

203. U.S. Senate Select Committee on Intelligence, "Report of The Select Committee On Intelligence, United States Senate, On Russian Active Measures Campaigns And Interference In The 2016 US Election, Volume 2: Russia's Use Of Social Media With Additional Views," *United States Senate,* October 8, 2019, https://www.intelligence.senate.gov/sites/default/files/documents/Report_Volume2.pdf

from coming to a vote in the Senate by Mitch McConnell.[204] This has earned McConnell the moniker, "#Moscow Mitch."

There are eight states that will have no paper record as to how a vote was cast in the presidential election. These are called the "paperless" ballot states. *The Hill* reported in August 2019 that New York University's Brennan Center for Justice found that "around 12 percent of Americans, or about 16 million people, will vote on paperless machines in 2020 and will have no paper record of how they voted. Many of these Americans will vote in the eight states that will use some form of paperless voting in 2020."[205] Those states are Texas, Louisiana, Tennessee, Mississippi, Kansas, Indiana, Kentucky, and New Jersey. *The Hill* article also stated, "Experts have long warned that these machines are a security risk because they do not allow election officials or the public to confirm electronic vote totals."

KS-03-Sharice Davids (D) is in a heavily Republican district in a paperless ballot state. This seat would be an easy one to steal by GRU hackers with no real method to audit the theft.

Those paperless ballot states control 102 Electoral College votes. How easy would it be for the GRU cyber experts to hack into those eight states and manipulate the election results? We already know that young eleven-year-old children can do it. We can thank #MoscowMitch for wondering if our vote was even counted.

---

204. Jordain Carney, "Senate GOP blocks three election security bills," *The Hill*, February 11, 2020, https://thehill.com/homenews/house/482569-senate-gop-blocks-three-election-security-bills

[205] Maggie Miller, "Report says eight states to use paperless voting in 2020 despite security concerns," *The Hill*, August 13, 2019, https://thehill.com/policy/cybersecurity/457168-report-says-eight-states-to-use-paperless-voting-in-2020-despite

Republican-controlled states, Russian hacking, and simple Electoral College math can force the election into the House of Representatives under the 12th Amendment.

If the presidential election goes to the House, who do you think will win? You'll have an idea after November 3, 2020, when you can analyze for yourself how many states are controlled by which party. Then you can do the math, knowing that each state has only one vote as to who becomes president of the United States. But, because people can die, or be coerced to resign for some reason, following the November 3, 2020 election. We won't know for sure who our next president will be until January 6, 2021, when Trump's "Nuclear Option" to win the 2020 election has fully played itself out.

◆ ◆ ◆

Defenses Against Trump's "Nuclear Option"

There are defenses against Trump's "Nuclear Option" that I would like to review with Mike Bloomberg and Tom Steyer.

Follows are a few of the foundational details of how to defeat Trump's "Nuclear Option" to steal the 2020 election.

A savvy campaign strategist would have the Democrats immediately embark on four tactics. Space does not allow reviewing those necessary actions in this article. I will review them in greater detail with Tom Steyer and Biden campaign strategists who contact this writer. Here is an outline of some of the required strategies to defeat a man unbound by ethics or legality.

One, pre-emptively sue Wisconsin, Michigan, New Mexico, Florida, Kansas, and a few other select states, seeking a mandatory injunction ordering the Secretaries of State to prove that the election preparations meet certain standards and criteria. You do this to assure the public in advance that they will experience a smooth and accurate vote process and count. One element of a mandatory injunction is to stop existing harm or imminent harm. It would be easy to find plaintiffs who have lost their voting privilege for various reasons, including five-hour-long voting lines when the Federal guideline maximum is 30 minutes.[206] Other plaintiffs can be enrolled who have been illegally purged from voting polls like the 4,000 plus voters, as shown in a NAACP Florida lawsuit.[207] The specific metrics are too long to list here but suffice it to say this was not done prior to the last two Georgia election debacles, where equipment was lost, undelivered and broken. Many waited in lines for more than five hours. Others couldn't wait in a line that long and went home without voting. That's called voter suppression. The June 9, 2020, NBC News headlines stated, "Georgia election 'catastrophe' in largely minority areas sparks investigation. Long lines, lack of voting machines, and shortages of primary ballots plagued voters."[208] Past PTSD caused by denial of the right to vote could be alleged. Current and potential physical and emotional stress caused by lack of confidence in being able to vote in a timely manner, etc. are just a few of the damage types, in this author's opinion, that could be listed in a mandatory injunction to protect a US citizens most sacred right, the right to vote freely and easily.

---

206. The Conversation, "It takes a long time to vote," *The Conversation*, July 7, 2020, https://theconversation.com/it-takes-a-long-time-to-vote-141267

207. Katie Sanders and PolitiFact, "Florida voters mistakenly purged in 2000," *TampaBay.com*, June 14, 2012, https://www.tampabay.com/news/politics/stateroundup/florida-voters-mistakenly-purged-in-2000/1235456/

208. Kevin Collier, Cyrus Farivar, Dareh Gregorian and Ben Popken, "Georgia election 'catastrophe' in largely minority areas sparks investigation. Long lines, lack of voting machines and shortages of primary ballots plagued voters." *NBC News*, June 9, 2020, https://www.nbcnews.com/politics/2020-election/georgia-secretary-state-launches-investigation-after-unacceptable-voting-problems-n1228541

Two, knowing that Trump may pull the "Nuclear Option" and conduct activity that may be unethical or illegal, what can the Democrats do pro-actively in advance? They can realize that currently, four states in the House of Representatives have a Republican majority of only one vote. They are FL, MI, MN, and WI. And one state, Pennsylvania, has a 9-9 tie.

The Democrats need a commitment from only 1 House Republicans in each of those five states listed above who say they will not participate in a Trump "Nuclear Option" that reeks of underhandedness, and possible illegal activity. With those five committed Republicans who publicly state they will not vote for Trump if the election goes to the House. That should provide a solid block preventing Republicans from having a 26 state voting majority in a 12th Amendment House vote. If that happens then, American democracy and the Democrats can relax a bit. If the announcements are public, it might cause certain Republican-controlled state legislatures to reconsider any smelly shenanigans. Again, those five key states are FL, MI, MN, PA, and WI. Readers in those states should start lobbying their Republican Congressional Representatives right now. Make them commit one way or the other. Will they participate in a suspicious scuttling of the Electoral College vote? Yes or No? If "no," then will they also commit to voting "present" in any 12th Amendment House vote if that vote is a result of suspicious behavior? Yes or No? Then you go public with that information to your local paper. This gives you an excuse to educate your community on Trump's possible "Nuclear Option."

Three, Trump has said the Republicans will spend $20 million dollars to send in 50,000 off-duty police and other volunteers to patrol precincts in 15 battleground states. That's $4,000 per precinct worker. That's a lot of money. And for that big bucks payday, the "volunteer" will have to produce results. The Republicans are playing a no-holds-barred strategy to win. Their primary role will be to wear their security outfits, and their guns and their job will be to intimidate, and raise so many questions on as many voters as possible so that the lines get so long people give up and go home. Many people with an outstanding parking ticket, unpaid child support, a joint of medicinal grass in their pocket will not want to encounter an off-duty police officer checking their IDs. They may think those "off-duty" police cars are there for them and will turn right around and go home. That's voter suppression. It's wrong, but it works. You have to remember George Bush won the 2000 election by 537 votes. That minuscule number of votes gave Bush Florida and the White House. It's up to the Dems to bring in 100,0000 volunteers of their own to make sure these 50,000 off-duty cops and Republican volunteers are not acting inappropriately.

Four, the Democrats need to embarrass #MoscowMitch McConnell to the point where he will stop blocking legislation designed to protect American Democracy from being undermined by Russian hacking.

Five, in a strange plot twist don't be surprised if the Russian hackers deliberately leave clues that specific electoral systems have been hacked. This provides easy "cover" for a Republican-controlled legislative body to say, "See, we have absolute evidence of election system hacking proving that we cannot arrive at an accurate vote count. Therefore, we must send a neutral slate of electors to the Electoral College. To further obfuscate the matter, the Russians will leave evidence that a Democrat received "fake" votes. This would give "cover" to Trump declaring a national emergency and disavow the November 3, 2020 elections altogether. In a bizarre Faustian psychological mind war game, Trump would say, "Obviously, China was colluding to help Biden." Democrats must expose this ruse early and often between now and November 3, 2020.

Six, there are various sections within Title 3[209] of the United States Code that come into play if there are any controversies regarding the Electoral College vote. The Democrats need to recruit a team of attorneys right now who are experts in this area of the law. In researching this section of the book, this author interviewed a number of election and Electoral College legal experts, including Jack Young, who was a lead attorney in the Gore v Bush 2000 legal battles contesting Florida's method of assigning Electoral College Electors in Florida.

Now you know Trump's "Nuclear Option" to steal the 2020 election and steps you can take to prevent it.

---

209. Cornell Law, "3 U.S. Code Chapter 1—Presidential Elections And Vacancies," *Cornell Law*, Retrieved July 9, 2020,
https://www.law.cornell.edu/uscode/text/3/chapter-1

CHAPTER 6

POLITICAL CARTOONS

Obama Warning: Democrats in Circular Firing Squad

Chicken Coward Trump

Coward Trump

U.S. Presidential Candidates fearlessly release their tax returns
to prove they have nothing to hide.
Except Coward(I'm-hiding-something)Trump.

Trump Tax Heist – Pumping Our Tax $ to $B Corps

Women-You Have No Choice- Surrender Your Body

Two-Faced Liar Trump on Wall

Donald Trump Admits U.S. Taxpayers Will Pay For The Wall. (2017)
https://bit.ly/2VDjVJo

Taxpayers will pay for wall, White House aide acknowledges. (2019)
https://cnn.it/39bp1R5

Two-Faced Liar Trump

Tax Heist Trump - Corporate Sponsored Get-away Car

Two-Faced Liar Trump on Presidential Golfing

Trump Tax Heist: Robbing Us Giving $ To $B Corps

Trump's Tax ~~Cut~~ Theft

Two-Faced Trump

Trump's tax law takes from the poor gives to rich.

Trump Heist: Angry Truckers See $B Corps Take Their $

Jail Traitor Trump – "Stole" U.S. Tax Payer Money and is a Russian "Agent" Spewing Putin Propaganda--"Lock'em up!"

Traitor Trump!

Putin Puppet Trump

Putin Puppet Trump

Voter Suppression

CHAPTER 7

CONCLUSION

In conclusion, this is just the beginning. We have much to do to correct the damage caused to our United States by Donald Trump both here and abroad. The Democrats can win by including the *12-Steps To Victory* outlined in this book as part of a larger strategy within the Democratic 2020 campaign.

As to the Electoral College, the Democrats "only" need to flip Wisconsin, Pennsylvania, and Michigan from the 2016 loss column to the 2020 victory column while retaining all the states won in 2016 to win with a total of 278 Electoral College votes. Well above the minimum needed of 270.

Wisconsin, Michigan, and Pennsylvania all narrowly went into the Trump win column with very small margins. WI-1.6% with a 22,748 margin. PA- 1.5% with a 44,292 margin. MI-1.6% with a 22,748 margin. That total margin of difference for the three states was 77, 863, or just ½ of 1% out of a total of 13,940,912 votes cast in those three states.

Trump and Russia know this, so you can expect the equivalent of a nuclear attack in those three states against Biden. The lies, deep fake videos, deep fake audios, and a kamikaze-like attack utilizing all the major social media platforms will be brought in as weapons. Why? Because for the Putin-Trump-SPIDER Party group, this is World War Three.

I say "kamikaze" because no legal or ethical boundary will restrain the Russian and Republican forces. This will be Trump in a death-throe.

To echo AG Barr when asked how the future will look back on his attempt to unilaterally overturn the conviction of Michael Flynn, he said, "History is written by the winners." Recall in the companion book to this one, and earlier in this book, where I refer to a lawsuit that showed over 4,000 African-Americans were denied their legal right to vote in Florida in the 2000 election. This voter suppression was illegal and unethical, but it worked, and that's all that mattered. That racist attack on black voters allowed Bush to beat Gore by 537 votes and gave Bush the presidency. So, illegal and unethical tactics prevailed, and the history books show that the winner was Bush. You will not find an asterisk next to President Bush's name that says, "Oh, by the way, an NAACP lawsuit proved beyond any reasonable doubt that Al Gore actually won." Trump and Russia know that illegal and unethical tactics can put you in the winner circle, and you can deal with the investigations and lawsuits later from the vantage point of the White House and controlling the Department of Justice.

Trump and Russia have but one goal, to win at all costs.

And Russia is being enabled by Moscow Mitch, who refuses to allow the Senate to vote on bipartisan legislation passed by the House to protect the 2020 election from a Pearl-Harbor-like attack by Russia on our democracy.

That's why I wrote this book, to save our democracy from Russia and "Putin's Puppet."

I end where I began in book one of this two-book series. My evidence is that The Republicans are approaching the 2020 election at a much more sophisticated and multi-pronged level than the Democrats—three-dimensional chess versus checkers to use a game metaphor. The Democrats did not anticipate the Russian's powerful use of social media to help Trump win in 2016. And the Democrats should be prepared to be surprised, again, by what Russia rolls out in 2020.

I further conclude that the Republicans under Trump with Russian support are playing at an Ultimate Fighting Championship Mixed Martial Arts (UFC MMA) no-holds-barred must-win-at-any-cost World War Three level. While the Democrats seem to be using the 2016 playbook with some new faces and a little more outrage sprinkled into the mix. The Democrats' biggest allies are the Republican groups against Trump, like the Lincoln Project, Republicans for the rule of law, the 43 alumni, and Vets against Trump.

My comments are certainly not the last word on these topics. Please let me know your thoughts via email.

Please read the "Afterward" about communicating with the author.

In the spirit of the highest ideals that created the United States of America, may we work together to continue to shape a more perfect Union.

David King Keller, PhD
DrDavidKingKeller@gmail.com

APPENDIX 1
DEMOCRATIC VICTORY NUMBERS BY STATE

Trump - 265; Biden - 273

AZ, Fl, GA, and NC go Trump as in 2016.

NM (5 EC) goes Trump, which Dems won in 2016.

Biden wins MI (16 EC), PA (20 EC), and WI (10 EC).

(Go to the next page for a detailed table.)

Appendix 1 - Democratic 2020 Victory Numbers: State by State						
STATE		EC	EC	2020	2020	Pop Vote	Pop Vote
	EC	T	B	Trump (R)	Biden (D)	All Others	Total Vote
AL	9	9		1,515,993	838,979	75,570	2,430,542
AK	3	3		187,895	133,922	38,767	360,584
AZ	11	11		1,440,261	1,335,342	159,597	2,935,200
AR	6	6		787,603	437,568	65,310	1,290,481
CA	55		55	5,156,386	10,066,861	943,998	16,167,245
CO	9		9	1,382,857	1,539,701	238,893	3,161,450
CT	7		7	774,197	1,032,208	74,133	1,880,538
DE	3		3	212,896	270,943	23,084	506,924
DC	3		3	14,631	325,255	15,715	355,601
FL	29	29		5,310,569	5,180,721	297,178	10,788,468
GA	16	16		2,402,470	2,159,657	147,665	4,709,792
HI	4		4	148,174	306,925	33,199	488,298
ID	4	4		470,413	218,230	91,435	780,078
IL	20		20	2,467,917	3,554,338	299,680	6,321,936
IN	11	11		1,790,879	1,188,095	144,546	3,123,520
IA	6	6		921,130	751,719	111,379	1,784,229
KS	6	6		771,671	491,056	86,379	1,349,105
KY	8	8		1,383,417	723,182	92,324	2,198,923
LA	8	8		1,355,434	897,177	70,240	2,322,851
ME	4	1	3	385,932	411,395	54,599	851,926
MD	10		10	1,084,644	1,929,617	160,349	3,174,611
MA	11		11	1,254,527	2,294,475	238,957	3,787,959
MI	16		16	2,507,497	2,586,476	250,902	5,344,876
MN	10		10	1,521,394	1,572,873	254,146	3,348,413
MS	6	6		805,821	557,901	23,512	1,387,234
MO	10	10		1,833,688	1,231,728	143,026	3,208,442
MT	3	3		321,126	204,365	40,198	565,689
NE	5	5		570,355	327,168	63,772	961,295
NV	6		6	588,867	620,149	74,067	1,283,083
NH	4		4	397,659	400,805	49,980	848,443
NJ	14		14	1,842,223	2,470,520	123,835	4,436,578
NM	5	5		383,600	365,972	93,418	842,991
NY	29		29	3,242,463	5,239,536	345,791	8,827,790
NC	15	15		2,717,026	2,517,713	189,617	5,424,356
ND	3	3		249,313	107,822	33,808	390,943
OH	18	18		3,267,156	2,753,289	261,318	6,281,762
OK	7	7		1,091,506	483,431	83,481	1,658,419
OR	7		7	899,763	1,152,422	216,827	2,269,012
PA	20		20	3,119,270	3,219,085	268,304	6,606,659
RI	4		4	207,624	290,404	31,076	529,104
SC	9	9		1,328,697	983,679	92,265	2,404,641
SD	3	3		261,879	135,077	24,914	421,870
TN	11	11		1,751,364	1,001,299	114,407	2,867,070
TX	38	38		5,387,804	4,459,548	406,311	10,253,663
UT	6	6		592,516	357,277	305,523	1,255,316
VT	3		3	109,674	205,359	41,125	356,158
VA	13		13	2,034,859	2,278,694	233,715	4,547,268
WA	12		12	1,405,009	2,004,126	352,554	3,761,689
WV	5	5		562,777	217,113	36,258	816,148
WI	10		10	1,586,077	1,601,916	188,330	3,376,323
WY	3	3		200,582	64,369	25,457	290,408
Total	538	265	273	72,007,485	75,497,484	7,830,934	155,335,903
				46.4%	48.6%	5.04%	100.00%

David King Keller, PhD

APPENDIX 2
TRUMP 2020 VICTORY NUMBERS BY STATE

Trump - 275; Biden – 263

Same results as Appendix 1 except:

WI (10 EC) goes Trump as in 2016

(Go to the next page for a detailed table.)

Appendix 2 - Trump's 2020 Victory Numbers: State by State						
STATE	EC	EC T	EC B	2020 Trump (R)	2020 Biden (D)	Pop Vote All Others	Pop Vote Total Vote
AL	9	9		1,515,993	838,979	75,570	2,430,542
AK	3	3		187,895	133,922	38,767	360,584
AZ	11	11		1,440,261	1,335,342	159,597	2,935,200
AR	6	6		787,603	437,568	65,310	1,290,481
CA	55		55	5,156,386	10,066,861	943,998	16,167,245
CO	9		9	1,382,857	1,539,701	238,893	3,161,450
CT	7		7	774,197	1,032,208	74,133	1,880,538
DE	3		3	212,896	270,943	23,084	506,924
DC	3		3	14,631	325,255	15,715	355,601
FL	29	29		5,310,569	5,180,721	297,178	10,788,468
GA	16	16		2,402,470	2,159,657	147,665	4,709,792
HI	4		4	148,174	306,925	33,199	488,298
ID	4	4		470,413	218,230	91,435	780,078
IL	20		20	2,467,917	3,554,338	299,680	6,321,936
IN	11	11		1,790,879	1,188,095	144,546	3,123,520
IA	6	6		921,130	751,719	111,379	1,784,229
KS	6	6		771,671	491,056	86,379	1,349,105
KY	8	8		1,383,417	723,182	92,324	2,198,923
LA	8	8		1,355,434	897,177	70,240	2,322,851
ME	4	1	3	385,932	411,395	54,599	851,926
MD	10		10	1,084,644	1,929,617	160,349	3,174,611
MA	11		11	1,254,527	2,294,475	238,957	3,787,959
MI	16		16	2,507,497	2,586,476	250,902	5,344,876
MN	10		10	1,521,394	1,572,873	254,146	3,348,413
MS	6	6		805,821	557,901	23,512	1,387,234
MO	10	10		1,833,688	1,231,728	143,026	3,208,442
MT	3	3		321,126	204,365	40,198	565,689
NE	5	5		570,355	327,168	63,772	961,295
NV	6		6	588,867	620,149	74,067	1,283,083
NH	4		4	397,659	400,805	49,980	848,443
NJ	14		14	1,842,223	2,470,520	123,835	4,436,578
NM	5		5	383,600	365,972	93,418	842,991
NY	29		29	3,242,463	5,239,536	345,791	8,827,790
NC	15	15		2,717,026	2,517,713	189,617	5,424,356
ND	3	3		249,313	107,822	33,808	390,943
OH	18	18		3,267,156	2,753,289	261,318	6,281,762
OK	7	7		1,091,506	483,431	83,481	1,658,419
OR	7		7	899,763	1,152,422	216,827	2,269,012
PA	20		20	3,119,270	3,219,085	268,304	6,606,659
RI	4		4	207,624	290,404	31,076	529,104
SC	9	9		1,328,697	983,679	92,265	2,404,641
SD	3	3		261,879	135,077	24,914	421,870
TN	11	11		1,751,364	1,001,299	114,407	2,867,070
TX	38	38		5,387,804	4,459,548	406,311	10,253,663
UT	6	6		592,516	357,277	305,523	1,255,316
VT	3		3	109,674	205,359	41,125	356,158
VA	13		13	2,034,859	2,278,694	233,715	4,547,268
WA	12		12	1,405,009	2,004,126	352,554	3,761,689
WV	5	5		562,777	217,113	36,258	816,148
WI	10	10		1,616,077	1,589,916	188,330	3,394,323
WY	3	3		200,582	64,369	25,457	290,408
Total	538	270	268	72,037,485	75,485,484	7,830,934	155,353,903
				46.4%	48.6%	5.04%	100.00%

APPENDIX 3
17 BATTLEGROUND STATES

Percentage used is the 2016 difference in the 2 candidate's votes divided by Trump's votes in that State. Based on the 2016 Presidential election results.

Example: Michigan:
Total votes cast in 2016:   4,799,284
Trump received: 2,279,543 votes
Clinton received: 2,268,839 votes
Difference: Trump votes minus Clinton: 10,704 votes
Percentage: Difference/ Trump's votes = 0.5%.

Using Difference/ Total votes cast gives you the same battleground states.

First Tier: 0% - 5% Percentage separating winner's votes from loser's votes.
MI (16EC) 0.5% - Trump won by
PA (20EC) 1.5% - Trump won by
WI (10EC) 1.6% - Trump won by
FL (29EC) 2.4% - Trump won by
NH (4EC) 0.8% - Clinton won by
MN (10EC) 3.4% - Clinton won by
NV (6EC) 5.3% - Clinton won by

Second Tier: 5% - 10% Percentage separating winner's votes from loser's votes.
ME (4EC) 6.6% - Clinton won by
AZ (11EC) 7.3% - Trump won by
NC (15EC) 7.3% - Trump won by

Third Tier: 10% - 20% Percentage separating winner's votes from loser's votes.
GA (16EC)) 10.1% - Trump won by
OH (18EC) 15.7% - Trump won by
TX (38EC) 17.2% - Trump won by
IA (6EC) 18.4% - Trump won by
CO (9EC) 11.3% - Clinton won by
VA (13EC) 12.0% - Clinton won by
NM (5EC) 20.5% - Clinton won by

Folding in the 2018 mid-term election results puts key battleground states as MI, PA, WI, FL, AZ, NC, and GA. Current trends are placing TX and OH in the battleground mix. The author adds in NM based on probable Russian hacking.

APPENDIX 4
PREDICTIONS

Can Reliably Blue New Mexico Go Red?

In a close race, Republicans have historically turned to third parties to win. Republicans can duplicate their 2016 victory by getting the third parties in nine battleground states to pull just enough votes away from their opponent to assure victory. So, of course, millions upon millions went into supporting third parties in Michigan, Pennsylvania, Wisconsin, Florida, Arizona, North Carolina, Minnesota, Georgia, and New Mexico. New Mexico? Yes, this author believes there is a "secret" Trump strategy taking place in New Mexico.

Why is New Mexico a "secret" strategy? Because the Republican Party wants the Dems sleeping at the wheel when it comes to New Mexico. It's also secret because it may involve Russian hacking.

Even though New Mexico had been considered a safe and reliable Democratic blue state since 2004, the following three facts change that landscape.

Fact one, it is common knowledge reported in the *New York Times* and elsewhere that Russia has penetrated election computers in all 50 states.[210]

This fact about Russia isn't too surprising since we know an 11-year-old hacked into a replica of a popular election computer system used in Florida and elsewhere in ten minutes changing names and tallies![211]

---

210. David E. Sanger & Catie Edmondson, "Russia Targets Election Systems in All 50 States, Report Finds," *New York Times,* July 25, 2019, https://www.nytimes.com/2019/07/25/us/politics/russian-hacking-elections.html
211. Brendan O'Brien & Andrew Heavens, "Boy, 11, hacks into replica U.S. vote website in minutes at convention," *Reuters*, August 14, 2018,

Imagine what a superpower could do and would do if they absolutely needed to make sure "their man" won the US national election again.

Fact two, as CBS News and other media outlets have reported, we know that Senate Republican leader "Moscow Mitch" McConnell has unpatriotically blocked all legislation to protect our electoral process from further and continued penetration by Russia.[212]

Fact three, Trump held rallies in New Mexico, claiming that he can make New Mexico a red Republican-voting state.[213]

Where does Trump get the confidence that he can convert New Mexico from blue to red?

This author predicts that Trump will, indeed, win New Mexico, and that prediction is based on history. US and Russian both have a history of internal political meddling in other countries. Based on Fact #1, Russian hacking, this author believes New Mexico will go red. Russia has already penetrated the New Mexico election computers according to the above New York Times article.

We also know that Trump and Putin have had secret meetings and secret phone calls with no American national security people on the call or in the meeting. As of January 2019, a New York Times article stated,

---

https://www.reuters.com/article/us-usa-election-cyber/boy-11-hacks-into-replica-u-s-vote-website-in-minutes-at-convention-idUSKBN1KZ0O2

212. Kathryn Watson, "Mitch McConnell blocks election security legislation," *CBS News,* July 26, 2019, https://www.cbsnews.com/news/mitch-mcconnell-blocks-election-security-bill/

213. Associated Press Staff, "Trump tells supporters he can turn New Mexico red, warns of Green New Deal," *Market Watch*, September 16, 2019, https://www.marketwatch.com/story/trump-tells-supporters-he-can-turn-new-mexico-red-warns-of-green-new-deal-2019-09-16

"Trump and Putin Have Met Five Times. What Was Said Is a Mystery."[214]

[Warning, if you read the above referenced NYT article, you may get depressed at the historically unprecedented level of secrecy and the volume of secret discussions between Trump and Putin.]

Remember, Trump admitted on May 30, 2019, at 7:57 am, in a Tweet that he owed Putin for "helping me get elected."

The <u>Republican-led</u> Senate Intelligence Committee says Russia interfered in the 2016 election on Trump's behalf and that Russia is still continuing to pursue election interference tactics.

So, it's no secret to anyone who reads a newspaper that Russia will do as much or more than they did in 2016 to help re-elect their preferred candidate, Donald Trump, again. Is there anyone who is aware of all of Russia's activities to help Trump, including their three thousand five hundred Facebook ads in the 2016 campaign, who believes that in all those hours of secret discussions between Putin and Trump that not one word is spoken of their mutual desire to have Trump win in 2020?

Did Putin and Trump discuss what is already public knowledge, that Russia has hacked the New Mexico election computer systems? Might they both have agreed that wouldn't it be nice if Trump won New Mexico's 5 Electoral College votes?

Can we all agree that it is a safe bet that a large portion of Trump's prefrontal cortex activity is dedicated to his being inaugurated in January 2021 to his second term? Yes, all first-term Presidents obsess about winning a second term (except Joe Biden, who has stated if he

---

214. Peter Baker, "Trump and Putin Have Met Five Times. What Was Said Is a Mystery," *New York Times*, January 15, 2019, https://www.nytimes.com/2019/01/15/us/politics/trump-putin-meetings.html

becomes President, he will not be campaigning for a second term. But that is a rare exception.)

Ask yourself what is it worth to Putin for his man Trump to be President another four years? Is it worth trillions? What land grabs by Russia might be easier if Putin has a compliant US President who doesn't have to worry about getting re-elected? What will Russia do if they have an ally in the White House who believes that he no longer has a need for public approval? Does Eastern Ukraine become another Crimea? Are their Russian populations in other small countries who "vote" to join Russia?

Moscow is working hard to elect Trump again. That is easy to accept, right? It also helps to make sense out of Fact #2, above, Moscow Mitch stopping election protection bills from coming to the floor for a vote. Why is Moscow Mitch so aggressively blocking all efforts to prevent Russia from manipulating our election computers? Is it because he knows that a Republican victory may depend on those election computer compromises being acted upon by Russia?

Below we address one battleground state that can turn the election around with just one Electoral College vote. Because of that, New Mexico's five EC votes become a nice safety cushion in Trump's Electoral College math strategy.

Yes, there are a number of battleground states that impact Electoral College math and can decide who wins and who loses.

But there is one battleground state that most people don't think about. Maine.

Maine Could Decide Who Wins The 2020 Election.

Maine has four Electoral College votes. One for each of its two congressional districts. And two for its two US Senators. Maine is one of two states that does not follow the winner-take-all approach to awarding the Electoral College votes. Maine awards one Electoral College vote to the winner of each of its two congressional districts. And then the candidate who won the most votes across the entire state receives the two remaining Electoral College votes. In 2016, Trump won Maine's second congressional district, ME-02, with the other three Electoral College votes going to Clinton. In the scenario where we use 2016 with no faithless electors as our base (Trump - 306, Clinton - 232), and the difference is that in 2020 Trump loses Pennsylvania and Michigan's 36 Electoral College votes, Trump still wins with 270 Electoral College votes. In that scenario, Trump again won ME-02. But wait, in 2018 ME-02 flipped from Republican to Democrat with the Democrat winning by just under 4,000 votes. So, in 2020, in the above scenario where Trump won with 270 votes, the bare minimum, we were counting ME-02 with its one Electoral College vote staying in the Trump column. But in 2020, if that district, ME-02, votes Biden, then, here's what happens. Trump drops to 269 votes, and Biden bumps up to 269 Electoral College votes. A tie. In that case, neither candidate wins, and the 12th amendment kicks in. When that happens, the decision as to who becomes president gets moved to the House of Representatives. In this election cycle that House vote would occur on January 6, 2021.

So, one congressional district in the state of Maine could decide the fate of the 2020 election.

Michael Pence Becomes The 46th US President

Just follow these facts:

Fact 1: As of May 30, 2019, as reported in USA Today, over 1,000 former prosecuting attorneys said that, but for a Department of Justice office of legal counsel (OLC) guideline memo, Trump would've been indicted for crimes against the United States.[215] [216] [217]

Fact 2: Trump's alleged 25 Federal crimes have a total of over 100 years in possible jail time.

Knowing that he can be tried for federal crimes once he is no longer President, then it's reasonable for Donald Trump to take protective and prophylactic action that would prevent him from ever being tried in a federal criminal court, and possibly going to jail.

It would be reasonable, then, learning from the Nixon experience that Trump would want to work a deal with Vice President Mike Pence. That deal would say, in essence, "I will resign before my term is up, making you the 46th President of the United States of America, subject to you granting me an unconditional pardon." I will do this with the understanding that you will do for me what Gerald Ford did for Richard Nixon. When Richard Nixon resigned under multiple charges of criminal misconduct (where his impeachment was a virtual certainty), his Vice President, Gerald Ford, became President of the United States. And one of the first official acts taken by Gerald Ford was to grant an unconditional pardon for Richard Nixon for any, and all, federal crimes. The excuse given by Ford was that this would be in the best interest of

215. Eric Tucker, "Ex-prosecutors: Trump would've been charged if not President," *ABC News,* May 6, 2019, https://abcnews.go.com/Politics/wireStory/prosecutors-trump-wouldve-charged-president-62857640

216. Dartunorro Clark, "Hundreds of former prosecutors say Trump would have been indicted if he were not President," *NBC News,* May 6, 2019, .https://www.nbcnews.com/politics/politics-news/hundreds-former-prosecutors-say-trump-would-have-been-indicted-if-n1002436

217. Nicholas Wu, "Robert De Niro, 1,000+ prosecutors make the case for indicting President Trump in new video," *USA TODAY*, May 30, 2019, https://www.usatoday.com/story/news/politics/onpolitics/2019/05/30/robert-de-niro-prosecutors-say-trump-committed-obstruction-justice/1284763001/

the United States because it would allow the Country to heal from the past and focus on moving forward.

So, Trump will take a lesson right out of Watergate and secure a commitment from Michael Pence. In fact, he will already have had the pardon written up by his attorney and prepared for Mike Pence's signature. When Donald Trump resigns, and Michael Pence becomes President, President, Michael Pence will grant a full and unconditional pardon of citizen Donald J. Trump.

Now, whenever this happens, Trump will come up with a good excuse that requires a necessity that he resign. The excuse may be for his health, possibly, and for the good of the Country, since he always puts America first, he will offer to step aside as he addresses his medical concerns. I will let your imagination run. You can create a dozen scenarios where Trump is the poor victim of something garnering sympathy, and because of that, something he must (under Doctor's orders?) immediately step aside to address this (life-threatening (fill in the blank.)

Even though Trump believes President Trump can pardon citizen Trump, he won't take the chance that a Supreme Court challenge might go against him.

This resignation will occur before January 20, 2021, if he loses the 2020 election. This resignation will occur before January 20, 2025, if he wins the 2020 election, and someone other than Mike Pence wins the 2024 election. In this last scenario, if Mike Pence wins in a 2024 election, then Trump might wait till after a Pence is inaugurated, assuming certain understandings are in place. This date of resignation will change if Trump wins in 2020. But a Trump 2020 victory would be followed by another more successful Nixon-like impeachment endeavor.

You might say, well, Michael Pence's moral, ethical, and evangelical background would not allow him to get into petty politics like this, right? Pence was allegedly involved in far more scurrilous activities than that predicted here. All I have to do is point you to the alleged act of withholding $400 million from a new democracy that was under attack by an enemy of Western society and Western democracies. Pence was allegedly in on the decision to sacrifice life and limb in Ukraine to advance the political agenda of Trump-Pence.

Pence could not pass up the chance to become the 46th President, and like Gerald Ford, for all years going forward to be known as "President Pence." Pence, for the rest of his life, would have secret service protection, and all the other goodies that flow out of that honorary position. Who would not want to add "President of the United States" on their resume?

Everyone to whom I have mentioned this prediction, at first scoffed at the idea, and then after hearing my logic, have all said, "Yep, that does make sense."

November 4, 2020, Constitutional Crisis

There is a strong likelihood that if Trump loses the 2020 election, he will challenge that decision, based on "fraud" or "voting equipment malfunction." You will remember Trump repeatedly claimed fraudulent voters gave Hillary Clinton her nearly 3 million popular vote win over him. He said he was going to set up a commission to investigate that voter fraud. No 2016 voter fraud was ever found. He claimed "fraud" when he won. You can imagine what he'll claim if he loses.

I have a longer memo on this prediction but will leave that possible scenario to your imagination for now.

Last 100 Days of Campaign Will Be A Nightmare

The last 100 days of the 2020 campaign will be a nightmare web of lies, deep fake videos, and misdirection headlines by the Trump campaign. Already by the first week in April 2020, Trump has personally, through his Twitter account, distributed doctored videotapes of Vice President Joe Biden that use splices and other artifacts to produce a presentation of unethical bold-faced lies.

The Independent publication made this statement on March 9, 2020, "Donald Trump has been criticized for retweeting a doctored video of Joe Biden supposedly endorsing his re-election – spurring Twitter to use its "manipulated media" warning tag for a video for the first time."[218]

Helen, an award-winning teacher in Tampa, Florida, says, "These are the actions of a man with no moral or ethical standards." When confronted, Trump makes no pretense that it was any kind of error by a junior staffer. Helen believes, he's saying, in essence, "Yea, I lied. So what? I can do whatever I want, and as long as it does damage to my opponent, then it's justified." She went on to say, "What are the morals and ethics of an individual who endorses and promotes a known blatant lie to his 75 million Twitter followers?" Where's the apology and embarrassment by his evangelical Vice President who is clearly aware of this unethical deception? WWJD Mr. Pence?"

Just Google "false Facebook posting by Trump."

Do you remember this 2019 headline, "Facebook confirms Donald Trump can lie in ads, but he can't curse."? Facebook owner Mark

---

218. Andrew Naughties, "Trump spreads fake video of Joe Biden," *The Independent,* March 9, 2020, https://www.independent.co.uk/news/world/americas/us-politics/trump-biden-video-bernie-sanders-dan-scavino-a9385917.html

Zuckerberg and friend of Trump, when called before a Congressional hearing on deceptive ads, doubled down on his refusal to remove any knowingly deceptive ads by Trump.[219]

Emboldened, Trump placed an ad on Facebook that was so egregious that even Facebook took it down because it involved a misleading ad purporting to be part of the US Government 2020 census. The headline said, "Facebook removes 'deceptive' Trump census ads."[220]

The adverts were "deceptive" and "unacceptable", said Vanita Gupta, President and CEO of The Leadership Conference on Civil and Human Rights, which helped Facebook craft its policy on census interference. Gupta said,

> If Trump says a fake census is 'official,' people are going to think its official," she said in a series of tweets. "Trump's deceptive ads will confuse people about how and when to participate in the 2020 Census, threatening their right to get counted and bring resources and political power to their communities.

Here's is the ad that was so deceptive even Facebook took it down:

---

219. Will Fischer, "Facebook confirms Donald Trump can lie in ads, but he can't curse, " *Business Insider*, Oct 8, 2019, https://www.businessinsider.com/trump-can-lie-in-facebook-ads-but-no-profanity-cursing-2019-10

220. Tom Gerken, "Facebook removes 'deceptive' Trump census ads," *BBC*, March 5, 2020, https://www.bbc.com/news/world-us-canada-51730185

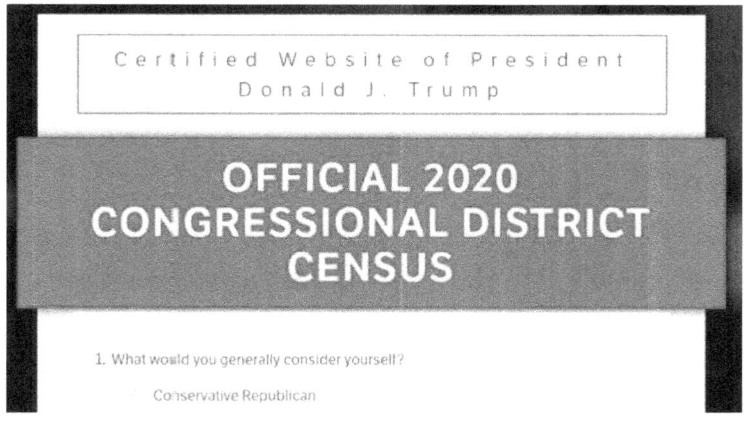

About social issues, elections or politics

Donald J. Trump
Sponsored · Paid for by TRUMP MAKE AMERICA GREAT AGAIN COMMITTEE

We need your help to defeat the Democrats and the FAKE NEWS, who are working around the clock to defeat President Trump in November. President Trump needs you to take the Official 2020 Congressional District Census today. We need to hear from you before the most important election in American history. The information we gather from this survey will help us cra...

This author teaches an ethics Continuing Learning Education (CLE) course for attorneys. Based on that experience this question must be asked, "What kind of ethical standards do you have that will allow you to deceive American citizens around something as serious and vital to American Democracy as the US Census?"

Trump's fake census ad was a narrowly-focused, heavily biased, political survey. Previously, we have reprinted a couple of Trump's surveys in this book. He knew using the words "official," "2020," and "census" coming from "President Donald J. Trump" instead of honestly stating this was a Trump campaign "survey" was a deliberate attempt at deception. The wording and visuals were designed to appeal to every American's patriotic duty to participate in the actual official 2020 census.

Remember, Trump is a man who says through his attorney that he can murder anyone (which would include your family in any gruesome way you can imagine), and he can't be held liable as long as he's President. Here's the audiotape of that claim in a Federal court: find a white audio arrow in the article:[221]

Watch for "created" headlines to distract the voters.

Don't be surprised if there is a terror attack that brings Donald Trump to the rescue to help polish his leadership image in the last 45 days of the campaign. Dare I say, "a made for TV scenario." When ethics and honesty are not in play, and Trump believes winning is all that matters, just let your imagination run on the kind of dirty tricks he might add to those he's already done.

---

221. Ian Millhiser, "Trump's lawyer: If Trump shoots someone on 5th Avenue, nothing could be done," *Vox*, October 23, 2019, https://www.vox.com/2019/10/23/20928680/nothing-could-be-done-trump-fifth-avenue-immunity-mazars-vance

Please send me a word or words that can convey the level of repulsion and disgust and nausea that this type of vileness conjures up inside a person with ethics and human values. DrDavidKingKeller@gmail.com.

Misrepresenting the US Federal Census Bureau and fraudulently impersonating official US Government business is a federal crime. Specifically, it is a violation of **Title 18 U.S. Code § 912. Officer or employee of the United States,** which states,

> Whoever falsely assumes or pretends to be an officer or employee acting under the authority of the United States or any department, agency or officer thereof, and acts as such, or in such pretended character demands or obtains any money, paper, document, or thing of value, shall be fined under this title or imprisoned not more than three years, or both.[222]

Cousin Helen, a respected teacher in Florida, believes that this act alone, deceptively pretending to represent official US Government Census business, is such a despicable violation of the United States of America and for which it stands, that Trump should be removed from office forthwith.

This is Trump's 25th alleged federal crime by my count. Would reasonable Americans support a second impeachment vote prior to the election? Why not put out the facts of these alleged criminal acts on YouTube, websites, social media, and press conferences and then ask Gallup and Pew Research to conduct a poll.

Shielded by the "six headlines theory," in this case, the horrific Covid-19 pandemic ravaging America and America's lifestyle, the media haven't had the time or bandwidth to cover this apparent "heinous" federal crime by Trump.

---

222. Legal Information Institute, "18 U.S. Code § 912.Officer or employee of the United States," *Cornell Law School*, March 20, 2020, https://www.law.cornell.edu/uscode/text/18/912

United Post Office Bankruptcy

If Trump wins, he will put the United States Post Office into Bankruptcy. Trump is on record as saying if Americans can vote by mail, Republicans will never win another election.[223]

The biggest threat to the Republican Party, according to Trump, is the US Postal Service (USPS). Why? Because the USPS delivers mail. More specifically, the USPS delivers ballots cast in an election. Making it easy for people to vote will reduce Republican voter suppression at the precinct voting booth. Eliminating voting booths and their associated computers means less computers for the Russians to hack in favor of their preferred victor(s). The USPS might be purchased by a private enterprise that was more susceptible to political influence.

Attorney General William Barr will pull a "Comey"

The May 3, 2017, fivethirtyeight.com headline read, "The Comey Letter Probably Cost Clinton The Election."[224] On October 28, 2016, just ten days before the November 8, 2016, presidential election, FBI Director James Comey sent a letter to Congress. The letter said, "the FBI had 'learned of the existence of emails that appear to be pertinent to the investigation' into the private email server that Clinton used as secretary of state [that] upended the news cycle and soon halved Clinton's lead in the polls."

---

223. The Guardian, "Trump says Republicans would 'never' be elected again if it was easier to vote," *The Guardian*, March 30, 2020, https://www.theguardian.com/us-news/2020/mar/30/trump-republican-party-voting-reform-coronavirus

224. Nate Silver, "The Comey Letter Probably Cost Clinton The Election," *fivethirtyeight.com*, May 3, 2017, https://fivethirtyeight.com/features/the-comey-letter-probably-cost-clinton-the-election/

The Trump Team knows the "Comey letter" may be the reason Trump won the 2016 election. Their thinking will be that maybe lightning can strike twice. On or about October 7, 2020, less than four weeks before the election, this author predicts that Atty. Gen. William Barr will probably file an indictment against VP Joseph Biden and his son Robert Hunter Biden. Or Barr will announce the formation of a grand jury to investigate Joseph Biden and his son. The premise will be that VP Joe Biden and his son misused government equipment and funds when Biden flew his son on Air Force One to Ukraine. It doesn't matter that Trump has done the same thing on a regular basis for his family. The only goal is to influence those independent voters who make up their minds in the last two or three weeks of the election, and as you learned from book one in this companion series that these independent voters vote for the person with the least unfavorable rating in their mind. This group makes up about 7% of the voting population, and that group decides who wins the presidential election when it's a hair-thin close election.

I have said over and over again that for Donald Trump this is World War III, no holds barred, anything goes, and ethics and legality are out the window because they will fight those fights later after the deed is done, and the election is over. The only goal is to win. And win at all costs.

Prediction:

Barr will pull a "Comey" and indict Biden on October 15, 2020 on charges stemming from Ukraine and China. Barr will claim Biden used "unlawful" influence to secure his son a position on Ukraine Power Company board and business in China and used US Federal funds (flying on Air Force One) to do so. It won't hold water, but it will give some Independents pause. And it provides "cover" for other nefarious deeds that will impact the vote count. Prognosticators will be directed toward the smoke and mirrors "Ukraine indictment" as the reason a number of votes swung over to Trump.

The groundwork is already being laid. On June 29, 2020, at 3:15 PM EST Sebastian Gorka, a well-known reactionary talk show host said that Biden's son flew 400 times on Air Force 2 to over 28 countries on self-promotion trips at the government expense. In one case, Hunter Biden sealed a billion-dollar deal in China leveraging his father's position to gain work and fees in areas in which Hunter had no experience. So, my prediction is already starting to come true.

APPENDIX 5A
$100 MILLION PROFIT CORPS: PAID NO TAXES.

55 Corps that made over $100 million in profit (net income) and paid no taxes.			
Company	**Profit Mil $**	**Company**	**Profit Mil $**
Amazon.com	10835	American Elec Pwr	1943
Delta Air Lines	5073	Kinder Morgan	1784
Chevron	4547	Public Service Ent Grp	1772
General Motors	4320	Principal Financial	1641
EOG Resources	4067	FirstEnergy	1495
Occidental Petroleum	3379	Prudential Financial	1440
Duke Energy	3029	Xcel Energy	1434
Dominion Resources	3021	PulteGroup	1340
Honeywell Intl	2830	Molson Coors	1325
Deere	2152	Devon Energy	1297

APPENDIX 5B
$100 MILLION PROFIT CORPS: PAID NO TAXES.

55 Corps that made over $100 million in profit (net income) and paid no taxes.			
Company	**Profit Mil $**	**Company**	**Profit Mil $**
Pioneer Natrl Res	1249	Whirlpool	717
DTE Energy	1215	MGM Res Intl	648
Wisconsin Energy	1139	Atmos Energy	600
PPL	1110	Eli Lilly	598
Halliburton	1082	Alaska Air Group	576
Ameren	1035	Cliffs Natrl Res	565
Netflix	856	UGI	550
Salesforce.com	800	IBM	500
CMS Energy	774	Celanese	480
Rockwell Collins	719	Activision Blizzard	447

APPENDIX 5C
$100 MILLION PROFIT CORPS: PAID NO TAXES.

55 Corps that made over $100 million in profit (net income) and paid no taxes.

Company	Profit Mil $	Company	Profit Mil $
Goodyear Tire & Rubber	440	Tech Data	203
United States Steel	432	Realogy	199
Owens Corning	405	Performance Food Group	192
Penske Automotive Group	393	Arrow Electronics	167
Ryder System	350	Trinity Industries	138
Arthur Gallagher	322	Total:	78,711
Aramark	315		
MDU Resources	314		
AECOM Technology	238		
JetBlue Airways	219		

Total: $79 Billion in profits.

Paid not one nickel in taxes.

Under Trump's new welfare-for-the-rich 2017 tax law.

How much in taxes did you pay?

How much infrastructure do you use compared to these corps?
Who benefits more from military and police costs? Yet who's paying?

Source: Multiple sources: CBS News; Institute on Taxation and Economic Policy; The Center For Public Integrity; FairTax.org.

APPENDIX 6
STATS: WE ARE ECONOMIC SLAVES-TO-THE RICH

Economic-Slaves-To-The-Rich Statistics Created By Trump's New 2017 Tax Law	
$ 268,000,000,000	Annual reduction in taxes for rich under new tax bill: $268 Billion
140,900,000	Total American workers
$ 1,902	Cost per working American
$ 32,000	Average income for majority of average Americans
$ 2,210	Annual tax paid by avg American
$ 4,658	Fed Tax + Medicare + Social Sec tax
86%	Percent of Fed tax to rich
5	5-day work week
86%	Percent of work week working to give rich
4.3	Days per week spent working to benefit rich, as an economic slave
60	60-minute work hour
51.6	Minutes /hr. worked to pay their fed tax dollars to the rich

How much infrastructure do you, the reader, damage compared to rich corps? Who benefits more from military and police costs? Yet, who's paying? *Multiple sources: American Progress :[225]
ITEP Institute on Taxation and Economic Policy (ITEP) says 2017 TCJA cost US Treasury **$324.2 billion in FY 2020**. ITEP also says 72% of this $324.2 billion went to richest 20%.[226] Per ITEP cost is much higher than the $268B/yr. example the author used. Americans For Fair Taxation (AFFT), also known as FairTax.org; The Center For Public Integrity, publicintegrity.org

---

225. Galen Hendricks & Seth Hanlon, "The TCJA 2 Years Later: Corporations, Not Workers, Are The Big Winners," *Center for American Progress*, December 19, 2019, https://www.americanprogress.org/issues/economy/news/2019/12/19/478924/tcja-2-years-later-corporations-not-workers-big-winners/
226. Institute On Taxation And Economic Policy, *"TCJA by the Numbers 2020,"ITEP*, March 4, 2020, https://itep.org/tcja-2020/

APPENDIX 7
SAD AND SCARY "TRUMP TAX HEIST" STATISTICS

U.S. Treasury $ going to rich corps and rich 1% due to Trump-Socialist-Republican-Welfare-For-The -Rich Party's new 2017 tax law by increasing national debt by $268 Billion per year. This forces U.S. to borrow money to fund this give-away putting pressure on average tax payer to pay this debt and now Trump party wants to take money from poor and middle class programs, Social Security and Medicare, to pay for this government welfare for the rich.	
$ 268,000,000,000	Per year – Treasury $ going to rich
$ 734,246,575	Per day
$ 30,593,607	Per hour
$ 509,893	Per minute

*Multiple sources: American Progress:[227]
ITEP Institute on Taxation and Economic Policy (ITEP) says 2017 TCJA cost US Treasury **$324.2 billion in FY 2020**. ITEP also says 72% of this $324.2 billion went to richest 20%.[228] Per ITEP cost is much higher than the $268B/yr. example the author used.

---

227. Galen Hendricks & Seth Hanlon, "The TCJA 2 Years Later: Corporations, Not Workers, Are The Big Winners," *Center for American Progress*, December 19, 2019, https://www.americanprogress.org/issues/economy/news/2019/12/19/478924/tcja-2-years-later-corporations-not-workers-big-winners/
228. Institute On Taxation And Economic Policy, "TCJA by the Numbers 2020,"*ITEP,* March 4, 2020, https://itep.org/tcja-2020/

APPENDIX 8
ELECTORAL COLLEGE VOTES BY STATE

State	Electoral Votes		State	Electoral Votes
Alabama	9		Missouri	10
Alaska	3		Montana	3
Arizona	11		Nebraska	5
Arkansas	6		Nevada	6
California	55		New Hampshire	4
Colorado	9		New Jersey	14
Connecticut	7		New Mexico	5
Delaware	3		New York	29
District of Columbia	3		North Carolina	15
Florida	29		North Dakota	3
Georgia	16		Ohio	18
Hawaii	4		Oklahoma	7
Idaho	4		Oregon	7
Illinois	20		Pennsylvania	20
Indiana	11		Rhode Island	4
Iowa	6		South Carolina	9
Kansas	6		South Dakota	3
Kentucky	8		Tennessee	11
Louisiana	8		Texas	38
Maine	4		Utah	6
Maryland	10		Vermont	3
Massachusetts	11		Virginia	13
Michigan	16		Washington	12
Minnesota	10		West Virginia	5
Mississippi	6		Wisconsin	10
Total EC Votes = 538 EC Votes needed to win = 270			Wyoming	3

MEGAN BETTS "MURDERED" BY GOP POLICIES

Megan Betts, 22, was murdered August 4, 2019 in Dayton, Ohio by an AK-47 with a 100-round magazine.

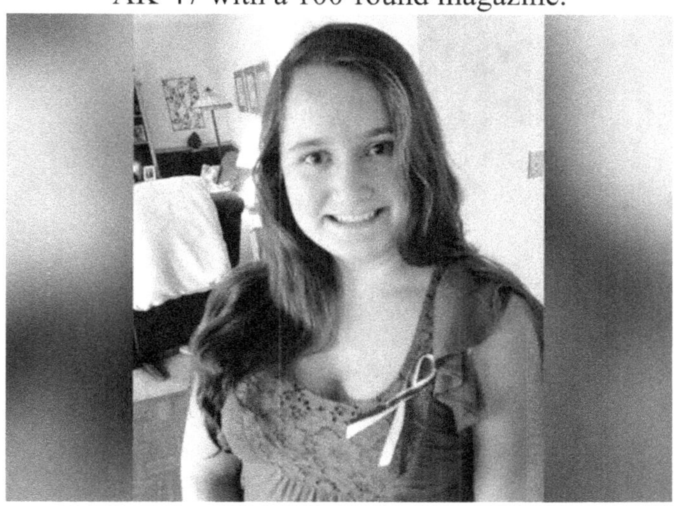

Murdered by a Republican-authorized military weapon of mass destruction.

The weapon of mass destruction, an assault rifle with 100-round capacity, was illegal to purchase under Democrat Bill Clinton from 1994 to 2004 but legalized by Republicans in 2004.

Vote to Murder More Megan Betts

Vote Republican

Republicans Turned 48,000 Americans Into Economic Slaves For This Man

Jeff Bezos
The richest man alive.

The Republican-run government gave Bezos' company $129,000,000 in hard-earned American taxpayer dollars as a 2018 tax "refund" even though his company, Amazon, made over $10 Billion in profit.

48,000 average Americans worked an entire year to pay the US Government $129,000,000 in taxes, which were then given to Bezos.

The rest of us work all year to pay taxes, so, 55 Corporations can make $79 Billion in profit, yet, receive $4.3 Billion in cash refunds of our paid-in tax dollars.

Vote to be a slave for the rich.
Vote Republican.

*[1] U.S. Median income = $36,000; Federal tax on $36,000 = $2,662.
$129,000,000 tax refund divided by $2,662 = 48,459 taxpayers.
https://en.wikipedia.org/wiki/Median_income; https://smartasset.com/taxes/income-taxes#bAETUfiszP
Amazon profit and refund: https://cnb.cx/2Il4Owx

APPENDIX 11
ADDITIONAL INFORMATION AVAILABLE

www.KellerResearchInstitute.com

1. Third Rail Social Security Threatened by Trump
2. The Bernie Sanders Socialist "Virus" That Infected Dems
3. A 2 Page Open Letter To Bernie Sanders On His Myopic Adherence To A Word That Damages
4. An 8 Page Open Letter to Bernie Sanders Suggesting He Drop Socialist As A Descriptor
5. A Review of Socialism In America
6. Website Analysis: Democratic Party
7. Images: Trump's TV Spot On Democratic Socialists Giving Free Healthcare to Illegal Immigrants
8. Medicare-for-All Job Loss
9. A New Health Care Plan ONLY For Those That Need It
10. 2016 Election Results in 5 Charts
11. More Info on Electoral College
12. Answering Electoral College Electors Questions
13. Stockholm Syndrome
14. Reason #13 Out Media-ed – Part 2
15. Where Do Trump Supporters Get Their Information?
16. Trump Admin Is Scrubbing Obamacare From Government Sites
17. Impact of Third Parties
18. Russian Assets in U.S.
19. The 2021 Trump Amendment to the U.S. Constitution.
20. Fixing the F'd-Up DNC Primary Process
21. Voter Suppression (continued).
22. Voter Suppression: Purging Voter Rolls With Postcards
23. Voter Suppression – Gerrymandering
24. Voter Suppression- continued
25. 2016 Election Results in 5 Charts
26. How To Scam Electoral College With Third Parties

APPENDIX 12
PANDEMIC'S IMPACT ON VOTER TURNOUT

The impact of the COVID-19 coronavirus pandemic on voting depended on how well it was under control by October 2020. The hard-core base for both sides were passionate and would probably find a way to vote no matter what. But there is a large group looking for a reason to avoid voting, and the virus became an unknown factor at the beginning of Summer 2020, which was when this book was in its final edit phase. In early June 2020 what the logistical environment would be for voting in the November 3, 2020 election was anybody's guess. Medical professionals were worried about a "Fall resurgence" of COVID-19. The other factor weighing on the November 3, 2020 election was the Trump-Republican desire to suppress mail-in voting options[229] and force people to get in line to vote.[230] Taking away the vote-by-mail option was done for the Wisconsin vote in April of 2020 where people were forced to get in line to vote and at least 52 of them came down with COVID-19.[231]

---

[229] Reid J. Epstein, Nick Corasaniti and Annie Karni, "Trump Steps Up Attacks on Mail Vote, Making False Claims About Fraud," *New York Times*, May 20, 2020, https://www.nytimes.com/2020/05/20/us/politics/trump-michigan-vote-by-mail.html

[230] Lisette Voytko, "Trump Rails Against Mail-In Voting, Threatening Michigan and Nevada," Forbes, May 20, 2020, https://www.forbes.com/sites/lisettevoytko/2020/05/20/trump-threatens-to-cut-off-michigans-federal-funds-over-mail-in-voting/#50ab674e1529

231. SCOTT BAUER and Associated Press, "52 who worked or voted in Wisconsin election have COVID-19," *ABC* News, April 29, 2020, https://abcnews.go.com/Health/wireStory/52-worked-voted-wisconsin-election-covid-19-70406317

AFTERWORD

You are reading a "live" book. Your input will help me create version 2.0. You are invited to participate in a booklogue, a dialogue between author and reader. Research indicates this is the first use of the word "booklogue" within this context. It's a portmanteau. To contribute information, comments, or ideas, please send this author an email.

The book's price is low to allow you to send copies to people who would appreciate learning about presidential politics.

To donate funds or other resources to the Keller Research Institute and its educational goals, please contact the author.

If you know Tom Steyer, or someone who knows Tom, please him or your contact to ask him to contact me. It's important.

At the end of the 2020 election cycle, this book will be updated and converted into a college PoliSci textbook. Please submit your comments to help our students.

If you found this book of value, please go to Amazon and leave a positive review. If you do, please let us know so that we can thank you personally. If, for any reason, you were unhappy with some aspect of the book, please tell us before anyone else so that we have a chance to address it with you and make any appropriate changes. Thank you for that courtesy.

With gratitude to all who are helping our country in some way,

David King Keller, PhD

DrDavidKingKeller@gmail.com

PUBLISHER'S NOTICE

Publisher's Terms and Conditions

Readers and Users of This Book's Content Accept These Publisher's Terms and Conditions As a Pre-condition To Reading or Using This Book or Any Portion Thereof In Any Manner or For Any Reason and Use of This Book or Its Contents In any Manner Is Agreement To a Complete Release of Liability For Any Harm of Any Type Including Reputational Harm. Reviewers may use accredited excerpts. Free rights to use of political cartoons. This book is about education and encouraging dialogue. Changes in future versions of this book will be based on new research and feedback. In order to protect the First Amendment rights and other rights of the author, publisher, and other contributors, the user of any element of this book or portion thereof for any reason (User) accepts these Publisher's Terms and Conditions as a pre-condition of use. These Publisher's Terms and Conditions are not separable from any of the Book's content. User agrees with David King Keller, PhD (Author) and Keller Research Institute (Publisher) that nothing in this Book is intended to, or does, cause harm or damage of any type to anyone, or any group or organization, and User further agrees not to participate in any action making any claim to the contrary (Participant), but if a User becomes a Participant, that Participant / User now agrees to assume all costs incurred by Author or Publisher in defense of any action or claim if same is brought about by and related actions of the Participant/User. Simply possessing this Book or any of its contents does not release the User of any obligations pursuant to these Terms and Conditions herein. The User holds Author and Publisher harmless of any and all loss or damage of any type. User agrees not to share any of the Book's content with anyone prior to that party agreeing to these same Terms and Conditions, and violation of this last-mentioned term makes the User a Participant. User agrees any claimed harm may be satisfactorily resolved by an edit of the current manuscript, which impacts all future releases utilizing that edited manuscript. This book is for educational purposes intended to encourage thoughtful dialogue about the issues reviewed herein. Legally protected parody is included. Thank you for engaging in this all-American process of political discourse.

IN GRATITUDE

To My Partner, My Wife

ABOUT THE AUTHOR

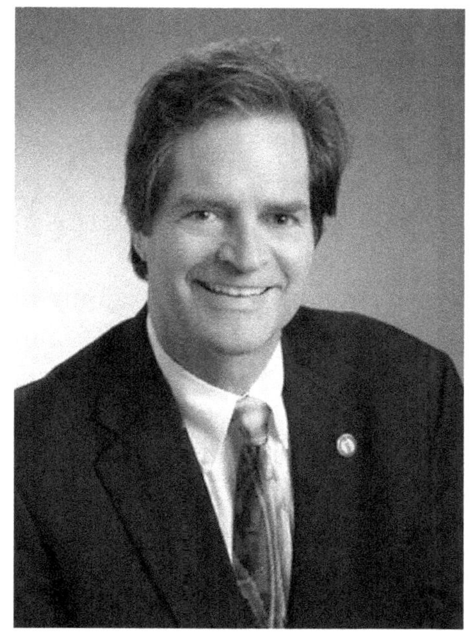

Best-selling legal author, political analyst, and communication strategist, David King Keller, PhD, brings a wide range of experience to this book.

Dr. Keller's political activism began when he worked with Dr. Martin Luther King's Poor People's Campaign as Chairman of the University of Maryland support committee. In that same year, he was the organizing Chairman of a U.S. Congressional Campaign.

Dr. Keller has supported several political campaigns. He drafted, launched, and successfully led a California proposition campaign.

As National Co-Director of a program to feed starving children in Africa, David worked with numerous politicians, movie stars, and the press. To help bring awareness to that crisis, he drafted memorialization legislation that was unanimously approved in a number of states.

Dr. Keller is an award-winning co-producer of a short film on the Nez Perce Native Americans titled, *Legend Days Are Over.* He is a TV commercial writer-director, and has been interviewed many times on radio and TV. He teaches an ethics course for lawyers and has addressed regional and national conferences of the American Bar Association.

Dr. Keller is the Founder of the Keller Research Institute, which is a non-profit educational organization that seeks donations to fund humanitarian projects.

Dr. Keller was a Trustee of a graduate school and served on many non-profit boards, including Meals on Wheels, Center for Attitudinal Healing, and a group to help ex-prisoners avoid recidivism. He has taught at the University of California extension system and brought educational programs into Federal prisons, including San Quintin.

His last legal business book is endorsed by five Presidents of the American Bar Association.

Drawing on his years of media, marketing, advertising, and training in the neuroscience of communication, Keller, with an MBA and PhD in East-West psychology, states, *"How Democrats Win The 2020 Election,* and its predecessor companion book, *Why Trump Won The 2020 Election,* is a wake-up call to Democrats and Republicans who want to see a new President replace Trump. Both books offer a detailed educational journey on the process and circumstances involved in electing a 21st century United States President."

Dr. Keller recently released a book dedicated to Black Lives Matter titled, *Racism and Racial Resentment, Their Role In Trump's Election.*

Dr. Keller is available for interviews, speaking engagements, and consulting.

The author wishes to speak with Tom Perez, Joseph Biden, Tom Steyer, Mike Bloomberg, Meryl Streep, Rob Reiner, Jon Stewart, and Stephen Colbert on key strategies to #DumpTrump.

DrDavidKingKeller@gmail.com

INDEX